Let's have a QUIZ Night

Let's have a QUIZ Night

Christopher Rigby

BARDFIELD
PRESS

First published by Bardfield Press in 2004

Bardfield Press is an imprint of
Miles Kelly Publishing Ltd
Bardfield Centre, Great Bardfield, Essex, CM7 4SL

2 4 6 8 10 9 7 5 3 1

Editorial Director: Belinda Gallagher
Editorial Assistant: Rosalind McGuire
Copy Editor: Louisa Somerville
Design Concept: Jo Brewer
Designer: Louisa Leitao
Picture Researchers: Rosalind McGuire/Liberty Newton
Production Manager: Estela Boulton

British Library Cataloguing-in-Publication Data
A catalogue record of this book is available from the British Library

ISBN 1-84236-456-1

Printed in China

www.mileskelly.net
info@mileskelly.net

Introduction

See Quiz 53

Let's Have a Quiz Night has something for everyone. The questions cover ten different subject areas and are presented in five levels, each one becoming progressively more difficult. Level 1 is just right for children and the images provide simple clues to guide them to the correct answer. Level 5 is the trickiest – designed for the supremely confident!

You can play in pairs, in teams, or individually. Work your way through the book, quiz by quiz, or choose a subject you feel confident about – it's up to you how you play. The answers are at the bottom of each quiz for quick reference – they'll also solve any disputes! However you decide to play, have fun. Remember – this isn't just a quiz book, it's also a brilliant source of information.

See Quiz 200

Level 1 QUIZZES 1–57

Level 2

QUIZZES 58–119

Level 3

QUIZZES 120–178

Level 4

QUIZZES 179–242

Level 5

QUIZZES 243–249

Picture Quizzes

How to use this book

Your book is split into five levels, each containing more than 50 quizzes. Level 1 is the easiest, with each level becoming progressively more difficult. The quizzes cover ten subject areas ranging from Music to Sport. The answers can be found at the end of each quiz.

Different Subjects
Each of the ten subject areas has its own tinted strip. Look for the red strips if you want to play the Total Trivia quizzes.

Levels 1 to 5
Each right-hand page tells you which level you are playing in.

Background Bonus
Look out for the Background Bonus panels. The large background image acts as a clue to the answer.

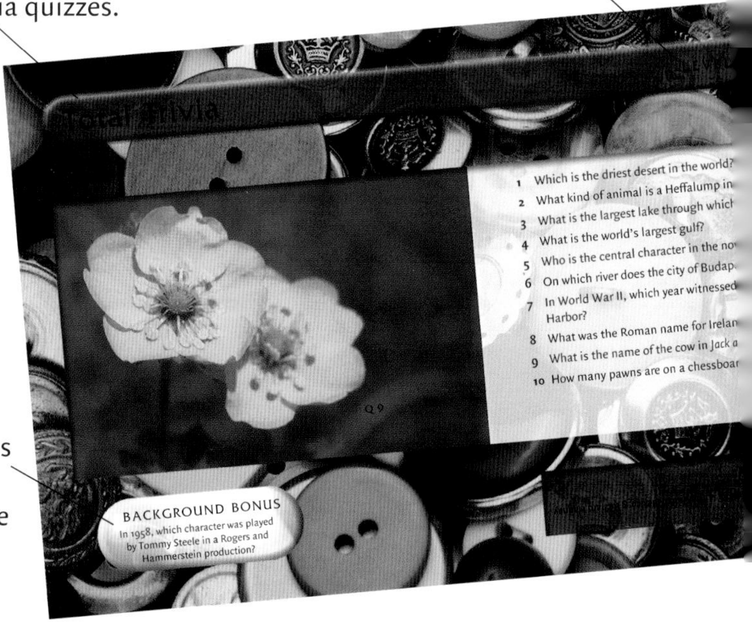

Total Trivia
1 Which is the driest desert in the world?
2 What kind of animal is a Heffalump
3 What is the largest lake through
4 What is the world's largest gulf?
5 Who is the central character in the
6 On which river does the city of
7 In World War II, which year
Harbor?
8 What was the Roman name for
9 What is the name of the cow in
10 How many pawns are on a
BACKGROUND BONUS
In 1958, which character was played by Tommy Steele in a Rogers and Hammerstein production?

Picture Quizzes

Look out for the picture quizzes with the blue backgrounds. These are pages dedicated to photographic quizzes.

Quiz Numbers

Each quiz is clearly numbered. There are 249 quizzes in total.

Feathers and Fur
LEVEL 2 · QUIZ 72
Can you identify these animals by their feathers, fur and skin?
1
2
3
4
5
6
7
8
ANSWERS
1 Penguin 2 Fawn 3 Parrot 4 Peacock 5 Chameleon 6 Butterfly 7 Snake 8 Cheetah

Picture Quiz Clues

The picture quizzes are made up of eight close-up shots of anything from animals to everyday objects. They can be tricky!

Answers

The answers to each quiz are positioned upside down on the right-hand pages.

Lights, Camera, Action!

1 Which popular children's TV characters live on Home Hill?

2 What is the name of the cowboy in the movie *Toy Story*?

3 Who travels through time in the TARDIS?

4 What is the last name of the vampire-slaying character, Buffy?

5 Which family lives in the town of Springfield next door to the Flanders family?

6 In the 2003 Disney movie *Finding Nemo*, what kind of fish is Bruce?

7 Is Barney the Dinosaur purple, pink or yellow?

8 What is the name of Mickey Mouse's girlfriend?

9 In the *Star Wars* movies, what is the name of Han Solo's Wookie co-pilot?

10 On which street is the Rover's Return pub?

LEVEL 1 • QUIZ 1

Q 6

ANSWERS
1 The Teletubbies **2** Woody **3** Dr. Who **4** Summers **5** The Simpsons
6 A great white shark **7** Purple **8** Minnie Mouse **9** Chewbacca **10** *Coronation Street*

Natural Selection

1 Which animal has a tail called a brush?

2 If the male is a bull and the female is a cow, what is the young called?

3 According to a popular saying, which animal can't change its spots?

4 Which has the longer ears, a rabbit or a hare?

5 What do fish breathe through?

6 Which part of an elephant's body contains approximately 40,000 muscles?

7 In which animal is the female a sow and the male a boar?

8 What is the world's largest mammal?

9 What is a joey?

10 What does the letter T stand for in T rex?

LEVEL 1 • QUIZ 2

ANSWERS

1 Fox **2** Calf **3** Leopard **4** Hare **5** Gills **6** The trunk **7** Pig **8** Blue whale **9** A young kangaroo **10** *Tyrannosaurus*

Written Word

LEVEL 1 · QUIZ 3

1 Which is the longer, the Bible's Old Testament or New Testament?

2 Who started his diary when he was age 13 and three-quarters?

3 In a popular fairytale, what is the name of Gretel's brother?

4 In the novel *Peter Pan*, where do the Lost Boys live?

5 Which animal knocked on the doors of the three little pigs?

6 In a nursery rhyme, which king is entertained by a trio of fiddlers?

7 What did the Grinch steal in December?

8 Which of the Seven Dwarfs is very shy?

9 What kind of bird is Captain Flint in *Treasure Island*?

10 What does the ugly duckling turn into?

ANSWERS

1 The Old Testament **2** Adrian Mole **3** Hansel **4** Never Never Land **5** The big bad wolf **6** Old King Cole **7** Christmas **8** Bashful **9** A parrot **10** A swan

Making History

1 Which king married three Catherines, two Annes and a Jane?

2 Which famous battle was fought at Senlac Hill, England, in 1066?

3 In which mythology is Zeus the king of the gods?

4 What is the first name of Captain Cook, the English sailor who discovered Australia?

5 Which English highwayman rode a horse called Black Bess?

6 Which Roman emperor was murdered on the Ides of March?

7 In which forest in England did Robin Hood live?

8 Name any year in which World War II was fought.

9 What name did Vikings give to their large sailing ships?

10 Who is Queen Elizabeth II's eldest child?

BACKGROUND BONUS

Which 1919 treaty forced Germany to accept responsibility for World War I?

LEVEL 1 · QUIZ 4

ANSWERS

1 Henry VIII **2** The Battle of Hastings **3** Greek **4** James **5** Dick Turpin **6** Julius Caesar **7** Sherwood Forest **8** 1939–1945 **9** Longboats **10** Charles

Background Bonus The Treaty of Versailles

Music Mania

1 Which Christmas song was released by the 12 finalists of the 2003 *Pop Idol* TV contest?

2 Is a tambourine a woodwind or a percussion instrument?

3 Which boy band teamed up with Elton John on the hit "Sorry Seems To Be The Hardest Word"?

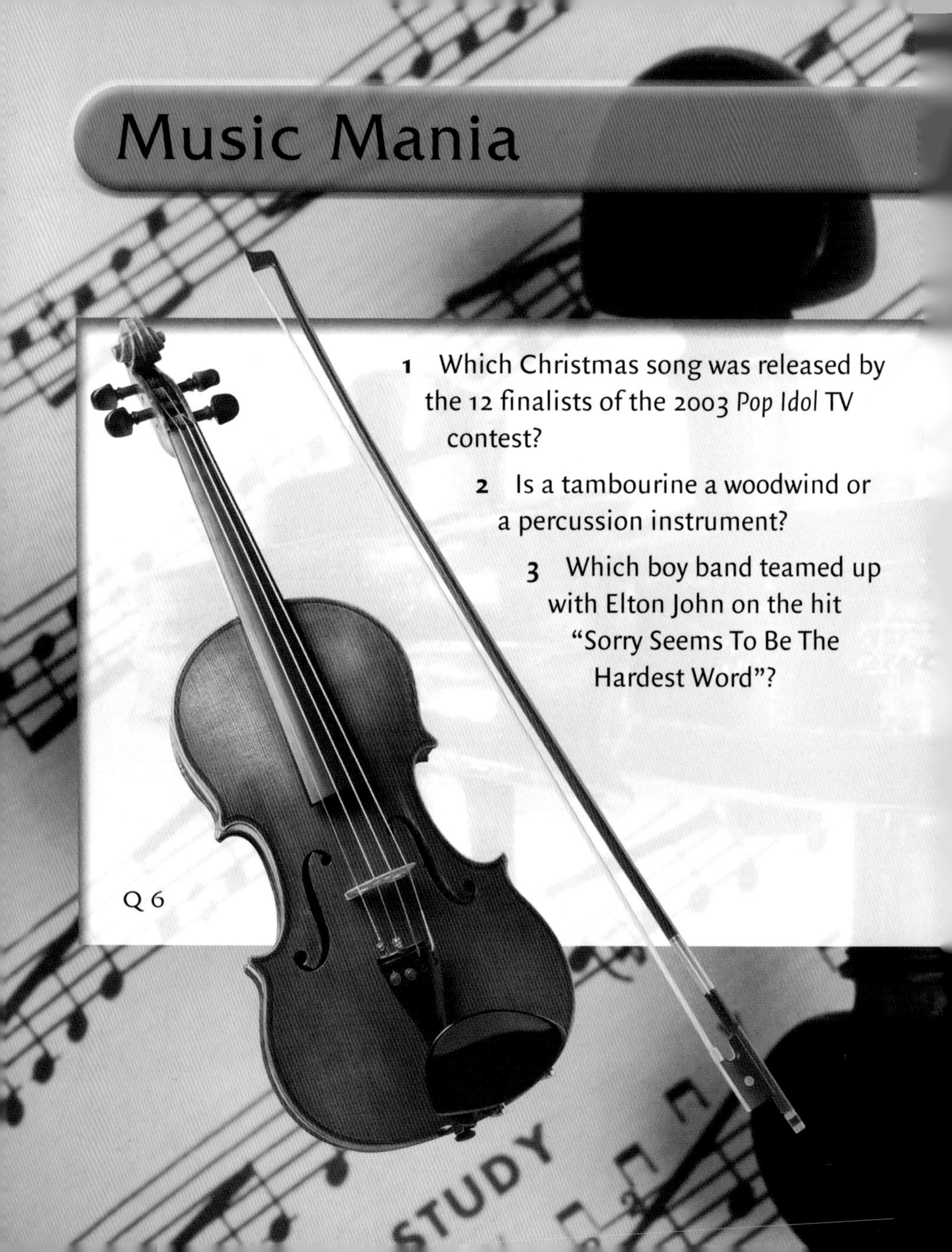

4 What nationality was the classical composer Ludwig Van Beethoven?

5 Which boy band was Justin Timberlake in before launching his solo career?

6 How many strings are on a violin?

7 Which U.S. pop goddess starred in the movie *Crossroads*?

8 Which former member of Take That recorded the album "Sing When You're Winning"?

9 Which English city do the pop group Oasis come from?

10 "Swing Low Sweet Chariot" is a traditional anthem sung by England supporters when watching which sport?

ANSWERS

1 "Happy Christmas War Is Over" 2 Percussion 3 Blue 4 German 5 N Sync 6 Four 7 Britney Spears 8 Robbie Williams 9 Manchester 10 Rugby union

Total Trivia

Q 10

1 What is the official language of the Netherlands?

2 What does the letter "e" stand for in email?

3 Which Spanish soccer club did David Beckham join in 2003?

4 "Pinkie" is a slang term for which part of the body?

5 Which TV soap is set in Walford?

6 What is the equivalent of 3 p.m. on a 24-hour clock?

7 Who joined Michael Jackson on the hit record "Scream"?

8 What kind of animal is Disney's Bambi?

9 According to a popular saying, what comes before a fall?

10 In the United States what is sometimes referred to as Old Glory or the Stars and Stripes?

ANSWERS

1 Dutch **2** Electronic **3** Real Madrid **4** The little finger **5** *Eastenders* **6** 15.00 (15.00 Hours) **7** His sister **8** A deer **9** Pride **10** The national flag

Global Matters

1 Which capital city surrounds the Vatican City?

2 What is the national flower of Scotland?

3 In which ocean do the British Isles lie?

4 Which is the only U.S. state that is an island?

5 In which country is the city of Barcelona?

6 What bird is the official national symbol of the United States?

7 What is the longest river in Africa?

8 In which city is the Eiffel Tower?

9 What is the world's largest continent by area?

10 Which is the most recent bridge to be built over the river Thames in London?

LEVEL 1 • QUIZ 7

Q 6

ANSWERS

1 Rome **2** Thistle **3** Atlantic Ocean **4** Hawaii **5** Spain **6** Bald eagle **7** River Nile **8** Paris **9** Asia **10** The Millennium Bridge

Scientifically Speaking

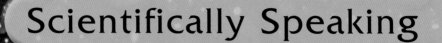

BACKGROUND BONUS

Which element makes up a large percentage of our bodies?

Q 3

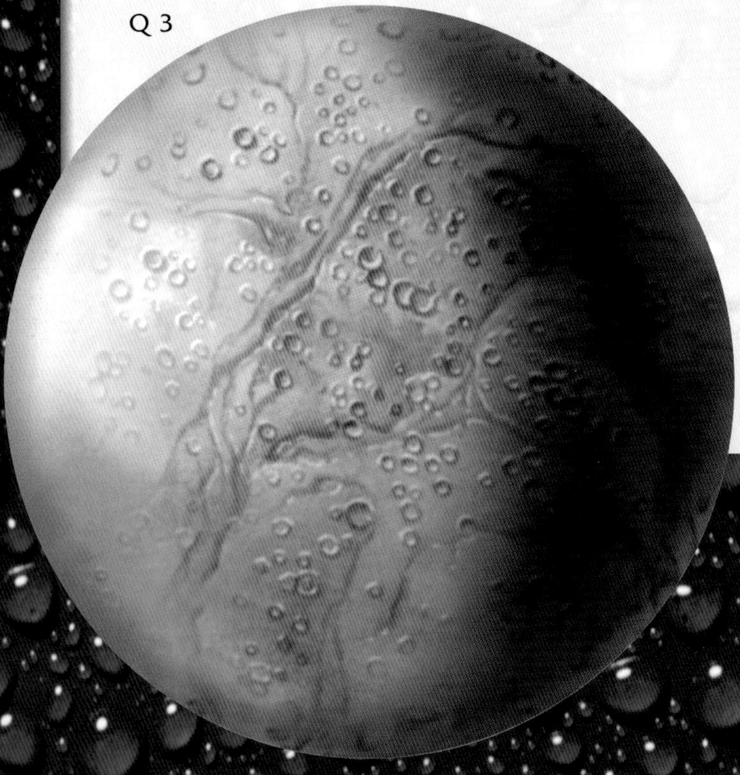

1 On which temperature scale is 100 degrees the boiling point of water?

2 What gas makes up most of the atmosphere?

3 What planet shares its name with Mickey Mouse's pet dog?

4 What is the chemical symbol for water?

5 What travels at 300,000 km (186,000 miles) per second?

6 What is one-sixtieth of a minute called?

7 How many legs does a tripod have?

8 What nationality was the first man in space?

9 What does most of the brain consist of?

10 Which part of the body is treated by an ophthalmologist?

ANSWERS

1 Centigrade or Celsius **2** Nitrogen **3** Pluto **4** H_2O **5** Light **6** A second **7** Three **8** Russian **9** Water **10** The eyes

Background Bonus Water

Great and Famous

1 Who replaced Bill Clinton as president of the United States?

2 Who directed the movies *E.T.* and *Jurassic Park*?

3 What kind of snake killed Cleopatra?

4 Who created the fictional character of Harry Potter?

5 What is the name of Queen Elizabeth II's husband?

6 Who asks the questions on *Who Wants To Be A Millionaire?*

7 Who was deposed as leader of Iraq in 2003?

8 Who founded the Virgin record label?

9 What is the name of Tony Blair's youngest son?

10 Who does Clark Kent become when he dons a red cape?

Q 10

ANSWERS
1 George W. Bush **2** Steven Spielberg **3** An asp **4** J.K. Rowling **5** Philip **6** Chris Tarrant **7** Saddam Hussein **8** Richard Branson **9** Leo **10** Superman

Sporting Chance

Q 7

LEVEL 1 · QUIZ 10

1 What does the word “love” mean in tennis?

2 Which C word means a golfer’s assistant?

3 What does the A stand for in FA Cup?

4 In the game of darts what is the highest score possible with one dart?

5 In which Scottish city do Celtic and Rangers play a soccer derby?

6 Which snooker ball has the highest value?

7 Which nation won the 2003 Rugby Union World Cup?

8 In which sport are dogs released from traps?

9 In which part of a motor racing track are re-fuels carried out?

10 Excluding extra time, how many minutes is a soccer match?

ANSWERS

1 Zero **2** Caddie **3** Association **4** 60 (treble 20) **5** Glasgow **6** Black ball **7** England **8** Greyhound racing **9** The pits **10** 90 minutes

Lights, Camera, Action!

Q 10

LEVEL 1 • QUIZ 11

1 Who is Miss Piggy madly in love with on *The Muppet Show*?

2 The sitcom *Bread* and the soap opera *Brookside* were both set in which English city?

3 Who does Robbie Coltrane play in the *Harry Potter* movies?

4 In which movie did John Travolta sing of his love for Sandy?

5 What type of transport is shown on a Blue Peter badge?

6 Who does Dr. Bruce Banner turn into when he is angry?

7 What is the dog's name in *The Magic Roundabout*?

8 What is the dog's name in *The Tweenies*?

9 In the Disney movie *Lilo And Stitch*, was the alien Lilo or Stitch?

10 In *The Jungle Book*, who is the bear who befriends Mowgli?

ANSWERS

1 Kermit the Frog **2** Liverpool **3** Hagrid **4** *Grease* **5** A ship **6** *The Incredible Hulk* **7** Dougal **8** Noodles **9** Stitch **10** Baloo

Eye Contact

Can you identify these animals by looking at their eyes?

1

2

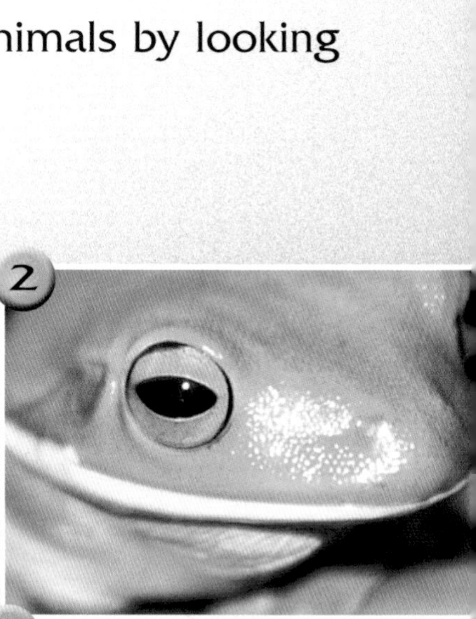

3

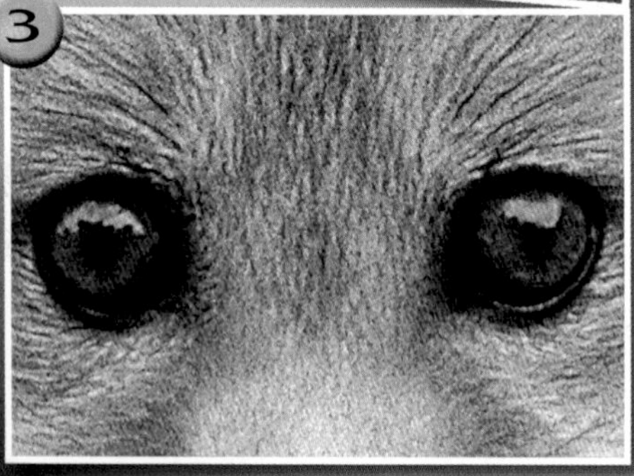

4

LEVEL 1 • QUIZ 12

5

6

7

8

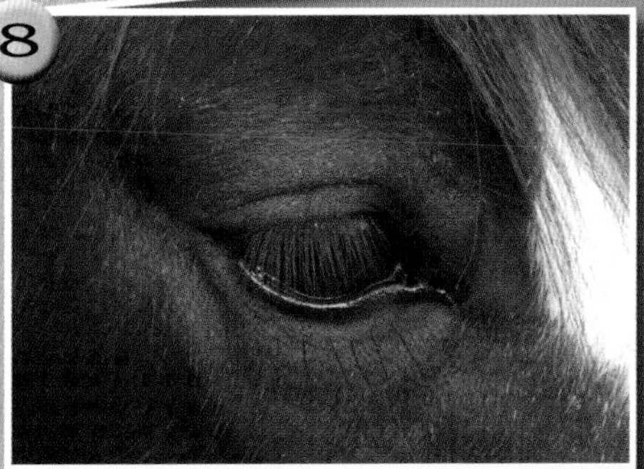

ANSWERS

1 Koala 2 Frog 3 Fox 4 Snake 5 Elephant 6 Jaguar 7 Owl 8 Horse

Natural Selection

1 Which T word is the name for a bird of prey's claws?

2 Which animal rears its young in a drey?

3 A boa constrictor is a species of what?

4 Which wild dogs are native to Australia?

5 Dorsal and tail are both types of what on a fish?

6 Is a hippopotamus a meat eater or a herbivore?

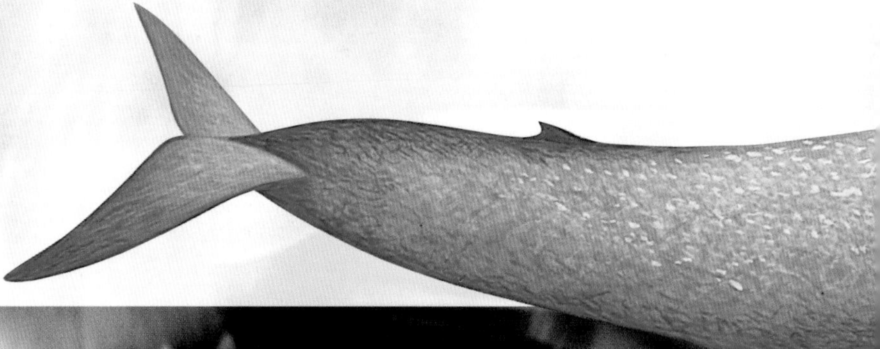

BACKGROUND BONUS

Which animal can reach speeds of over 120 km (60 mi) per hour and is the fastest animal on land?

7 What is the official national bird of Great Britain?

8 Are mammals cold or warm blooded?

9 What is a female peacock called?

10 What word can come before bell, whale and bird to give the name of three living things?

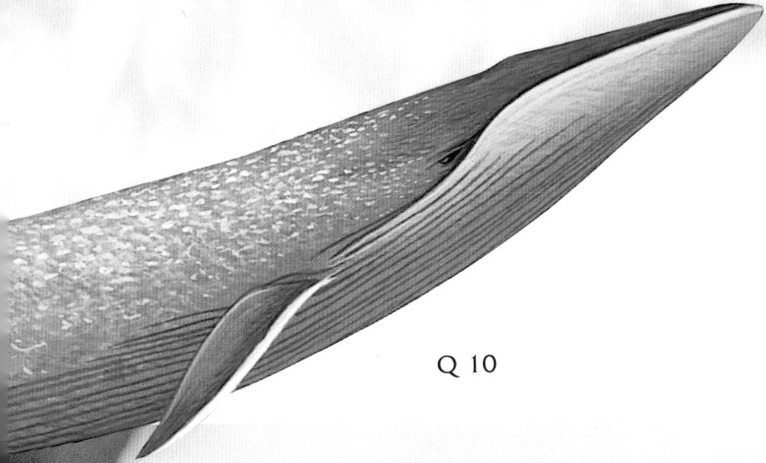

Q 10

ANSWERS

1 Talons **2** Squirrel **3** Snake **4** Dingoes **5** Fins **6** Herbivore **7** Robin **8** Warm blooded **9** Peahen **10** Blue

Background Bonus Cheetah

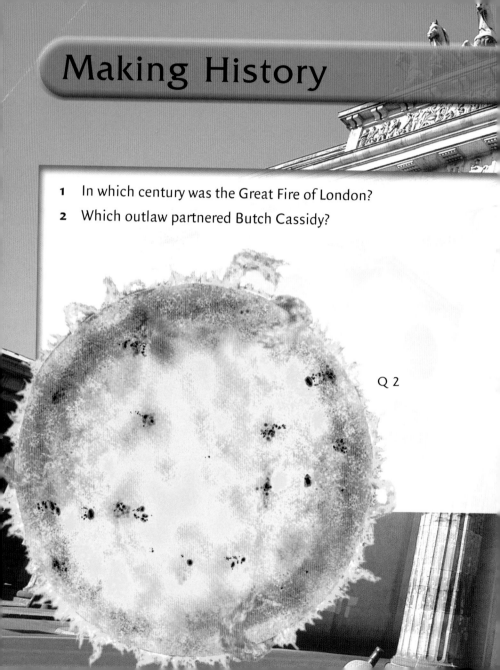

Making History

1 In which century was the Great Fire of London?

2 Which outlaw partnered Butch Cassidy?

Q 2

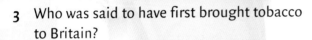

3 Who was said to have first brought tobacco to Britain?

4 Who committed the first murder in the Bible?

5 Which G word was a fighting slave trained to entertain the citizens of ancient Rome?

6 Who sailed to the land of Colchis with his Argonauts, in search of the Golden Fleece?

7 In which decade did man first walk on the Moon?

8 In which of the World Wars were tanks first used in battle?

9 What was invented by John Logie Baird, and is watched by most people every day?

10 In which country were the ancient Olympic Games held?

ANSWERS

1 The 17th century 2 The Sundance Kid 3 Walter Raleigh 4 Cain 5 Gladiator 6 Jason 7 1960s (1969) 8 World War I 9 Television 10 Greece

Music Mania

1 Which musical instrument is the national emblem of Ireland?

2 What does the B stand for in the name of Spice Girl Mel B?

Q 6

3 Which Andrew Lloyd Webber musical features a famous coat?

4 Which pop group was named after Debbie Harry's hair tone?

5 Who recorded the best-selling album "Bat Out Of Hell"?

6 Which P word is the name for an implement used to pluck guitar strings?

7 Who is introduced in the United States by a piece of music entitled "Hail To The Chief"?

8 Which teenage pop star married the broadcaster Chris Evans?

9 In which movie did Julie Andrews sing "My Favourite Things"?

10 Who won The Eurovision Song Contest singing about the Battle of Waterloo?

ANSWERS

1 Harp 2 Brown 3 *Joseph and The Technicolour Dreamcoat* 4 Blondie 5 Meat Loaf 6 Plectrum 7 The U.S. president 8 Billie Piper 9 *The Sound Of Music* 10 Abba

Total Trivia

Q 9

LEVEL 1 · QUIZ 16

1 Is the cross of St. George red, blue or green?

2 In the *Peanuts* cartoon strip what is Charlie Brown's dog called?

3 How many years are celebrated by a silver anniversary?

4 Who "picked a peck of pickled pepper"?

5 How is one-fifth expressed as a percentage?

6 Which card game features Mr. Bun the Baker?

7 Alphabetically, who is the first of the Teletubbies?

8 What animal is the symbol for the star sign of Cancer?

9 Who is the patron saint of Ireland?

10 What day follows Shrove Tuesday?

ANSWERS

1 Red **2** Snoopy **3** 25 years **4** Peter Piper **5** 20 percent **6** Happy Families **7** Dipsy **8** Crab **9** St. Patrick **10** Ash Wednesday

Global Matters

Q 8

BACKGROUND BONUS

In which art gallery is Leonardo da Vinci's *Mona Lisa* displayed?

1 On which continent is Kenya?

2 Eurodisney is in which country?

3 Which member of the Commonwealth has a maple leaf as its symbol?

4 Mount Snowdon is the highest peak in which country?

5 Which Australian state is an island?

6 Albion was the Roman name for England, Scotland, Ireland or Wales?

7 Which Scandinavian country begins with the letter F?

8 What is the name of the largest canyon in North America?

9 What is the world's largest ocean?

10 In which river was Jesus baptized?

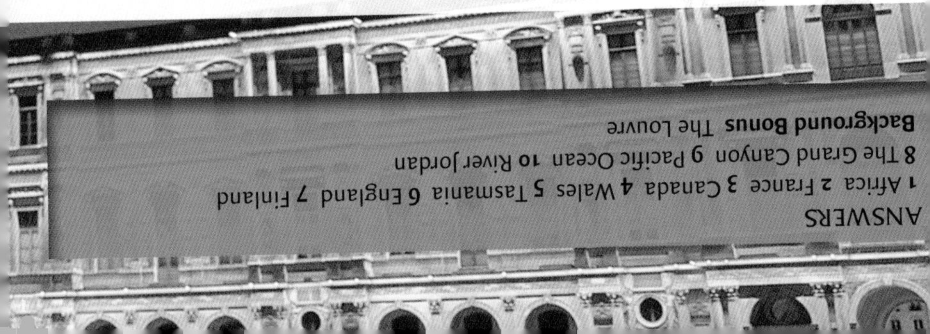

ANSWERS

1 Africa **2** France **3** Canada **4** Wales **5** Tasmania **6** England **7** Finland **8** The Grand Canyon **9** Pacific Ocean **10** River Jordan

Background Bonus The Louvre

Scientifically Speaking

1 Which god of war gave his name to the Red Planet?

2 Which vitamin does a person lack if they are suffering from scurvy?

3 Which A word means the smallest part of an element?

4 How many degrees are in a right angle?

5 What is another name for acetic acid?

6 Is the femur bone found in the arm or the leg?

7 Does litmus paper change to red or blue when it touches an alkali substance?

8 What does the computer acronym WYSIWYG stand for?

9 Which D word is the name for a line that bisects a circle?

10 Which process for heating milk was named after the scientist Louis Pasteur?

Q 3

ANSWERS

1 Mars **2** Vitamin C **3** Atom **4** 90 degrees **5** Vinegar **6** The leg **7** Blue **8** What you see is what you get **9** Diameter **10** Pasteurisation

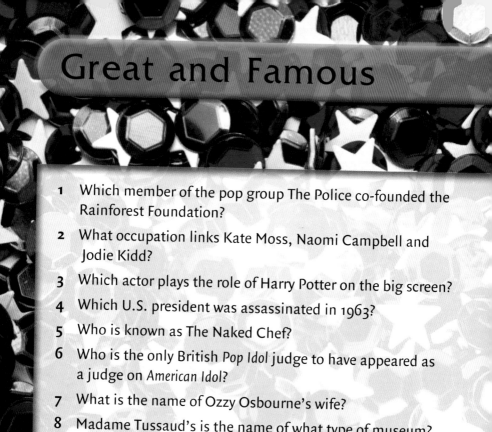

Great and Famous

1 Which member of the pop group The Police co-founded the Rainforest Foundation?

2 What occupation links Kate Moss, Naomi Campbell and Jodie Kidd?

3 Which actor plays the role of Harry Potter on the big screen?

4 Which U.S. president was assassinated in 1963?

5 Who is known as The Naked Chef?

6 Who is the only British *Pop Idol* judge to have appeared as a judge on *American Idol?*

7 What is the name of Ozzy Osbourne's wife?

8 Madame Tussaud's is the name of what type of museum?

9 On TV who plays the Vicar of Dibley?

10 What nationality is soccer manager Sven Goran Eriksson?

Q 2

ANSWERS
1 Sting 2 They are models 3 Daniel Radcliffe 4 John F. Kennedy 5 Jamie Oliver
6 Simon Cowell 7 Sharon 8 Wax works 9 Dawn French 10 Swedish

Written Word

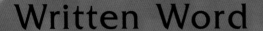

1 The prefix "quad" refers to which number?

2 Which word meaning "to become smaller" is also a slang term for a psychiatrist?

3 Which five-letter A word means a mixture of two or more metals?

4 Which month of the year can come before pole, or and fly to make three new words?

5 If a person is cantankerous, are they in a good or bad mood?

6 Which is the only number that is spelt the same in French and English?

7 Cantilever, arch and suspension are all names for what type of structure?

8 Which P word means the high point at the front of a horse's saddle?

9 Which letter of the alphabet can be added to "came" to make it a three-syllable word?

10 What is the name for the director of an orchestra?

Q 10

ANSWERS

1 Four **2** Shrink **3** Alloy **4** May **5** Bad mood **6** Six **7** Bridge **8** Pommel **9** O – to make cameo **10** Conductor

Sporting Chance

BACKGROUND BONUS

In which sport can you score with a lay-up, a leaning jumper and a hook shot?

1 Which birds are the pet name for Sheffield Wednesday?

2 Which British sport is governed by the Jockey Club?

3 What does a cricket umpire mean by a raised vertical forefinger?

4 Which four-a-side sport is played on horseback in periods of play called chukkas?

5 How long is the break between each round of a boxing match?

6 Who was crowned Formula One World Champion in 2003?

7 In which martial art is a bamboo sword called a shinai used?

8 Does Ian Thorpe compete on the track, in water, or on a horse?

9 What is the highest possible score for a gymnastics exercise?

10 What would a golfer's score be if taking three shots to complete a par five hole?

ANSWERS

1 Owls **2** Horse racing **3** That a batsman is out **4** Polo **5** One minute **6** Michael Schumacher **7** Kendo **8** In the water **9** Ten **10** Two

Background Bonus Basketball

Lights, Camera, Action!

1 Which cartoon rodent was the fastest mouse in all Mexico?

2 What kind of bird is Tweety Pie?

3 What does the movie rating PG signify?

4 In which movie did an ogre fall in love with Princess Fiona?

5 What insect bit Peter Parker to transform him into a superhero?

6 Which new TV channel was launched by The Spice Girls in 1997?

7 What is the name of Fred Flintstone's wife?

8 In which U.S. state was the soap *Dallas* set?

9 Which space-age hero was catapulted forward to the 25th century, where he befriended a robot called Twiki?

10 Who played the Beverly Hills Cop in three movies?

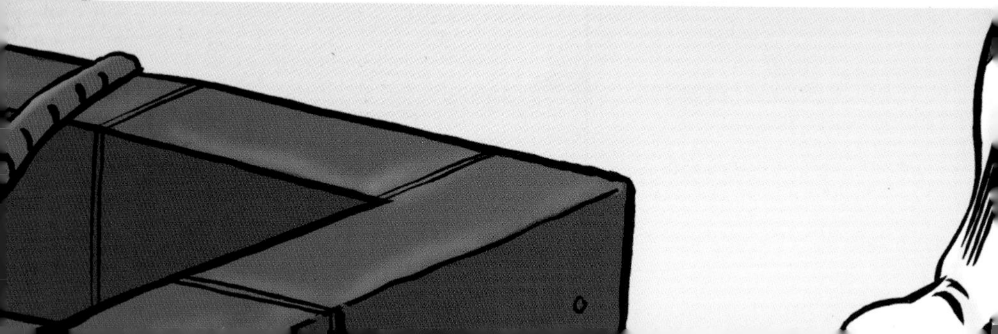

LEVEL 1 • QUIZ 22

ANSWERS

1 Speedy Gonzalez **2** A canary **3** Parental guidance **4** *Shrek* **5** A spider **6** Channel 5 **7** Wilma **8** Texas **9** Buck Rogers **10** Eddie Murphy

Natural Selection

1 Which four-letter word means a male foal?

2 Which planet completes the name of a carnivorous flytrap plant?

3 What substance makes up an elephant's tusk?

4 If the father is a billy and the mother a nanny, what is the young called?

5 What bird is the fastest land animal on two legs?

6 Which writing implement is also the name for a female swan?

7 Which Biblical character lends his name to the largest beetle?

8 What is a Rhodesian ridgeback?

9 Worker, drone and queen are three main types of which insect?

10 Which flower connects Remembrance Sunday and the drug opium?

Q 7

ANSWERS

1 Colt **2** Venus **3** Ivory **4** A kid **5** Ostrich **6** A pen **7** Goliath **8** A breed of dog **9** Bees **10** Poppy

Up Close

Can you identify these everyday objects?

1

2

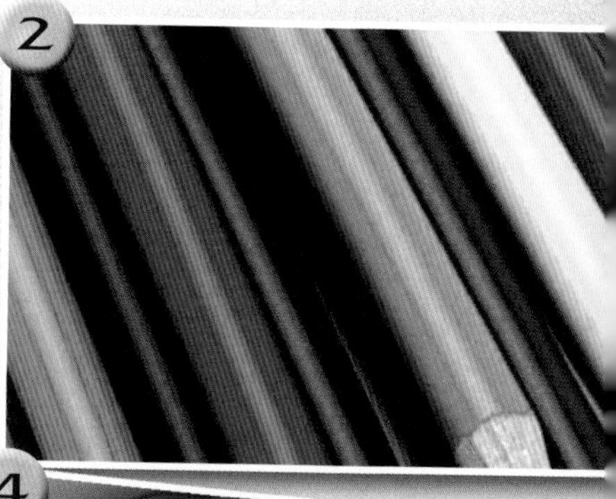

3

4

LEVEL 1 • QUIZ 24

5

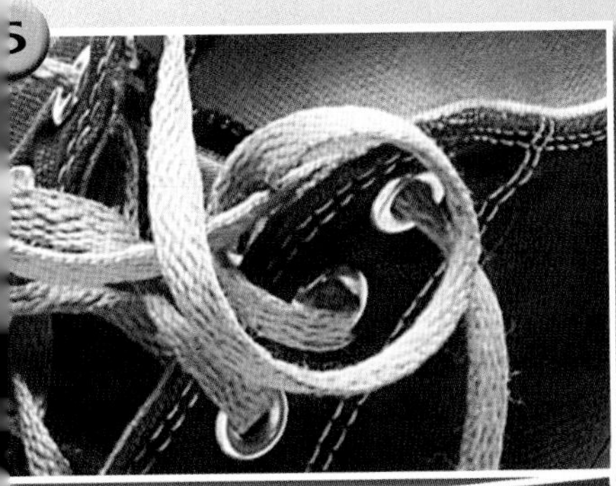

6

7

8

ANSWERS
1 Silver gift bow **2** Pencils **3** Dartboard **4** Kettle **5** Trainer **6** Balloons **7** CD **8** Alarm clock

Written Word

1 What was stolen by Tom the piper's son?

2 Where was Dr. Foster going?

3 What is the last animal in the rhyme "Hey Diddle Diddle"?

4 Which nursery rhyme character has an empty cupboard and a hungry dog?

5 Who went to sea with silver buckles on his knee?

6 How many men has the Grand Old Duke of York?

7 Which type of fruit is in Little Jack Horner's pie?

8 Which precious metal is mentioned in "Mary Mary Quite Contrary"?

9 In "Hickory Dickory Dock", what time is it when the mouse runs down the clock?

10 What is the only animal mentioned in "Humpty Dumpty"?

BACKGROUND BONUS

Where did Robin Hood and his band of merry men live?

Q 4

ANSWERS

1 A pig **2** Gloucester **3** A dog **4** Old Mother Hubbard **5** Bobby Shafto **6** 10,000 men
7 A plum **8** Silver **9** One o'clock **10** Horse
Background Bonus Sherwood Forest

Making History

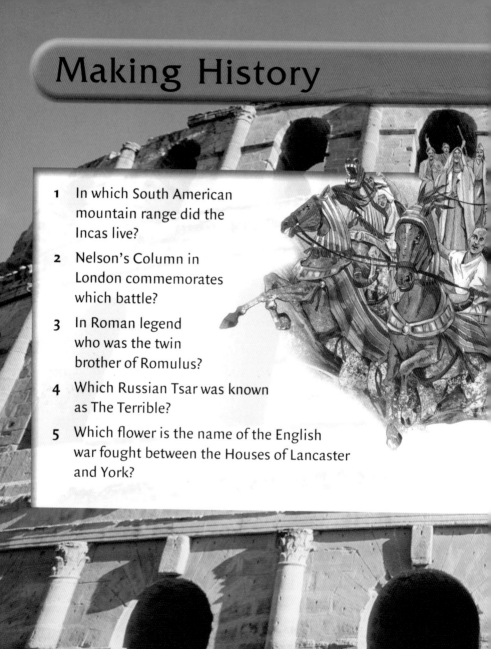

1 In which South American mountain range did the Incas live?

2 Nelson's Column in London commemorates which battle?

3 In Roman legend who was the twin brother of Romulus?

4 Which Russian Tsar was known as The Terrible?

5 Which flower is the name of the English war fought between the Houses of Lancaster and York?

6 In the Bible, who parted the Red Sea?

7 Which American dentist fought alongside Wyatt Earp at the OK Corral?

8 What name was given to the serial killer who terrorised London in the 1880s?

9 Was Rasputin known as The Barmy Bishop, The Mad Monk or The Deranged Deacon?

10 Which Roman general built a wall on the border of England and Scotland as a barricade against the Picts?

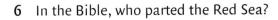

Q 6

ANSWERS

1 The Andes **2** The Battle of Trafalgar **3** Remus **4** Ivan the Terrible **5** War of the Roses **6** Moses **7** Doc Holliday **8** Jack the Ripper **9** The Mad Monk **10** Hadrian

Music Mania

1 For which movie did Bryan Adams record the song "Everything I Do, I Do It For You"?

2 Which girl band was formed as a result of the 2002 TV contest *Pop Idols The Rivals*?

3 Who sang the theme tune to the Bond movie *Die Another Day* and also played a fencing instructor in the movie?

Q 9

4 What is the name of the pop star son of Julio Iglesias?

5 "I'll Be There For You" is the theme tune for which TV comedy show?

6 Which Disney character sang, "Whistle While You Work" while cleaning a house?

7 What are there 88 of on a piano?

8 Which nationality is Luciano Pavarotti?

9 Which female trio had hits with the songs "Ladies' Night" and "The Tide Is High"?

10 The stage musical *We Will Rock You* features the songs of which pop group?

ANSWERS
1 Robin Hood Prince Of Thieves 2 Girls Aloud 3 Madonna 4 Enrique Iglesias
5 Friends 6 Snow White 7 Keys 8 Italian 9 Atomic Kitten 10 Queen

Total Trivia

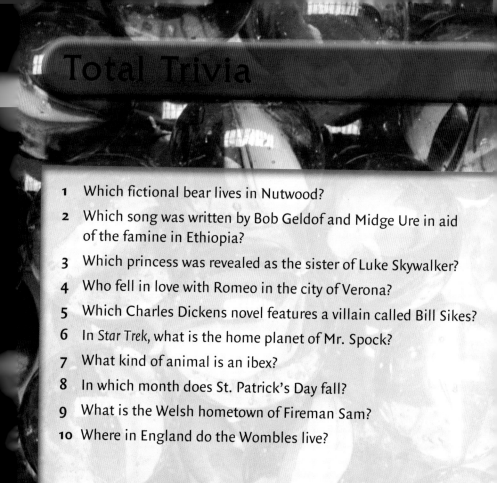

1 Which fictional bear lives in Nutwood?

2 Which song was written by Bob Geldof and Midge Ure in aid of the famine in Ethiopia?

3 Which princess was revealed as the sister of Luke Skywalker?

4 Who fell in love with Romeo in the city of Verona?

5 Which Charles Dickens novel features a villain called Bill Sikes?

6 In *Star Trek*, what is the home planet of Mr. Spock?

7 What kind of animal is an ibex?

8 In which month does St. Patrick's Day fall?

9 What is the Welsh hometown of Fireman Sam?

10 Where in England do the Wombles live?

Q 10

ANSWERS
1 Rupert 2 "Do They Know Its Christmas?" 3 Princess Leia 4 Juliet 5 Oliver Twist 6 Vulcan 7 A wild goat 8 March (March 17) 9 Pontypandy 10 Wimbledon Common

Global Matters

1 Which English city is home to Britain's oldest university?

2 Which P is a country that has a border with Brazil?

3 Which country has a border with Portugal?

4 In which country is the Taj Mahal?

5 What is the largest city by population in Australia?

6 In which Dutch city can tourists visit the house of Anne Frank?

7 In which country is the most northerly point of the British Isles?

8 KY is the zip code of which U.S. state?

9 In 1837, which building became the residence of the British sovereign?

10 What is the world's smallest ocean?

BACKGROUND BONUS

In which Italian city is Michelangelo's *David* exhibited?

Q 9

ANSWERS

1 Oxford **2** Paraguay **3** Spain **4** India **5** Sydney **6** Amsterdam **7** Scotland **8** Kentucky **9** Buckingham Palace **10** Arctic Ocean

Background Bonus Florence

Scientifically Speaking

Q 1

LEVEL 1 · QUIZ 30

1 Which English scientist discovered the theory of gravity?
2 Which body organ is protected by the cranium?
3 What name is given to a mountain made of ice?
4 What is measured on the Beaufort Scale?
5 In the eye, what controls the size of the pupil?
6 Is a shooting star a meteor or a comet?
7 Which D word describes a volcano that is sleeping?
8 What does a tornado become when it travels over water?
9 What are the nuts of oak trees called?
10 What is the nearest star to Earth?

ANSWERS
1 Isaac Newton 2 The brain 3 Iceberg 4 Wind speed 5 The iris 6 A meteor 7 Dormant 8 A waterspout 9 Acorn 10 The Sun

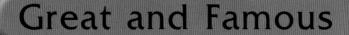

Great and Famous

1 In the Bible, who killed 1,000 Philistines with the jawbone of an ass?

2 According to the legend, who did Peeping Tom peep at?

3 In which garden did Adam and Eve live?

4 Of which game are Gary Kasparov and Nigel Short leading players?

5 What does the W stand for in the name of George W. Bush?

6 In 2003, which actor was appointed governor of California?

Q 4

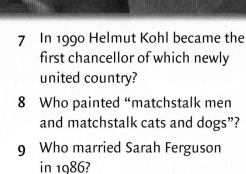

7 In 1990 Helmut Kohl became the first chancellor of which newly united country?

8 Who painted "matchstalk men and matchstalk cats and dogs"?

9 Who married Sarah Ferguson in 1986?

10 In which TV soap based in Denver did Joan Collins play the role of Alexis?

ANSWERS

1 Samson 2 Lady Godiva 3 The Garden of Eden 4 Chess 5 Walker
6 Arnold Schwarzenegger 7 Germany 8 L.S. Lowry 9 Prince Andrew 10 Dynasty

Sporting Chance

1 Which M is used to hit the ball in a game of croquet?

2 What number lies opposite the number 3 on a dartboard?

3 Is the bull's eye on an archery target red, white, yellow or blue?

4 Which Scottish city has twice hosted the Commonwealth Games?

5 Which was the first country to win soccer's World Cup four times?

6 What nationality is soccer player Patrick Viera?

7 Is the cap worn by the goalkeeper in water polo red, blue or green?

8 What name is given to an over in cricket in which no runs have been scored?

9 Which player won the most Men's Singles titles at Wimbledon Tennis Championships in the 1990s?

10 When England beat Argentina 1–0 in the 2002 Soccer World Cup, who scored England's goal?

Q 2

ANSWERS

1 Mallet **2** 20 **3** Yellow **4** Edinburgh **5** Brazil **6** French **7** Red **8** Maiden over **9** Pete Sampras **10** David Beckham

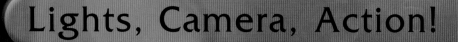

Lights, Camera, Action!

1 What animal completes the name of the movie company, 20th Century... ?

2 Which Disney animation tells of the legend of the young King Arthur?

3 What is the name of the clown, the comedy hero of Bart Simpson?

4 What is the secret identity of Batman?

5 The TV soap *Neighbours* is set in a suburb of which major Australian city?

6 Which basketball superstar is a teammate of Bugs Bunny in the movie *Space Jam*?

Q 2

7 In the movies, who fought Apollo Creed, Clubber Lang and Ivan Drago?

8 What do the initials E.T. stand for?

9 What name is shared by Snoopy's brother and the dog in the Tom and Jerry cartoons?

10 In which English city does Inspector Morse do his detecting?

BACKGROUND BONUS

Which movie saw Johnny Depp starring with Juliette Binoche and Dame Judi Dench?

ANSWERS

1 Fox 2 *The Sword in the Stone* 3 Krusty the Clown 4 Bruce Wayne 5 Melbourne 6 Michael Jordan 7 Rocky Balboa 8 Extra terrestrial 9 Spike 10 Oxford

Background Bonus *Chocolat*

Natural Selection

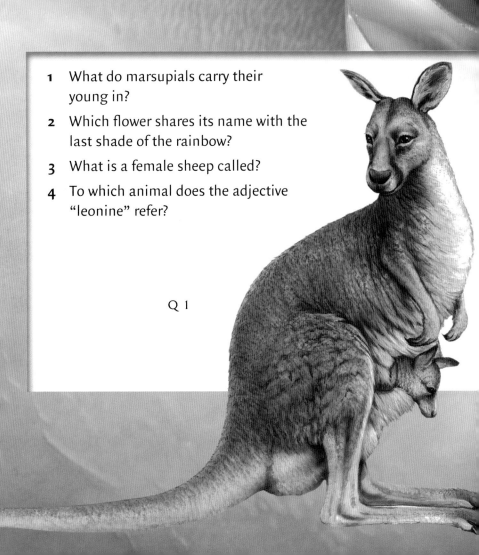

1 What do marsupials carry their young in?
2 Which flower shares its name with the last shade of the rainbow?
3 What is a female sheep called?
4 To which animal does the adjective "leonine" refer?

Q 1

LEVEL 1 · QUIZ 34

5 Which species of crab gets its name from its habit of living in empty seashells?

6 Is the skin of a polar bear black, white or pink?

7 Which G is another name for a eucalyptus tree?

8 How many humps does a bactrian camel have?

9 Which bird is another name for a castle in the game of chess?

10 What name is shared by a young beaver and a young cat?

ANSWERS

1 A pouch **2** Violet **3** Ewe **4** Lion **5** Hermit crab **6** Black, only the fur is white **7** Gum tree **8** Two **9** Rook **10** Kitten

Making History

1 Who were Britain's opponents in the Falklands War?

2 Which governor of Judea ordered the crucifixion of Jesus?

3 Which 15th-century French heroine was known as "the maid of Orléans"?

Q 4

LEVEL 1 • QUIZ 35

4 Which 19th-century U.S. president was assassinated while watching a play?

5 What war did Britain enter in March 1854?

6 Which Venetian explorer visited the court of Kublai Khan in the 1200s?

7 On which mountain did Moses receive the Ten Commandments?

8 Which English king ordered the compilation of the Domesday Book in 1085?

9 In which century did William Shakespeare die?

10 Which year followed 1BC?

ANSWERS

1 Argentina **2** Pontius Pilate **3** Joan of Arc **4** Abraham Lincoln **5** The Crimean War **6** Marco Polo **7** Mount Sinai **8** William the Conqueror **9** The 17th century (1616) **10** 1AD

Musical Madness

Can you identify these musical instruments?

1

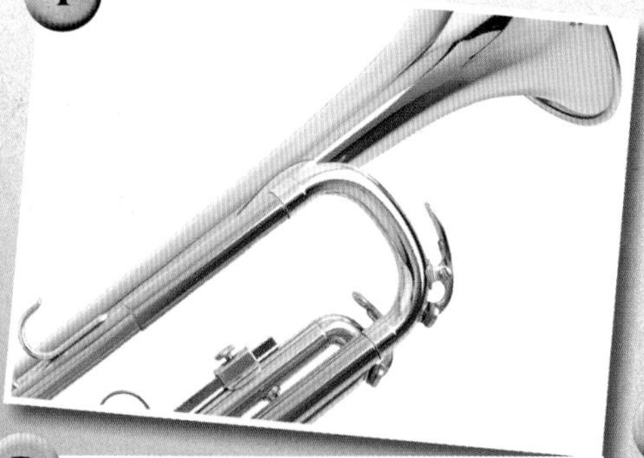

2

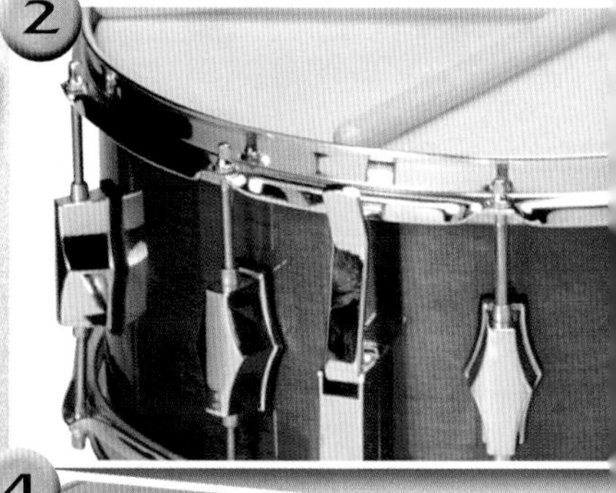

3

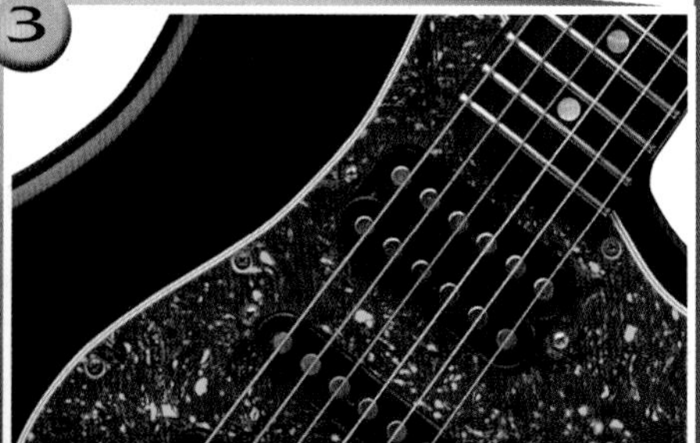

4

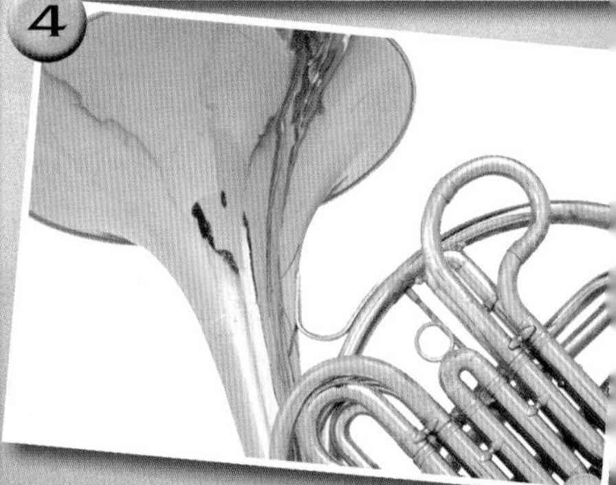

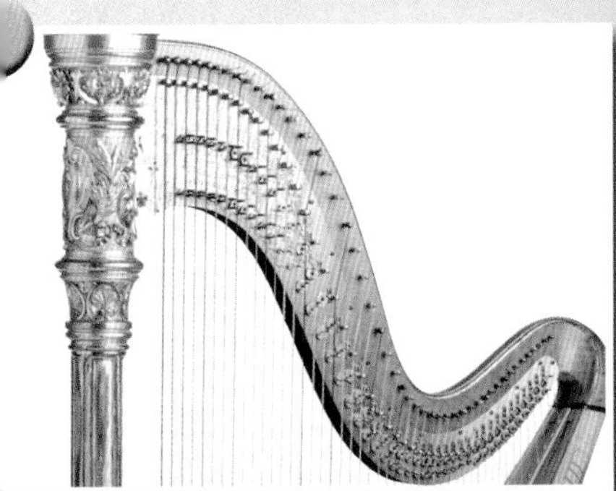

6

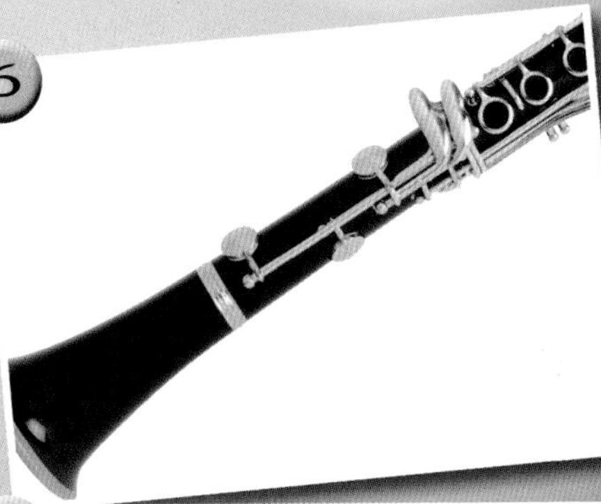

8

ANSWERS

1 Trumpet **2** Drum **3** Electric guitar **4** French horn **5** Harp **6** Clarinet **7** Violin **8** Saxophone

Music Mania

1 Which fountain in Rome, Italy, does the song "Three Coins In A Fountain" refer to?

2 On which Caribbean island did reggae music originate?

3 Which singer joined forces with Lil' Kim, Mya and Christina Aguilera on the 2001 hit "Lady Marmalade"?

4 How are Bryan, Nicky, Shane, Kian and Mark collectively known?

5 Which band's hit record "Teenage Dirtbag" was one of the best selling U.K. singles of 2001?

Q 2

6 Marshall Mathers is the real name of which controversial rap artist?

7 Which song provided the debut single of the short-lived pop group Hear'Say?

8 Bono is lead singer of which Irish rock group?

9 Which F word is the name for the metal ribs on a guitar's fingerboard?

10 Which Canadian singer declared, "Man, I Feel Like A Woman"?

BACKGROUND BONUS

Which 1962 song had Elvis experiencing problems with his mail?

ANSWERS

1 The Trevi Fountain **2** Jamaica **3** Pink **4** Westlife **5** Wheatus **6** Eminem **7** "Pure And Simple" **8** U2 **9** Frets **10** Shania Twain

Background Bonus "Return to Sender"

Total Trivia

1 Penfold is which animated rodent's assistant?

2 Which pachyderm "packed her trunk and said goodbye to the circus"?

3 What type of marine creature is the TV and movie hero, Flipper?

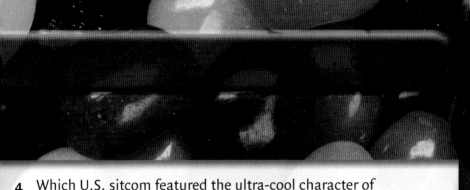

4 Which U.S. sitcom featured the ultra-cool character of the Fonz?

5 Which DC refers to the name given to a vicar's neckwear?

6 What is the first letter of the Greek alphabet?

7 What do the initials MA signify after a person's name?

8 What is Desperate Dan's hometown called?

9 How many different creatures make up the Chinese astrological calendar?

10 *Zwanzig* is German for which number?

ANSWERS

1 Dangermouse 2 Nelly the elephant 3 A dolphin 4 Happy Days 5 Dog collar 6 Alpha 7 Master of Arts 8 Cactusville 9 12 10 20

Global Matters

1 Which river flows beside the Luxor temple in Egypt?
2 The Italian flag is red, white and what?
3 What does the Statue of Liberty hold in her right hand?
4 Which mammal is depicted on the coat of arms of Australia?
5 What is the largest city in Egypt?
6 Which island is separated from the south coast of England by The Solent?
7 Which English county is known as the "red rose" county?
8 Which New Zealand city shares its name with an item of footwear?
9 The word louse is an anagram of which Asian capital city?
10 What is the capital of Iraq?

LEVEL 1 • QUIZ 39

Q 5

ANSWERS

1 The Nile **2** Green **3** A torch **4** Kangaroo **5** Cairo **6** Isle of Wight **7** Lancashire **8** Wellington **9** Seoul **10** Baghdad

Scientifically Speaking

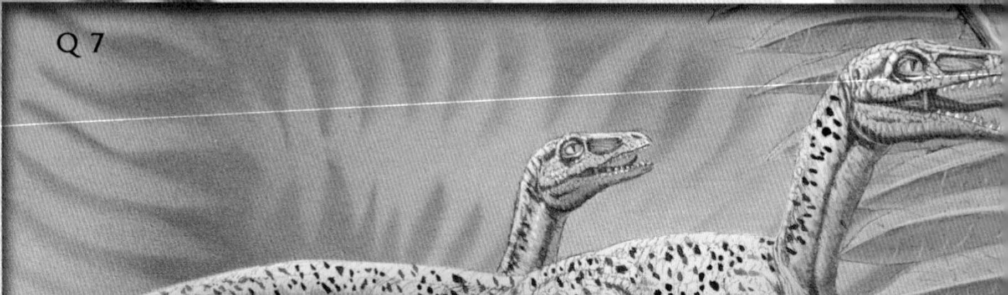

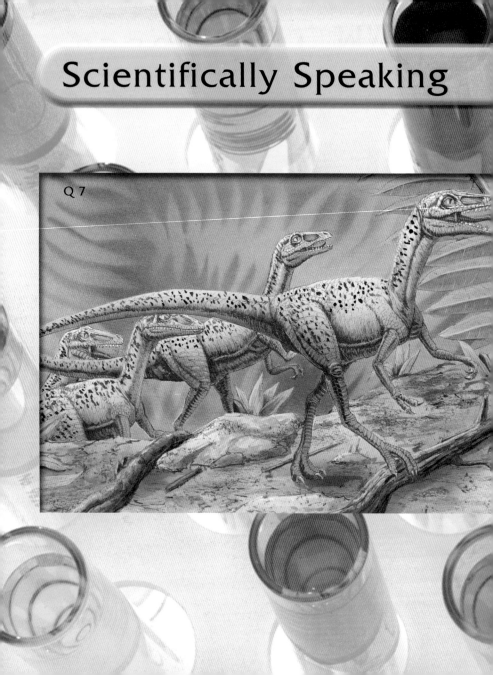

LEVEL 1 • QUIZ 40

1 Alphabetically, which is the first planet in our Solar System?

2 What do the initials REM stand for with regard to sleep patterns?

3 What is the "funnier" name for nitrous oxide?

4 In computing, what do the initials ROM stand for?

5 Which V word means the bones that make up the spine?

6 Cu is the chemical symbol for which metallic element?

7 Which extinct creatures' name means "terrible lizard"?

8 Which part of the body is affected by eczema?

9 Biceps and triceps are both names of what in the human body?

10 What is aeronautics the study of?

ANSWERS

1 Earth **2** Rapid Eye Movement **3** Laughing gas **4** Read Only Memory **5** Vertebrae **6** Copper **7** Dinosaur **8** The skin **9** Muscles **10** Aircraft and flying

Great and Famous

1 Which king of England was known as "the lionheart"?
2 In which movie did Madonna sing "Don't Cry For Me Argentina"?
3 What was Englishman Thomas Chippendale famous for designing?
4 Which musical instrument connects Vanessa Mae and Nigel Kennedy?
5 After which U.S. president were teddy bears named?
6 Which former soap star provides the love interest for Hugh Grant in the 2003 movie *Love Actually*?
7 Which king put his seal on the Magna Carta?
8 Which English soccer team do Ant and Dec support?

BACKGROUND BONUS

Which billionaire entrepreneur has been unlucky with world record attempts?

9 What is the full name of the singer and actress known as J-Lo?

10 What was the name of legendary King Arthur's wizard?

Q 3

ANSWERS

1 Richard I **2** Evita **3** Furniture **4** Violin **5** Theodore Roosevelt **6** Martine McCutcheon **7** King John **8** Newcastle United **9** Jennifer Lopez **10** Merlin

Background Bonus Richard Branson

Written Word

Q 4

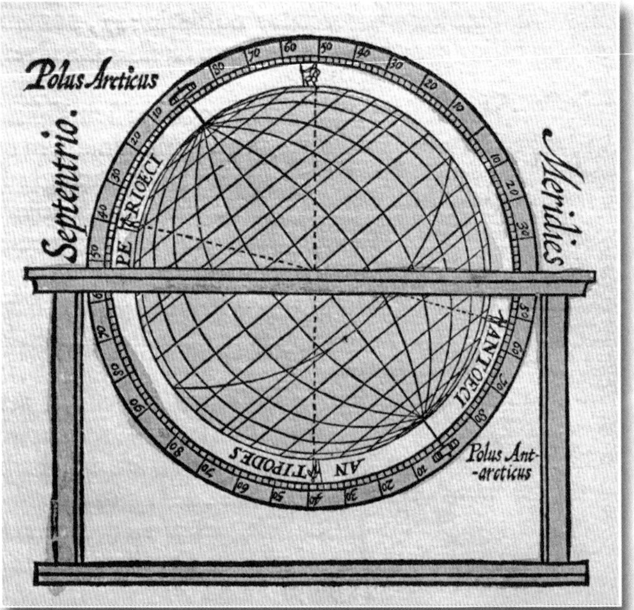

LEVEL 1 · QUIZ 42

1 Which H word can be a type of nut, a girl's name and a shade of brown?

2 Which A word means the ability to use both hands with equal skill?

3 Which number is represented by the prefix "mono"?

4 On a map, what is the opposite of longitude?

5 Which A word is the title given to the commander of a navy?

6 Which C word means the outside line of a circle?

7 What does the symbol % represent?

8 The fabled creature the centaur, is half man and half what?

9 Which M word can go before the words stroke, piece and mind?

10 Which S word is another name for bigfoot or yeti?

ANSWERS

1 Hazel **2** Ambidextrous **3** One **4** Latitude **5** Admiral **6** Circumference **7** Percentage **8** Horse **9** Master **10** Sasquatch

Sporting Chance

1 Which sport combines cross-country skiing and rifle shooting?

2 Which English soccer club does Elton John support?

3 In tennis, what score is known as deuce?

4 Who was sacked as manager of Leeds Utd in 2003?

5 Which horse won the English Derby in 1981 and was kidnapped two years later?

6 Who ended the 2003 Rugby Union World Cup as England's top points scorer?

7 In which Spanish city is the Nou Camp football stadium?

8 Who controversially bit the ear of Evander Holyfield?

9 Which country hosted the 2004 European Nations soccer championships?

10 Which Italian city is the home of Lazio FC?

ANSWERS

1 Biathlon **2** Watford **3** 40 all **4** Peter Reid **5** Shergar **6** Jonny Wilkinson **7** Barcelona **8** Mike Tyson **9** Portugal **10** Rome

Lights, Camera, Action!

1. In which English city is the soap *Hollyoaks* set?
2. Which cartoon series features the characters of Kenny and Chef?
3. In which decade did British families first watch colour TV?

Q 8

4 In which series of movies does Lawrence Fishburne play a character called Morpheus?

5 What is the name of Simba's father in *The Lion King*?

6 What kind of creature is the cartoon character Pepe le Pew?

7 What was the name of Dr. Who's mechanical dog?

8 Which animal was voiced by Eddie Murphy in *Shrek*?

9 Which dinosaur theme park was opened by the movie character of Dr. Hammond?

10 Which warrior princess is portrayed by Lucy Lawless?

ANSWERS

1 Chester **2** *South Park* **3** 1960s **4** *The Matrix* **5** Mustafa **6** Skunk **7** K9 **8** A donkey **9** *Jurassic Park* **10** Xena

Natural Selection

1 Which A word is another name for a viper?
2 Which breed of dog gets its name from the Alsace region of France?
3 Which species of whale is the fastest swimmer?
4 Which B is another name for deadly nightshade?
5 Which girl's name beginning with J is also a female donkey?
6 What is the largest species of ape?
7 How does a giraffe clean behind its ears?
8 What is the only bird that can fly backwards?
9 Which D word is the opposite of evergreen with regard to trees?
10 What do moles mostly eat?

BACKGROUND BONUS

Which animal's stripes can confuse predators?

ANSWERS

1 Adder **2** Alsatian **3** Killer whale **4** Belladonna **5** Jenny **6** Gorilla **7** It licks them with its own tongue **8** Hummingbird **9** Deciduous **10** Worms

Background Bonus Zebra

Written Word

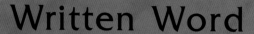

1 What is the name of the little boy in the Christmas story *The Snowman*?

2 Which house does Harry Potter belong to at Hogwart's School?

3 Which A word means a book written by a person about their own life?

LEVEL 1 · QUIZ 46

4 In which country is the novel *The Hunchback of Notre Dame* set?

5 Which children's comic features a bear called Biffo?

6 What is the last name of William in the *Just William* stories?

7 Who lost her sheep in a nursery rhyme?

8 Which tribe of Native Americans does Hawkeye belong to in a novel by James Fenimore Cooper?

9 In which novel is Big Brother watching you?

10 What do the initials BFG stand for in the novel by Roald Dahl?

ANSWERS

1 James **2** Griffindor **3** Autobiography **4** France **5** The Beano **6** Brown **7** Little Bo Peep **8** Mohicans **9** 1984 **10** Big Friendly Giant

Making History

1 Which English and Danish king failed to turn back the tide?

2 Which monk was a companion of Robin Hood?

3 Which Biblical event involving 13 people was painted by Leonardo da Vinci?

4 Whose wife was turned into a pillar of salt in the Bible?

5 Which warrior queen led the Iceni tribe?

6 Which British monarch was known as the Virgin Queen?

7 How many British prime ministers have been assassinated?

8 Which ancient Greek physician gave his name to the oath that is taken by doctors today?

9 What was the middle name of the inventor Thomas Edison?

10 Which C word is the name for knights that supported the king in the English Civil War?

ANSWERS

1 King Canute **2** Friar Tuck **3** The Last Supper **4** Lot's wife **5** Boudicca **6** Elizabeth I **7** One, Spencer Perceval **8** Hippocrates **9** Alva **10** Cavaliers

Name that Rhyme

Can you guess the titles of these nursery rhymes?

1

2

3

4

6

8

ANSWERS

1 I Had Little Nut Tree **2** Wee Willie Winkie **3** Mary Had a Little Lamb **4** Hey Diddle Diddle **5** Baa Baa Black Sheep **6** Mary Mary Quite Contrary **7** The Queen of Hearts **8** There Was an Old Woman

Music Mania

1 In the Christmas song "Jingle Bells", what is the name of the horse?

2 Which boy band had a hit with the song "It's What I Go to School For"?

3 Which Canadian rocker is known as "the groover from Vancouver"?

4 From which European country do the pop group Aqua come?

5 Under what name did Stephen, Shane, Keith, Mikey and Ronan perform?

6 Which Disney character sings "I've Got No Strings"?

7 Which W is the first name of the composer Mozart?

8 What was in a bottle in Christina Aguilera's first hit record?

BACKGROUND BONUS

Which song, released by Bruce Springsteen in 1984, tells the tale of a Vietnam war veteran?

9 What did my true love give to me on the seventh day of Christmas?

10 Which British singer, assisted by the Kumars, had a 2003 hit with "Spirit In The Sky"?

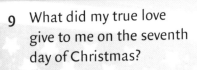

Q 4

ANSWERS

1 Bobtail **2** Busted **3** Bryan Adams **4** Denmark **5** Boyzone **6** Pinocchio **7** Wolfgang **8** A genie **9** Seven swans a-swimming **10** Gareth Gates

Background Bonus "Born in the USA"

Total Trivia

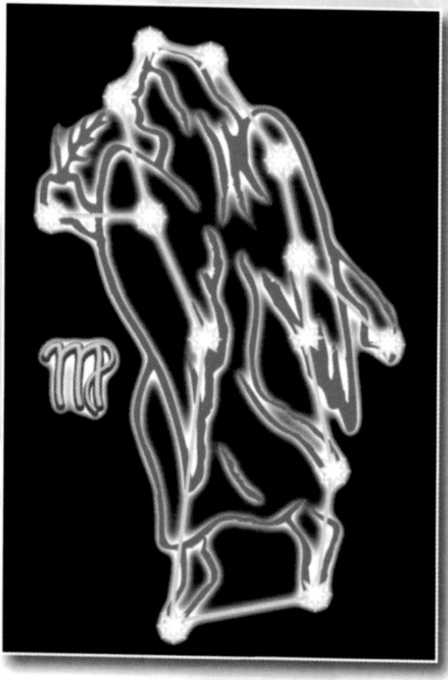

Q 1

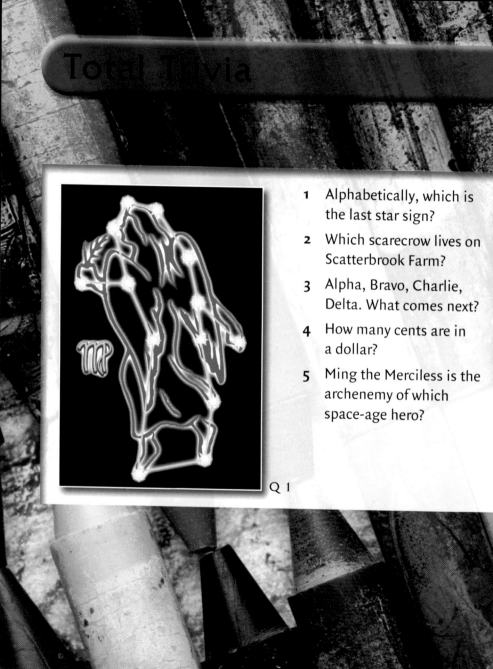

1 Alphabetically, which is the last star sign?

2 Which scarecrow lives on Scatterbrook Farm?

3 Alpha, Bravo, Charlie, Delta. What comes next?

4 How many cents are in a dollar?

5 Ming the Merciless is the archenemy of which space-age hero?

6 Which chess piece can only move diagonally?

7 In which U.S. city does Batman fight crime?

8 Which U word is the English equivalent of an American mortician?

9 Which number is represented in Roman numerals by the letter M?

10 Which enemies of Dr. Who were famous for the phrase "Exterminate, exterminate"?

ANSWERS
1 Virgo 2 Worzel Gummidge 3 Echo 4 100 5 Flash Gordon 6 The bishop 7 Gotham City 8 Undertaker 9 1,000 10 The Daleks

Global Matters

1 What is Spanish for "coast"?

2 In which country is the Aswan Dam?

3 What is the name of England's largest lake?

4 What is the name of the most highly populated city in Turkey?

5 Which is the only U.S. state beginning with the letter P?

6 What is the Arabic name for God?

7 Walloon, German and Flemish are the three official languages of which country?

8 Which is the world's largest desert?

9 What is the name of the chief river in the city of Rome, Italy?

10 Which language, related to Dutch, is spoken in South Africa?

LEVEL 1 • QUIZ 51

ANSWERS

1 Costa **2** Egypt **3** Lake Windermere **4** Istanbul **5** Pennsylvania **6** Allah **7** Belgium **8** Sahara Desert **9** Tiber **10** Afrikaans

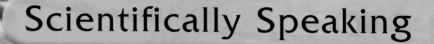

Scientifically Speaking

1 How many sides has a snowflake?
2 What is drawn by a cartographer?
3 Cirrus and cumulus are both types of what?
4 Which gas shares its name with the home planet of Superman?
5 Which P was the world's first antibiotic?
6 Which is the second closest planet to the Sun?
7 Which heavenly body is visible from Earth every 76 years?
8 Name any type of weather that can be described as precipitation.
9 Which prize is awarded annually in six different categories of medicine, chemistry, physics, peace, literature and economics?
10 In computing, what do the initials AOL stand for?

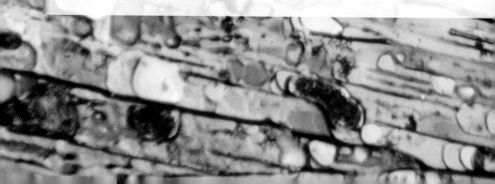

ANSWERS

1 Six **2** Maps **3** Clouds **4** Krypton **5** Penicillin **6** Venus **7** Halley's Comet **8** Rain, snow, hail or sleet **9** The Nobel Prize **10** America On Line

Great and Famous

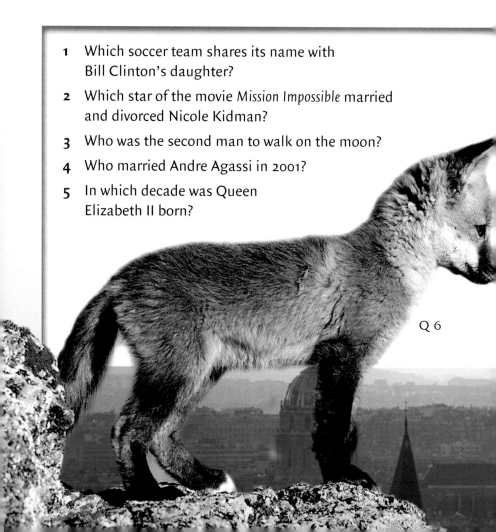

1 Which soccer team shares its name with Bill Clinton's daughter?

2 Which star of the movie *Mission Impossible* married and divorced Nicole Kidman?

3 Who was the second man to walk on the moon?

4 Who married Andre Agassi in 2001?

5 In which decade was Queen Elizabeth II born?

Q 6

6 What is the first name of the character played by David Duchovny in *The X Files*?

7 What is the first name of the character played by Gillian Anderson in *The X Files*?

8 What is the first name of George W. Bush's wife?

9 What was Victoria Beckham's last name before her marriage to David Beckham?

10 Which disciple of Jesus was known as "Doubting"?

BACKGROUND BONUS

Which movie musical stars Gene Kelly and and features the song "I've got rhythm?"

ANSWERS

1 Chelsea **2** Tom Cruise **3** Buzz Aldrin **4** Steffi Graf **5** 1920s (1926) **6** Fox **7** Dana **8** Laura **9** Adams **10** Thomas

Background Bonus *An American in Paris*

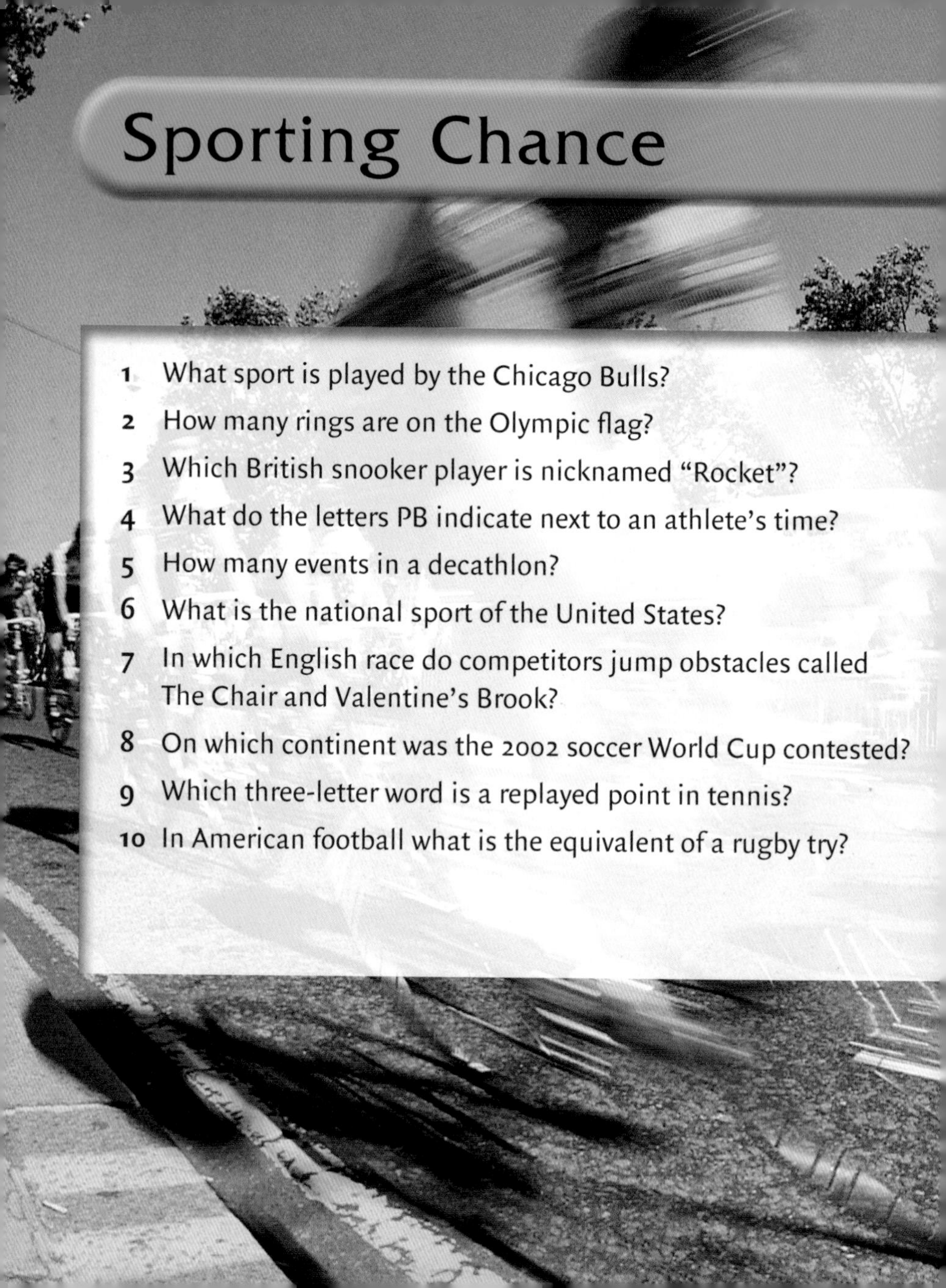

Sporting Chance

1 What sport is played by the Chicago Bulls?
2 How many rings are on the Olympic flag?
3 Which British snooker player is nicknamed "Rocket"?
4 What do the letters PB indicate next to an athlete's time?
5 How many events in a decathlon?
6 What is the national sport of the United States?
7 In which English race do competitors jump obstacles called The Chair and Valentine's Brook?
8 On which continent was the 2002 soccer World Cup contested?
9 Which three-letter word is a replayed point in tennis?
10 In American football what is the equivalent of a rugby try?

Q 1

ANSWERS

1 Basketball **2** Five **3** Ronnie O'Sullivan **4** Personal best **5** Ten **6** Baseball **7** The Grand National **8** Asia **9** Let **10** Touchdown

Lights, Camera, Action!

Q 2

LEVEL 1 · QUIZ 55

1 Which type of animal was forever trying to catch Roadrunner?

2 Which trio have been played in movies by Cameron Diaz, Lucy Liu and Drew Barrymore?

3 Who was the first actor to play James Bond in a movie?

4 What is the Flintstones' family pet called?

5 What is the name of the bear on the TV show *Rainbow*?

6 In which children's TV show were viewers invited to look through the round, square or arched window?

7 In *Coronation Street*, what is the last name of Vera, Jack and Terry?

8 Which musical features the song "Food Glorious Food"?

9 What does Ermintrude the cow always have in her mouth in *The Magic Roundabout*?

10 Who asks the questions on the TV game show *The Weakest Link*?

ANSWERS

1 Coyote **2** Charlie's Angels **3** Sean Connery **4** Dino **5** Bungle **6** Play School **7** Duckworth **8** Oliver! **9** A flower **10** Anne Robinson

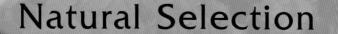

Natural Selection

1 Blue and seal are both varieties of which breed of domestic cat?

2 What animal has three hearts and a skirt?

3 What name is given to a young eel?

4 What animal provides the nickname of the U.S. state of Oregon?

5 The bootlace is the world's longest species of what?

6 What animal does the adjective lupine refer to?

7 Which bird family do robins belong to?

8 What is the name for the offspring of a cob and a pen?

9 Who created the character of Baloo the bear?

10 The name for which dance is also the collective term for a group of rattlesnakes?

LEVEL 1 • QUIZ 56

Q 6

ANSWERS

1 Siamese **2** Octopus **3** Elver **4** Beaver **5** Worm **6** Wolf **7** Thrush **8** Cygnet i.e. baby swan **9** Rudyard Kipling **10** Rumba

Making History

Q 8

BACKGROUND BONUS

Which ancient monuments can still be seen at the town of Giza in Egypt?

1 Who was the first Roman emperor, who gave his name to the eighth month of the year?

2 Which TV show starring Sean Bean was set in the Napoleonic War?

3 In which century did Billy the Kid live and die?

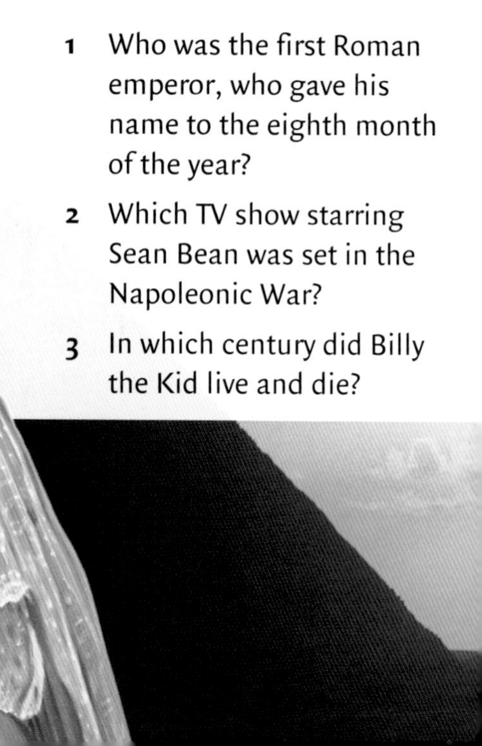

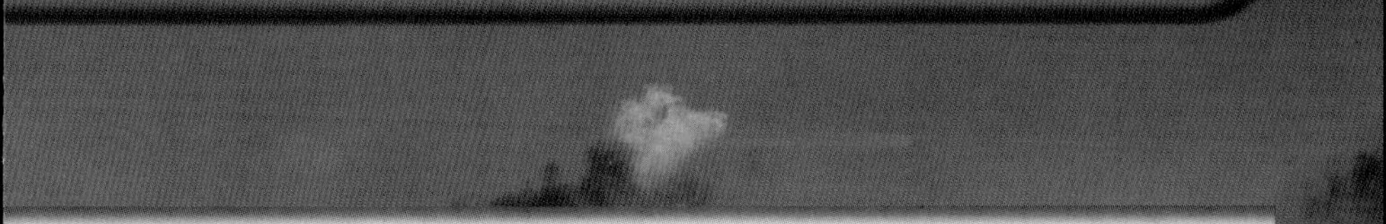

4 In which "flowery" bay was the first convict settlement established in Australia?

5 Was the Channel Tunnel officially opened in 1994, 1995 or 1996?

6 Which 42 km (26 mi) race was named after a battle fought in 490BC?

7 In which country were emperors given the title of Kaiser until 1917?

8 Which British monarch was proclaimed Empress of India in 1877?

9 Which gangster, who led the Chicago Mafia, was known as Scarface?

10 Who was the last wife of Henry VIII?

ANSWERS

1 Augustine **2** Sharpe **3** The 19th century **4** Botany Bay **5** 1994 **6** Marathon **7** Germany **8** Queen Victoria **9** Al Capone **10** Catherine Parr

Background Bonus The pyramids

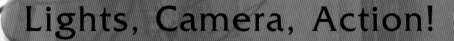

Lights, Camera, Action!

1 Who plays Chief Inspector Dreyfuss in the *Pink Panther* movies?

2 Which actress played Ryan O'Neal's lover in *Love Story*?

3 Sergeant Joe Friday is a character in which TV crime show?

4 In which sitcom did Gwen Taylor play Keith Barron's wife?

5 Which 1953 movie featured a famous love scene between Burt Lancaster and Deborah Kerr?

6 Who connects the movies *Silkwood* and *The Witches of Eastwick*?

7 Who plays the U.S. president in the movie *Mars Attacks*?

8 Which former *Coronation Street* star plays the role of Dolly in *Dinner Ladies*?

9 Which TV series was set in Oxbridge General Hospital?

10 In which movie did Terry Jones announce, "He is not the Messiah, he is a very naughty boy"?

LEVEL 2 · QUIZ 58

Q 5

ANSWERS

1 Herbert Lom **2** Ali McGraw **3** Dragnet **4** Duty Free **5** From Here to Eternity **6** Cher **7** Jack Nicholson **8** Thelma Barlow **9** Emergency Ward **10** The Life of Brian

Natural Selection

1 Which tree has varieties called English, white and slippery?

2 A Suffolk Punch is a breed of what?

3 What is the substance that the body overproduces as a result of allergic reaction to pollen?

4 A rearmouse was an old name for which mammal?

5 Which mammal has webbed feet, lays eggs and has a tail similar to a beaver?

6 The neutered male of which animal is called a barrow?

7 What is the name of the only sea without a coastline, a breeding place for eels?

8 What is apiphobia the fear of?

9 In Scotland, which bird is known as a bubbly jock?

10 Which plant's name is Italian for "beautiful lady"?

ANSWERS

1 Elm 2 Horse 3 Histamine 4 Bat 5 Duck-billed platypus 6 Pig 7 Sargasso Sea 8 Bees 9 Turkey 10 Belladonna

Wonders of the World

Can you identify these famous landmarks?

1

2

3

4

6

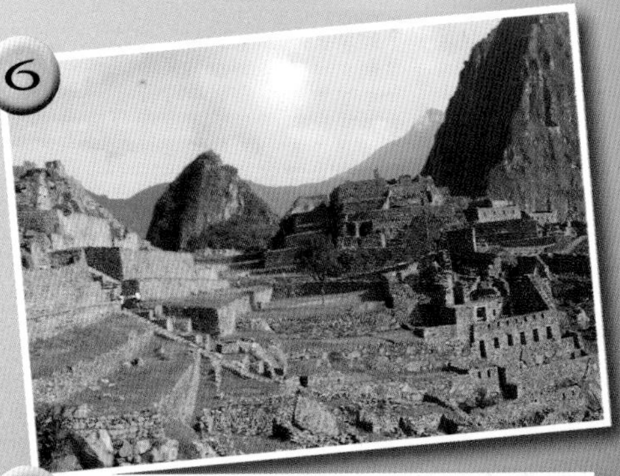

8

ANSWERS

1 Mont St. Michel **2** Niagara Falls **3** Uluru (Ayers Rock) **4** The Great Wall of China **5** Mount Fuji **6** Macchu Pichu **7** Monument Valley **8** Easter Island statues

Written Word

1 Who was the only Brontë sister to marry?

2 Which novel introduced readers to Jo, Meg, Beth and Amy?

3 Which novel by Truman Capote was adapted to a movie starring Audrey Hepburn?

4 Which P.G. Wodehouse character was fond of his Aunt Dahlia but frightened of his Aunt Agatha?

5 Which Shakespeare character died on a battlefield without a horse?

6 Whose first novel was *The Hunt for Red October*?

7 In the Bible, who ascended to heaven by climbing a ladder?

8 Who wrote the book *The History of the World* while captive in the Tower of London?

BACKGROUND BONUS

Which book, written by Francis Hodgson Burnett, features a spoilt little girl called Mary?

9 Under what name did Alfred Wight write several best-selling novels about a vet?

10 What is the title of the third book in *The Lord of the Rings* trilogy?

Q 3

ANSWERS

1 Charlotte Brontë **2** *Little Women* **3** *Breakfast at Tiffany's* **4** Bertie Wooster **5** Richard III **6** Tom Clancy **7** Jacob **8** Sir Walter Raleigh **9** James Herriot **10** *The Return of the King* **Background Bonus** *The Secret Garden*

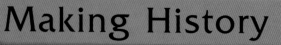

Making History

1 Name any year that the composer Frédéric Chopin was alive.

2 What does the M stand for in Richard M. Nixon?

3 After which historic explorer is Venice's international airport named?

4 Which mythological hero killed the gorgon Medusa?

5 Who was elected governor of California, United States, in 1966?

6 Sir Walter Raleigh and Sir Francis Drake were both born in which county?

7 Born in 1678, which composer was known as the Red Priest?

8 Who was king of Great Britain during World War II?

9 Oak Apple Day, on 29th May, commemorates the birthday of which British monarch?

10 Who was the first woman to be shot dead by the FBI?

Q 9

ANSWERS

1 1810 to 1849 **2** Milhouse **3** Marco Polo **4** Perseus **5** Ronald Reagan **6** Devon **7** Antonio Vivaldi **8** George VI **9** Charles II **10** Bonnie Parker

Music Mania

Q 10

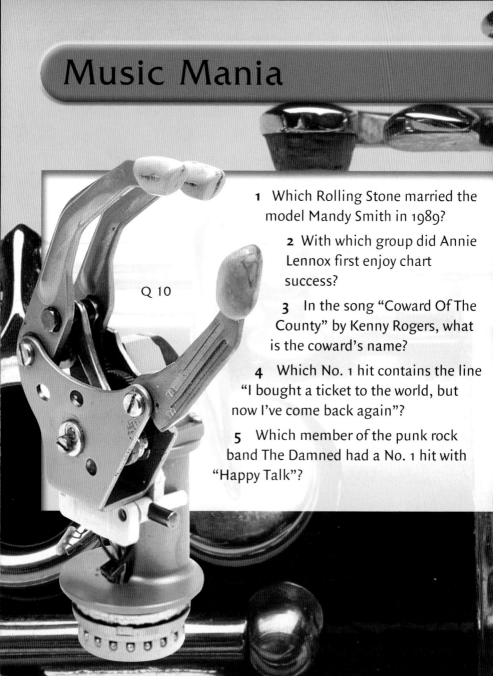

1 Which Rolling Stone married the model Mandy Smith in 1989?

2 With which group did Annie Lennox first enjoy chart success?

3 In the song "Coward Of The County" by Kenny Rogers, what is the coward's name?

4 Which No. 1 hit contains the line "I bought a ticket to the world, but now I've come back again"?

5 Which member of the punk rock band The Damned had a No. 1 hit with "Happy Talk"?

6 What is Elvis Presley's Memphis mansion called?

7 On which island was Freddie Mercury born?

8 What is the usual stage attire of rock guitarist Angus Young of AC/DC?

9 Who narrated the video for Michael Jackson's "Thriller"?

10 What was the first James Bond theme performed by Shirley Bassey?

ANSWERS

1 Bill Wyman 2 The Tourists 3 Tommy 4 "True" 5 Captain Sensible 6 Graceland 7 Zanzibar 8 A school uniform 9 Vincent Price 10 "Goldfinger"

Total Trivia

LEVEL 2 · QUIZ 64

1 Which is the only reptile to represent a year in the Chinese astrological calendar?

2 Which Dickens' novel features the character of Little Emily?

3 In the womb, which cord connects the baby to the placenta?

4 What is the American equivalent of the Victoria Cross?

5 Which newspaper was edited by Ken Barlow in *Coronation Street*?

6 What is the clergyman's name in the board game of Cluedo?

7 What is Britain's first nuclear power station called?

8 Which is the world's tallest bird?

9 Alphabetically, which is the last U.S. state?

10 Which Firth separates Scotland from the northwest coast of Cumbria?

ANSWERS

1 Snake **2** *David Copperfield* **3** Umbilical cord **4** Congressional Medal of Honors **5** *Weatherfield Recorder* **6** Reverend Green **7** Calder Hall **8** Ostrich **9** Wyoming **10** Solway Firth

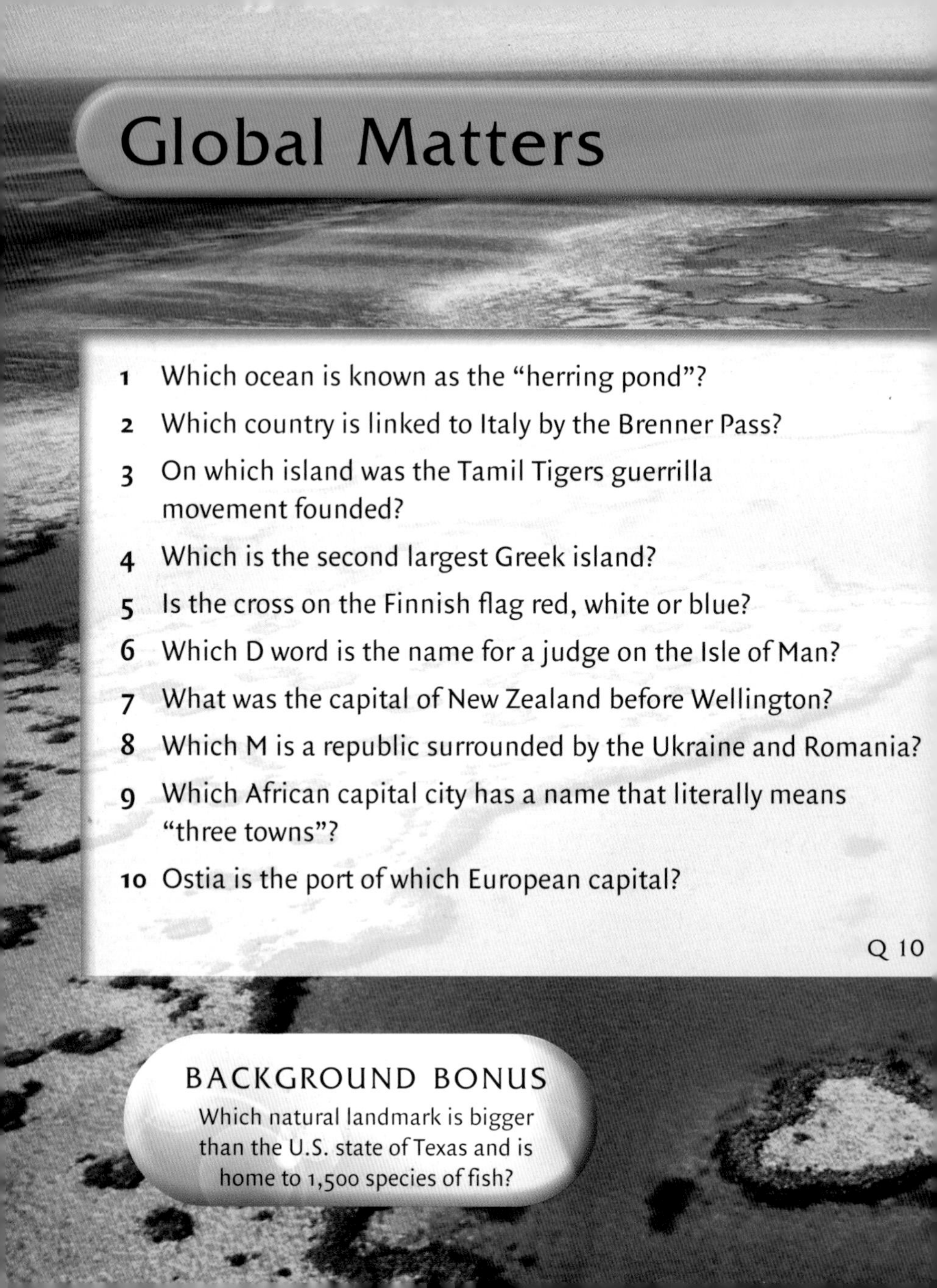

Global Matters

1 Which ocean is known as the "herring pond"?

2 Which country is linked to Italy by the Brenner Pass?

3 On which island was the Tamil Tigers guerrilla movement founded?

4 Which is the second largest Greek island?

5 Is the cross on the Finnish flag red, white or blue?

6 Which D word is the name for a judge on the Isle of Man?

7 What was the capital of New Zealand before Wellington?

8 Which M is a republic surrounded by the Ukraine and Romania?

9 Which African capital city has a name that literally means "three towns"?

10 Ostia is the port of which European capital?

BACKGROUND BONUS

Which natural landmark is bigger than the U.S. state of Texas and is home to 1,500 species of fish?

ANSWERS

1 Atlantic Ocean **2** Austria **3** Sri Lanka **4** Rhodes **5** Blue **6** Deemster **7** Auckland **8** Moldovia **9** Tripoli **10** Rome

Background Bonus The Great Barrier Reef

Scientifically Speaking

Q 2

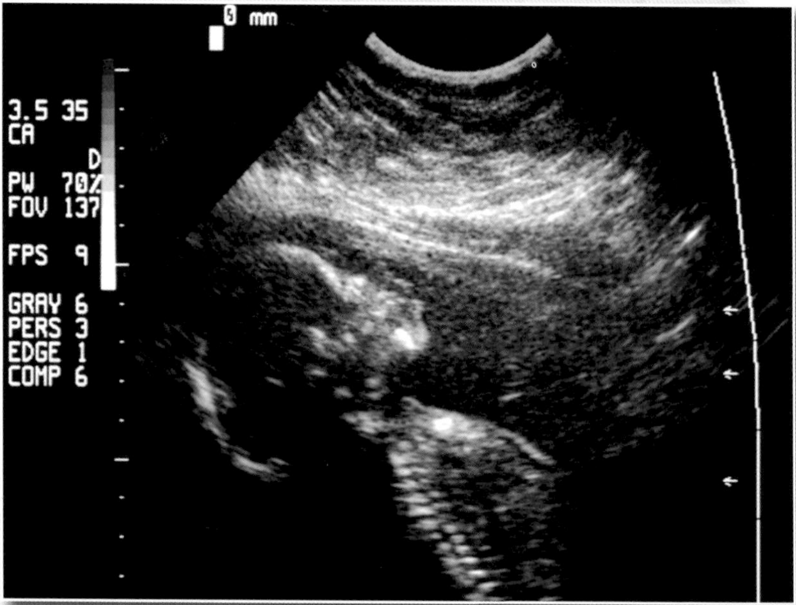

1 What forms in the body by the process of ossification?

2 What does a Gravindex test detect in women?

3 Which element is also known by the name of quicksilver?

4 What is the name of Jupiter's largest moon?

5 Which P word is a substance that is given in place of a drug?

6 The patella is the medical name for which bone?

7 In World War II, who invented the bouncing bomb?

8 NaCl is the chemical symbol for what?

9 Are the science and nature questions in a game of Trivial Pursuit red or green?

10 What is the name of the moon closest to the Autumn Equinox?

ANSWERS

1 Bones **2** Pregnancy **3** Mercury **4** Ganymede **5** Placebo **6** Kneecap **7** Barnes Wallis **8** Salt **9** Green **10** Harvest moon

Great and Famous

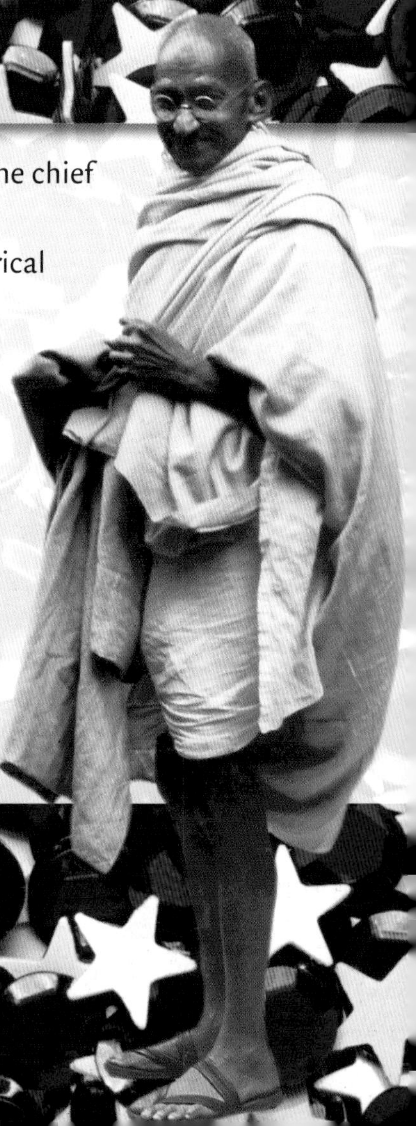

1 What nationality is Hans Blix, the chief weapons inspector in Iraq?

2 For his portrayal of which historical figure did Ben Kingsley win an Oscar?

3 Who designed Madonna's wedding dress for her marriage to Guy Ritchie?

4 Who was the first female speaker in the House of Commons?

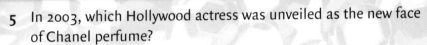

5 In 2003, which Hollywood actress was unveiled as the new face of Chanel perfume?

6 The autobiography of which entertainer is entitled *Its Hello From Him?*

7 Who was named director of the CIA in 1976 and went on to become U.S. president?

8 Who wrote the first book of the New Testament?

9 In which British city did the infamous body snatchers Burke and Hare operate?

10 Who wrote the poem *The Owl and the Pussycat?*

ANSWERS

1 Swedish 2 Gandhi 3 Stella McCartney 4 Betty Boothroyd 5 Nicole Kidman 6 Ronnie Barker 7 George Bush Snr. 8 Matthew 9 Edinburgh 10 Edward Lear

Sporting Chance

1. Which baseball star was known as the Yankee Clipper?
2. Who was the first woman to train a Grand National winner?
3. In cricket, what is a golden duck?
4. In which South American city is the Maracana soccer stadium?
5. In which sport is Bruce Penhall a former world champion?
6. Which nationality is the former snooker champion Cliff Thorburn?
7. In snooker, how many times is the black ball potted when making a maximum 147 break?
8. At Lords cricket ground, what is the name of the gallery where the Ashes are kept?
9. Which sports company is named after a South African antelope?
10. In which ball sport does the net stand 2.43 m (8 ft) high?

LEVEL 2 · QUIZ 68

Q 4

ANSWERS

1 Joe Di Maggio **2** Jenny Pitman **3** Out for zero off the first ball **4** Rio de Janeiro **5** Speedway **6** Canadian **7** 16 **8** Memorial Gallery **9** Reebok **10** Volleyball

Lights, Camera, Action!

BACKGROUND BONUS

In the 1996 movie *Jerry Maguire*, what was the profession of the central character, played by Tom Cruise?

1 Who played Clayton Farlowe in *Dallas*?

2 The movie *Out of Africa* is set in which country?

3 Which musical features the song "If I Were A Rich Man"?

4 Who played Forrest Gump's mother in the movie?

5 In which movie did Patrick Swayze play Sam, Demi Moore play Molly and Whoopi Goldberg play Oda Mae?

6 In which TV series did Nick Berry play the role of PC Rowan?

7 Rex Harrison played Professor Henry Higgins in which musical?

8 Which 1996 movie featured a striptease group called Hot Metal?

9 Name the actor, who died in 2002, famed for playing Dutch detective Van Der Valk.

10 At which German movie festival is the Golden Bear presented for the best movie?

ANSWERS

1 Howard Keel **2** Kenya **3** *Fiddler on the Roof* **4** Sally Field **5** *Ghost* **6** *Heartbeat* **7** *My Fair Lady* **8** *The Full Monty* **9** Barry Foster **10** The Berlin Film Festival

Background Bonus Sports agent

Natural Selection

1 What is a young zebra called?

2 Which three-letter R word is the mating season of deers?

3 What is an animal's spoor?

4 Which P word, pertaining to thick skin, describes elephants and rhinos?

5 Which bird has species called gold, green and zebra?

6 Which bird family does the jay belong to?

7 Which F word is the wide lobes of a whale's tail?

8 Is a Colorado beetle black and white or black and yellow?

9 Which plant is St. Peter said to have used to illustrate the Holy Trinity?

10 Which L word is a sticky wax obtained from sheep?

Q 6

ANSWERS

1 Foal **2** Rut **3** Its track or footprint **4** Pachyderm **5** Finch **6** Crow **7** Fluke **8** Yellow **9** Shamrock **10** Lanolin

Written Word

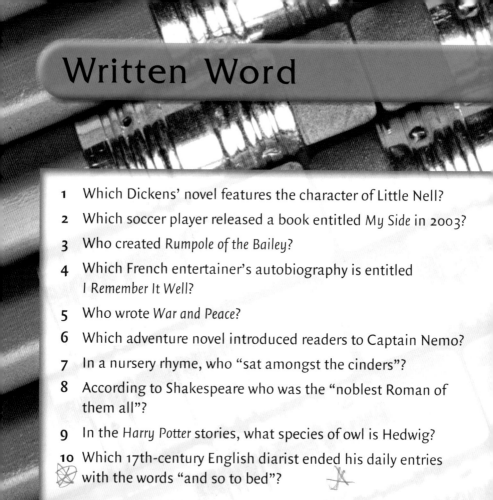

1 Which Dickens' novel features the character of Little Nell?

2 Which soccer player released a book entitled *My Side* in 2003?

3 Who created *Rumpole of the Bailey*?

4 Which French entertainer's autobiography is entitled *I Remember It Well*?

5 Who wrote *War and Peace*?

6 Which adventure novel introduced readers to Captain Nemo?

7 In a nursery rhyme, who "sat amongst the cinders"?

8 According to Shakespeare who was the "noblest Roman of them all"?

9 In the *Harry Potter* stories, what species of owl is Hedwig?

10 Which 17th-century English diarist ended his daily entries with the words "and so to bed"?

Q 9

ANSWERS

1 *The Old Curiosity Shop* **2** David Beckham **3** John Mortimer **4** Maurice Chevalier **5** Leo Tolstoy **6** *20,000 Leagues Under the Sea* **7** Little Polly Flinders **8** Brutus **9** Snowy owl **10** Samuel Pepys

Feathers and Fur

Can you identify these animals by their feathers, fur and skin?

1

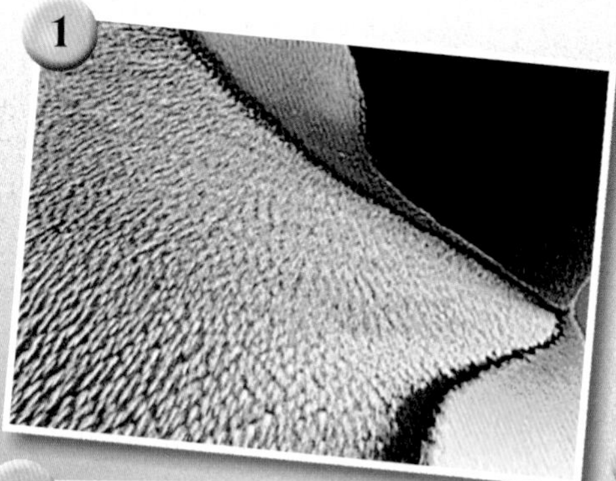

2

3

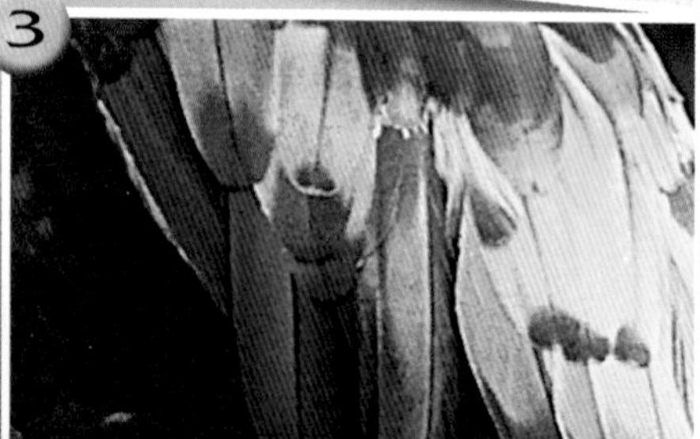

4

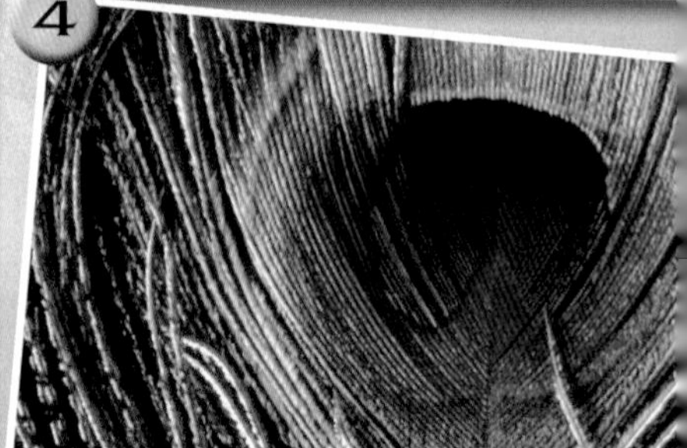

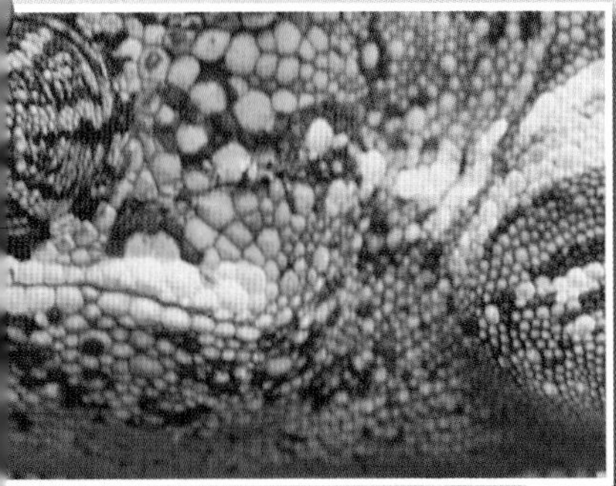

6

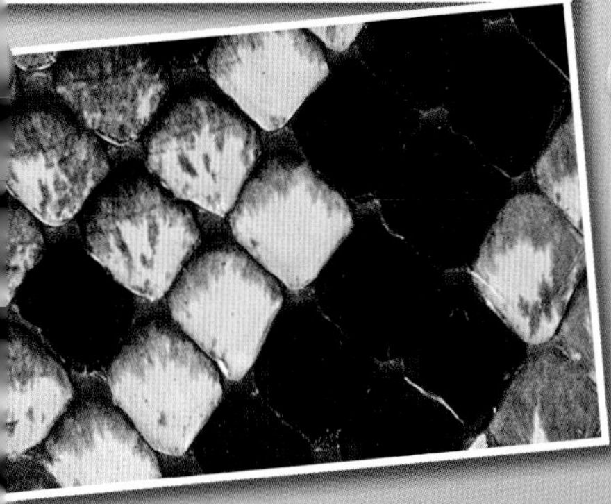

8

ANSWERS

1 Penguin 2 Fawn 3 Parrot 4 Peacock 5 Chameleon 6 Butterfly 7 Snake 8 Cheetah

Making History

1 What was the name of the outlawed brother of Jesse James?

2 In Arthurian legend who was the half sister of King Arthur?

3 Which financial crash occurred in the United States in 1929?

4 Who was assassinated in 1916 and became the subject of a hit record for Boney M?

5 Which robber was released by Pontius Pilate instead of Jesus?

6 In which month do the French celebrate Bastille Day?

7 Who is buried beneath the Arc de Triomphe?

8 *A Tale of Two Cities* by Charles Dickens is set in London and which other European city?

9 In which decade was William the Conqueror born?

10 Henry VII and Elizabeth I were members of which royal dynasty?

BACKGROUND BONUS

Which explosive invention is thought to have been developed by the Chinese in the 6th century?

LEVEL 2 • QUIZ 73

Q8

ANSWERS

1 Frank **2** Morgan le Fay **3** The Wall Street Crash **4** Rasputin **5** Barabbas **6** July **7** The Unknown Soldier **8** Paris **9** 1020s **10** Tudor

Background Bonus Fireworks

Music Mania

1 Ziggy Stardust was the alter ego of which rock star?
2 Which country and western singer married Julia Roberts?
3 Which F is a small flute and a region in Scotland?
4 Which song has been a hit for Little Eva and Kylie Minogue?
5 In which musical did Michael Crawford sing "Music Of The Night"?
6 Which hit for Madonna opens with the line "I made it through the wilderness"?
7 Who links the pop duos Erasure and Yazoo?
8 Which Elvis Presley hit took the Pet Shop Boys to No. 1 in 1987?
9 Which James Bond theme was performed by Gladys Knight?
10 What four words provide the title of a hit for 10CC and the motto of MGM studios?

ANSWERS

1 David Bowie **2** Lyle Lovett **3** Fife **4** "The Locomotion" **5** The Phantom of the Opera **6** "Like A Virgin" **7** Vince Clarke **8** "Always On My Mind" **9** "Licence to Kill" **10** "Art for Arts Sake"

Total Trivia

1 In which month is Thanksgiving Day celebrated in the United States?

2 *The Toronto Star* is the best-selling newspaper in which country?

3 What is the traditional occupation of a leprechaun?

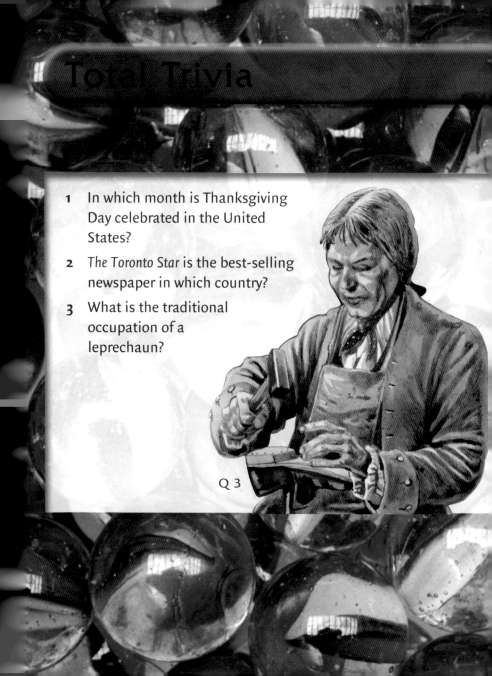

Q 3

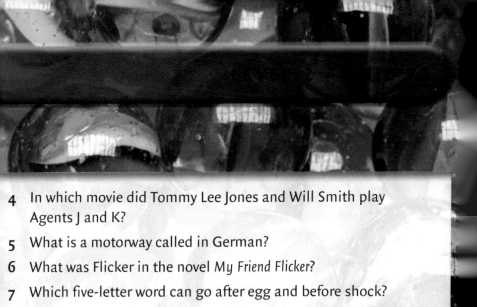

4 In which movie did Tommy Lee Jones and Will Smith play Agents J and K?

5 What is a motorway called in German?

6 What was Flicker in the novel *My Friend Flicker*?

7 Which five-letter word can go after egg and before shock?

8 What is a spectacular fall in the sport of surfing called?

9 Which was the first country to issue postage stamps?

10 Which word can link an item of clothing, a variety of potato and the name of an island?

[redacted]

Global Matters

1. In which country is the Islamic holy city of Mecca?
2. Which range of mountains separates the highlands and lowlands of Scotland?
3. Which African country was invaded by Italy in 1935 and aided by Bob Geldof 50 years later?
4. Which S is the capital of the Andalusia region of Spain?
5. In which country did denim originate?
6. Is the background of the Turkish flag white or red?
7. Which country is home to over half the world's tigers?
8. In which British city is Aston University?
9. MN is the zip code of which U.S. state?
10. Which is the only U.S. state to get its name from an English county?

Q 4

ANSWERS

1 Saudi Arabia **2** Grampians **3** Ethiopia **4** Seville **5** France **6** Red **7** India **8** Birmingham **9** Minnesota **10** New Hampshire

Scientifically Speaking

1 Which gas solidifies to form dry ice?
2 What is the medical name for the skull?
3 Which is the largest tendon in the human body?
4 Which organ of the body produces insulin?
5 What does the A stand for in DNA?
6 K is the chemical symbol for which element?
7 As used by a teacher, what is the common name for calcium carbonate?
8 Which R word describes the bending of light as it passes from one medium to another?
9 What does a seismograph record the intensity of?
10 What is the common name for a scapula?

BACKGROUND BONUS

What carries a current of 10,000 amps and is hotter than the surface of the Sun?

Q 7

ANSWERS

1 Carbon dioxide **2** Cranium **3** Achilles tendon **4** Pancreas **5** Acid **6** Potassium **7** Chalk **8** Refraction **9** Earthquakes **10** Shoulder blade

Background Bonus Lightning

Great and Famous

1 Who is the eldest of the Bee Gees?

2 What sort of animal was the artist George Stubbs famous for painting?

3 In the Bible, who was the younger brother of Cain and Abel?

4 Who commanded the losing forces at the Battle of the Little Big Horn?

5 What was the four-letter surname of Buffalo Bill?

Q 6

LEVEL 2 · QUIZ 78

6 Who has been played on the big screen by Judi Dench, Cate Blanchett and Glenda Jackson?

7 In which decade was Gerald Ford president of the United States?

8 Which American soccer player is known as The Refrigerator?

9 Which comedy duo's fan club members are known as The Sons of the Desert?

10 Which actor, who played James Bond, was born in Wales?

ANSWERS

1 Barry Gibb 2 Horses 3 Seth 4 General George Custer 5 Cody 6 Queen Elizabeth I
7 1970s 8 William Perry 9 Laurel and Hardy 10 Timothy Dalton

Written Word

1 *Down the Rabbit Hole* is the first chapter of which novel?

2 Speedwell, Holly, Hazel and Dandelion are all names of what?

3 Which lawyer made his literary debut in the 1933 story *The Case of the Velvet Claws?*

4 The movie *The Slipper and the Rose* was based on which popular fairytale?

5 Who owned a dog called Jip and a pig called Gub?

6 Which three-word phrase is the French term for a pen name?

7 Which Scottish-born novelist is commemorated by a statue on Prince Street in Edinburgh?

8 Which diarist connects the author Helen Fielding and the movie star Renee Zellweger?

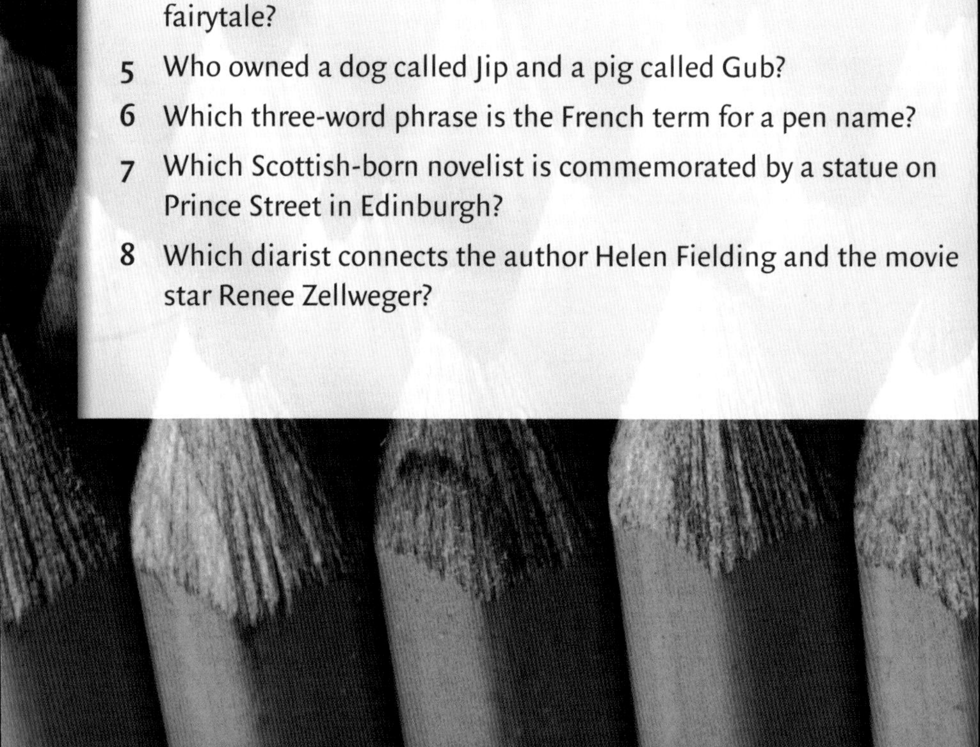

9 Which play contains the line, "Something rotten in the state of Denmark"?

10 Which series of tales begins with the *Knight's Tale* and ends with the *Parson's Tale*?

Q 1

ANSWERS

1 *Alice's Adventures in Wonderland* **2** *Rabbits in Watership Down* **3** Perry Mason **4** Cinderella **5** Dr. Doolittle **6** Nom de plume **7** Sir Walter Scott **8** Bridget Jones **9** Hamlet **10** *Canterbury Tales*

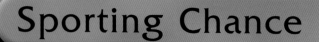

Sporting Chance

1 Which U.S. sport is governed by the Harvard Rules?

2 In which European country is Feyenoord soccer club based?

3 At the opening ceremony of the 2000 Sydney Olympics, which U.S. golfer carried the Olympic torch?

4 In ice hockey, what is a puck made from?

5 In which sport is a parachute known as a laundry used?

6 Which pet name is shared by Newcastle United and Notts County foorball clubs?

7 Who is the pop star nephew of the 1959 FA Cup winner Roy Dwight?

8 In which city did Australian Rules soccer originate?

9 Straddle and western roll are both styles of what?

10 Which metal is the alternative name for a golf club?

Q 6

ANSWERS

1 American football **2** Netherlands **3** Greg Norman **4** Vulcanised rubber **5** Drag racing **6** The Magpies **7** Elton John **8** Melbourne **9** High jump **10** Iron

Lights, Camera, Action!

Q 7

1 How old was Mickey Mouse in 2003?

2 Who played the title role in *Magnum PI*?

3 Which TV cop was famed for sucking lollipops?

4 *Holby City* was a spin off from which medical drama?

BACKGROUND BONUS

In which city are the movies *Notting Hill* and *Love Actually* both set?

5 Which biblical character has been played in movies by Charlton Heston, Burt Lancaster and Mel Brooks?

6 Who played the title role in the 1965 movie *Dr. Zhivago*?

7 Which police TV series is set at Sun Hill Station?

8 Which actor, who shot to fame as a TV cop, had a 1977 No. 1 hit with the song "Silver Lady"?

9 In Disney's animated version of *Robin Hood*, which animal represented Robin?

10 Who won a Best Actress Oscar for her role in the movie *Moonstruck*?

ANSWERS

1 75 **2** Tom Selleck **3** Kojak **4** *Casualty* **5** Moses **6** Omar Sharif **7** *The Bill*
8 David Soul **9** Fox **10** Cher
Background Bonus London

Natural Selection

1 What name is given to a young hippopotamus?
2 The quagga, now extinct, is related to which equine animal?
3 The branches of which tree appear on the United Nations flag?
4 What is a male duck called?
5 Which K is the staple diet of baleen whales?
6 Which marine creature provides the last name of Miami's American Football team?
7 Which breed of dog does Queen Elizabeth II seem to prefer?
8 From which flower is vanilla extracted?
9 Which W is the national flower of Australia?
10 What is an eel's young called?

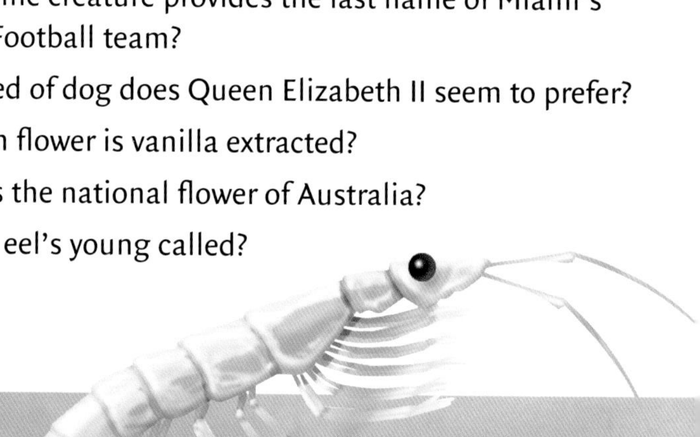

LEVEL 2 · QUIZ 82

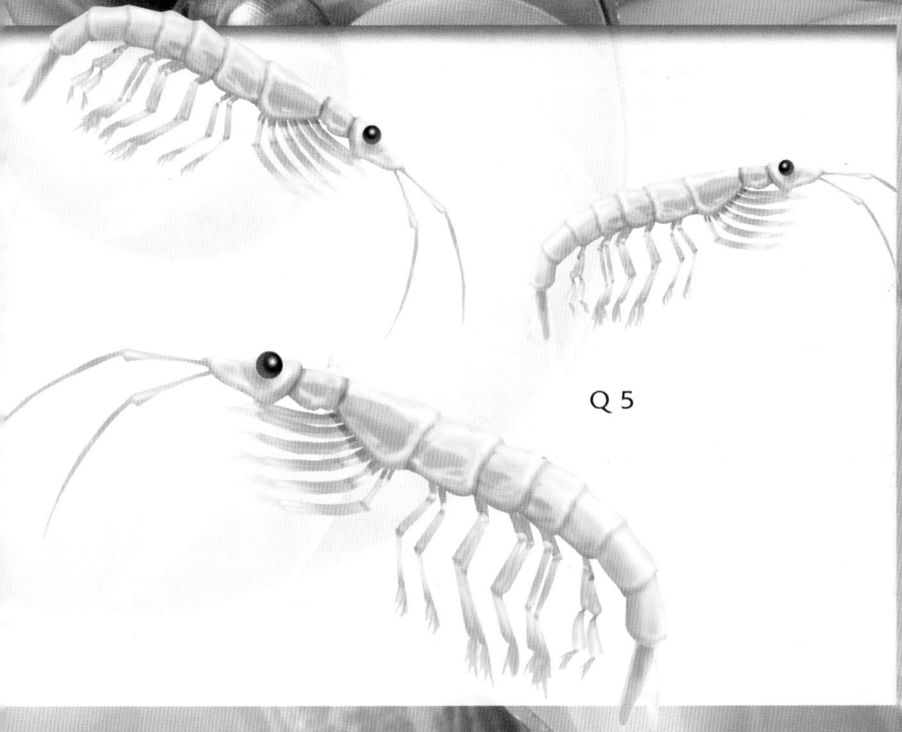

Q 5

ANSWERS

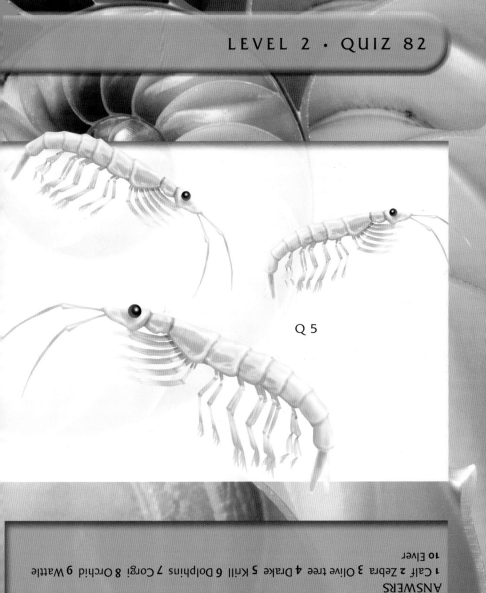

1 Calf **2** Zebra **3** Olive tree **4** Drake **5** Krill **6** Dolphins **7** Corgi **8** Orchid **9** Wattle **10** Elver

Written Word

1 Anne Shirley is the main character in which L.M. Montgomery novel?

2 Which adventure novel features Billy Bones and Long John Silver?

3 Which literary detective has been played in the movies by Peter Cushing, Peter Cook and Basil Rathbone?

4 On whose fairytale was the Disney movie *The Little Mermaid* based?

5 What type of animal is Jeremy Fisher in the Beatrix Potter stories?

6 What is the name of the professor who is Count Dracula's nemesis?

7 Which doctor created the Grinch?

8 What does the J stand for in J.R.R. Tolkien?

9 Which R is the last book of the Bible?

10 In which movie adaptation of a Stephen King novel did Jack Nicholson play the caretaker of the Overlook Hotel?

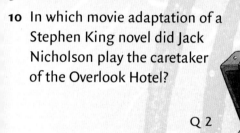

Q 2

ANSWERS

1 Anne of Green Gables 2 Treasure Island 3 Sherlock Holmes 4 Hans Christian Andersen 5 A frog 6 Professor Van Helsing 7 Dr. Seuss 8 John 9 Revelations 10 The Shining

Name the Sport

Can you identify the sports from these pictures?

1

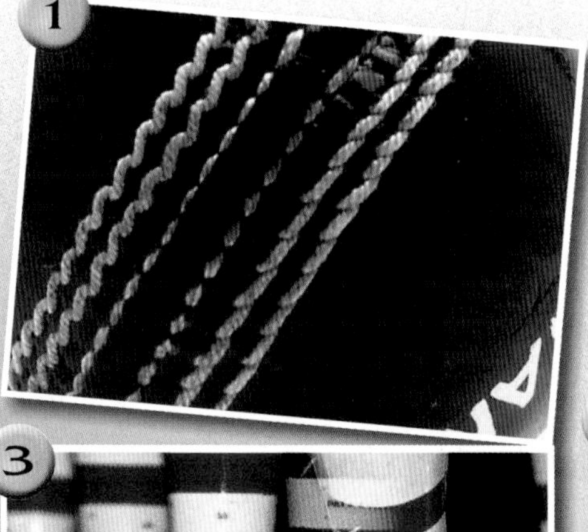

2

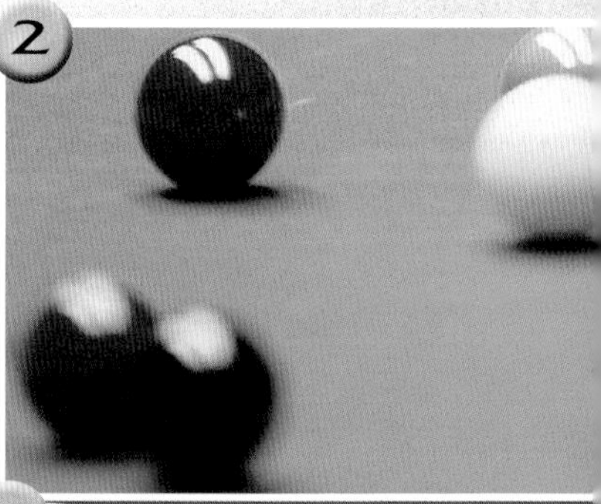

3

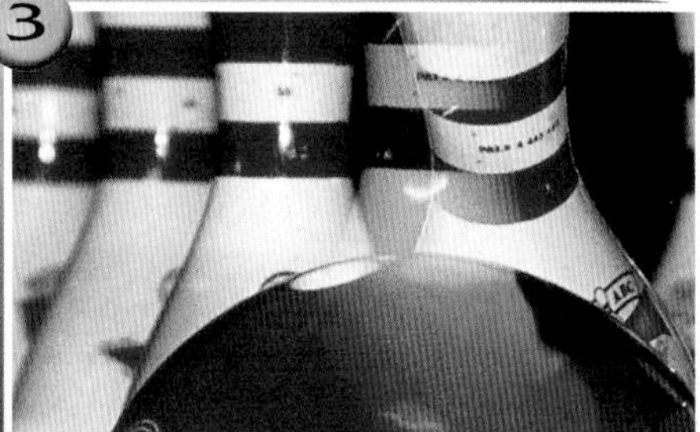

4

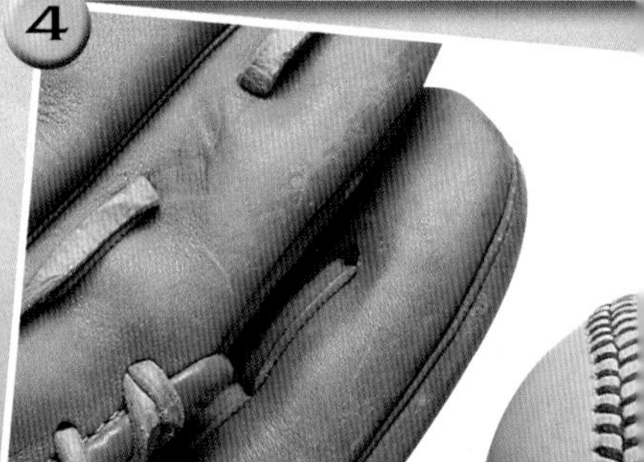

6

8
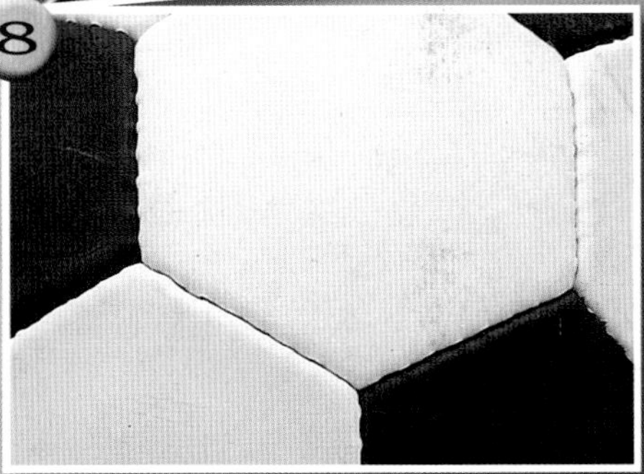

ANSWERS
1 Cricket 2 Snooker 3 Ten-pin bowling 4 Baseball 5 Golf 6 Tennis 7 Basketball 8 Soccer

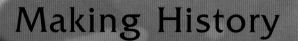

Making History

BACKGROUND BONUS

Which three political leaders became known as "The big three" during World War II?

1 What was the original name of Francis Drake's flagship *Golden Hind*?

2 From 1952 to 1999, which country was ruled by King Hussein?

3 Who played the role of Queen Elizabeth I in *Blackadder*?

4 In World War II, what was the second Japanese city to be devastated by an atomic bomb?

5 In which movie did Mel Gibson play William Wallace?

6 Which defender of the Alamo owned a rifle called Old Betsy?

7 Which English school was founded in 1440 by Henry IV?

8 Who married Prince Rainier of Monaco in 1956?

9 Who was the first person to see Jesus after his resurrection?

10 Who became president of the United States after John F. Kennedy's death?

ANSWERS

1 *The Pelican* **2** Jordan **3** Miranda Richardson **4** Nagasaki **5** *Braveheart* **6** Davy Crockett **7** Eton **8** Grace Kelly **9** Mary Magdalene **10** Lyndon B. Johnson

Background Bonus Churchill, Roosevelt and Stalin

Music Mania

1 In which country was Bob Marley granted a state funeral?

2 Who had a 1970s Christmas No. 1 hit with "When A Child Is Born"?

Q 4

LEVEL 2 · QUIZ 86

3 What was the first No. 1 hit for Tom Jones?

4 Which nationality was composer Giamaco Puccini?

5 Which singer's backing group is called The News?

6 In a song from the musical *My Fair Lady*, in which country does rain fall?

7 Which country and western star opened a theme park called Dollywood?

8 In which Italian city is La Scala opera house?

9 On whose poems was the stage musical *Cats* based?

10 Which record company was founded by Berry Gordy Jnr.?

ANSWERS

1 Jamaica 2 Johnny Mathis 3 "It's Not Unusual" 4 Italian 5 Huey Lewis 6 Spain 7 Dolly Parton 8 Milan 9 T.S. Eliot 10 Motown Records

Total Trivia

1 What does the J stand for in William J. Clinton?

2 Which English woman wrote *The Book of Household Management?*

3 Which is further north, the Tropic of Cancer or the Tropic of Capricorn?

4 *Consommé* and *gazpacho* are both types of what?

5 Which is the weakest piece in the game of chess?

6 Where on the body would a homburg be worn?

7 Which star of the movie *Spartacus* wrote an autobiography entitled *The Ragman's Son?*

8 Are pistachio nuts white or green?

9 What does amaretto liqueur taste of?

10 Traditionally, how many witches make up a coven?

Q 3

ANSWERS

1 Jefferson 2 Mrs. Beeton 3 Tropic of Cancer 4 Soup 5 Pawn 6 The head, it's a hat 7 Kirk Douglas 8 Green 9 Almonds 10 13

Global Matters

1 What is the capital city of Bulgaria?

2 Which country's flag contains the most stars?

3 From which country does the drink *ouzo* originate?

4 Which river rises in the Black Forest and flows into the Black Sea?

5 Which London building is home to the Whispering Gallery?

6 In which U.S. state is Las Vegas?

7 In which country does the river Amazon mainly flow?

8 Which is the only country to border Denmark?

9 Which group of islands does Ibiza belong to?

10 Which is the largest castle in Wales, and is also a cheese's name?

LEVEL 2 · QUIZ 88

ANSWERS

1 Sofia **2** United States **3** Greece **4** The Danube **5** St Paul's Cathedral **6** Nevada **7** Brazil **8** Germany **9** The Balearics **10** Caerphilly

Scientifically Speaking

1 What, with the atomic number of 1, is the lightest element?

2 Used for treating broken bones, what is the common name for hydrated magnesium sulphate?

3 What does the V stand for in DVT?

4 Which organ of the body beginning with S removes old red blood cells from circulation?

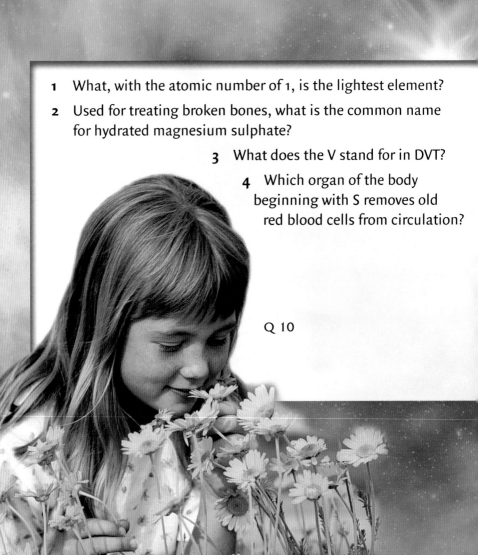

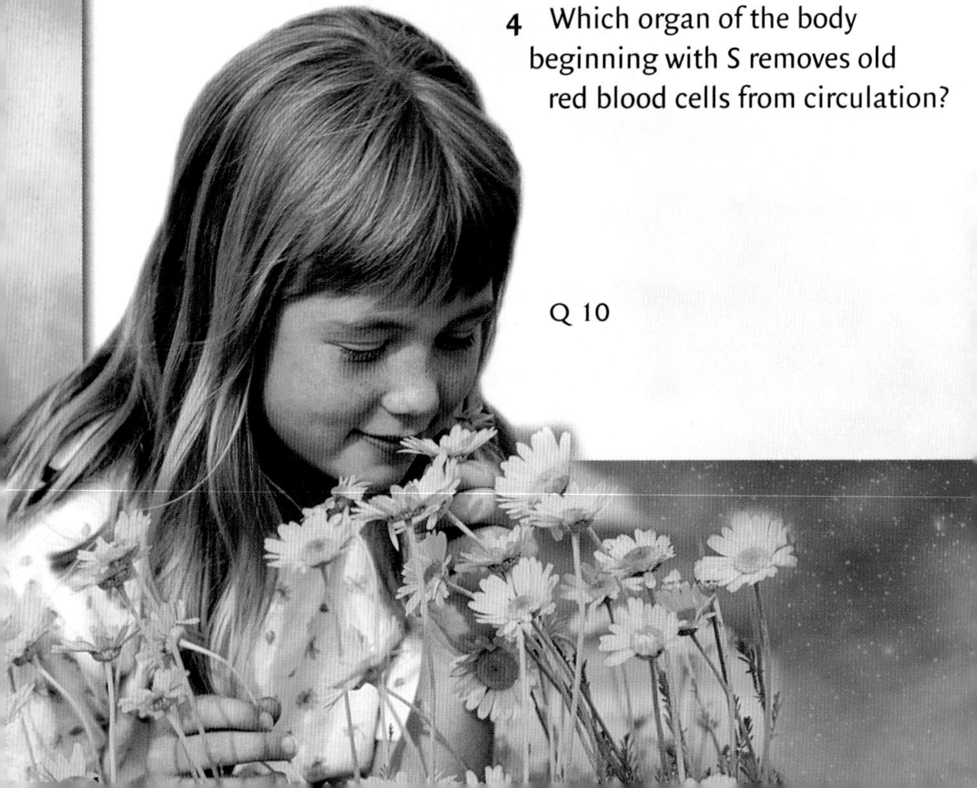

Q 10

LEVEL 2 · QUIZ 89

5 How many planets are there in our Solar System?

6 How many sides does a heptagon have?

7 Where in the human body is the carotid artery?

8 How is two-fifths expressed as a percentage?

9 How many equal angles are there in an isosceles triangle?

10 What is the common name for the olfactory organ?

BACKGROUND BONUS

What is the name for a star that explodes, emitting vast amounts of energy in the process?

ANSWERS

1 Hydrogen **2** Plaster of Paris **3** Vein (deep vein thrombosis) **4** Spleen **5** Nine **6** Seven **7** The neck **8** 40 percent **9** Two **10** The nose

Background Bonus Supernova

Great and Famous

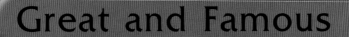

1 Which Wild West hero had a horse called Trigger and a dog called Bullet?

2 Who released an autobiography, a movie, an album and a single all entitled *Purple Rain*?

3 In which capital city was the Oscar-winning actor Russell Crowe born?

Q 9

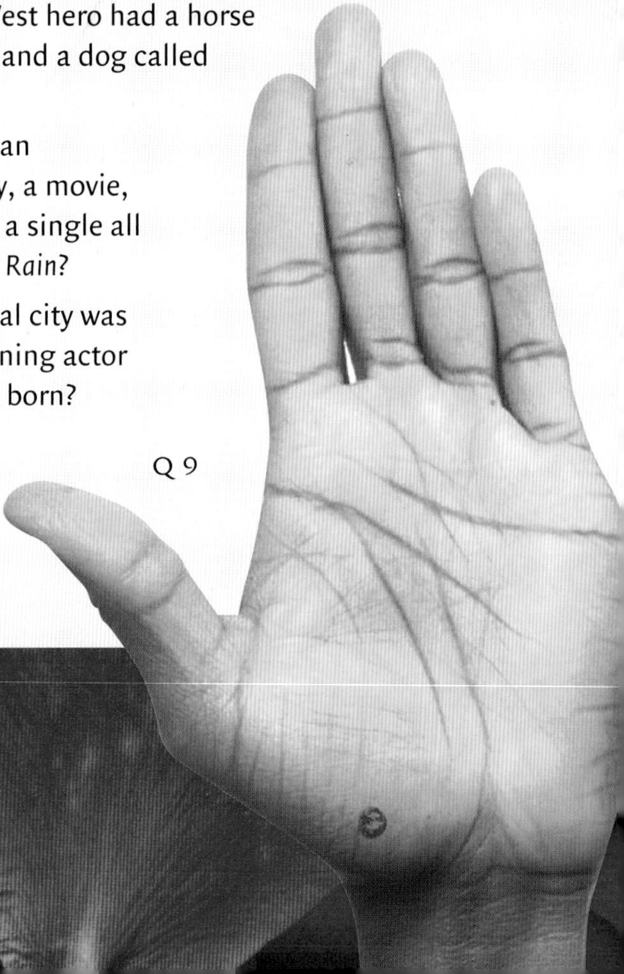

4 In 2003, who spent 44 days suspended in a glass cage over London's river Thames?

5 In which TV show did Clint Eastwood play Rowdy Yates?

6 *Eyes Wide Shut* was the last movie of which controversial director?

7 In which series of movies did Mel Gibson play a police detective called Martin Riggs?

8 What does the W stand for in the name of George W. Bush?

9 Which pop star, whose biggest hit was "Addicted To Love", died in 2003?

10 Which actor, famed for playing Dracula, wrote an autobiography entitled *Tall, Dark and Gruesome*?

ANSWERS

1 Roy Rogers **2** Prince **3** Wellington **4** David Blaine **5** *Rawhide* **6** Stanley Kubrick **7** *Lethal Weapon* **8** Walker **9** Robert Palmer **10** Christopher Lee

Sporting Chance

Q 9

1 Which country does soccer player Diego Forlan represent at international level?

2 Which nation finished third in the 2003 Rugby Union World Cup?

3 Which female Wimbledon winner of 1977 wrote an autobiography entitled *Courting Triumph?*

4 How many players are in a rugby union team?

5 What is the name of the ceremonial dance performed by the All Blacks called?

6 Which Scottish soccer club is nicknamed The Dons?

7 In golf, which number of wood is the driver?

8 Who screamed, "You cannot be serious" at Wimbledon Tennis Championships?

9 In which event did Britain's Sally Gunnell win Olympic gold?

10 Which squad number was David Beckham given when he joined Real Madrid?

ANSWERS

1 Uruguay **2** New Zealand **3** Virginia Wade **4** 15 **5** Haka **6** Aberdeen **7** Number 1 wood **8** John McEnroe **9** 400m hurdles **10** 23

Lights, Camera, Action!

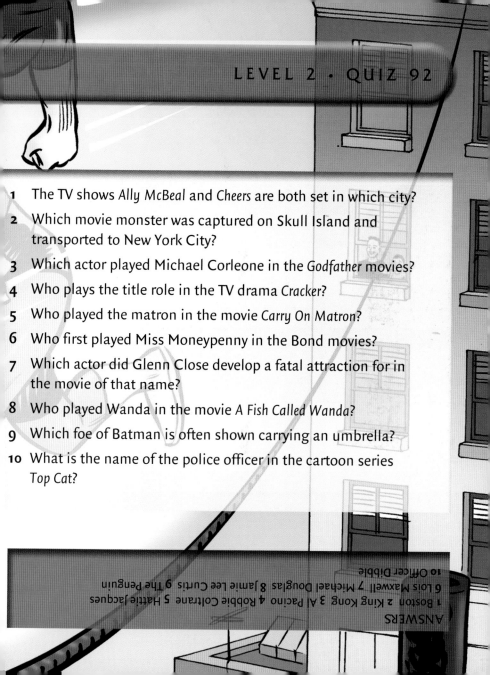

1 The TV shows *Ally McBeal* and *Cheers* are both set in which city?

2 Which movie monster was captured on Skull Island and transported to New York City?

3 Which actor played Michael Corleone in the *Godfather* movies?

4 Who plays the title role in the TV drama *Cracker*?

5 Who played the matron in the movie *Carry On Matron*?

6 Who first played Miss Moneypenny in the Bond movies?

7 Which actor did Glenn Close develop a fatal attraction for in the movie of that name?

8 Who played Wanda in the movie *A Fish Called Wanda*?

9 Which foe of Batman is often shown carrying an umbrella?

10 What is the name of the police officer in the cartoon series *Top Cat*?

ANSWERS

1 Boston **2** King Kong **3** Al Pacino **4** Robbie Coltrane **5** Hattie Jacques **6** Lois Maxwell **7** Michael Douglas **8** Jamie Lee Curtis **9** The Penguin **10** Officer Dibble

Natural Selection

1 From which tree's wood are cricket bats traditionally made?

2 What shape is a bee's honeycomb?

3 Which marsupials travel in mobs under the leadership of a boomer?

4 What is a Moorish Idol?

5 How many legs does a lobster have?

6 What is a female foal called?

7 Which is the largest wild carnivore native to the British Isles?

8 Which birds are associated with the Tower of London?

9 Where did bluebirds fly over according to Vera Lynn?

10 What is a group of wolves called?

BACKGROUND BONUS

Which is the largest of the big cats, with a roar that can be heard up to 2 km (1.5 mi) away?

ANSWERS

1 Willow **2** Hexagonal **3** Kangaroo **4** A tropical fish **5** Ten **6** Filly **7** Badger **8** Ravens **9** The white cliffs of Dover **10** A pack

Background Bonus Tiger

Making History

Q 6

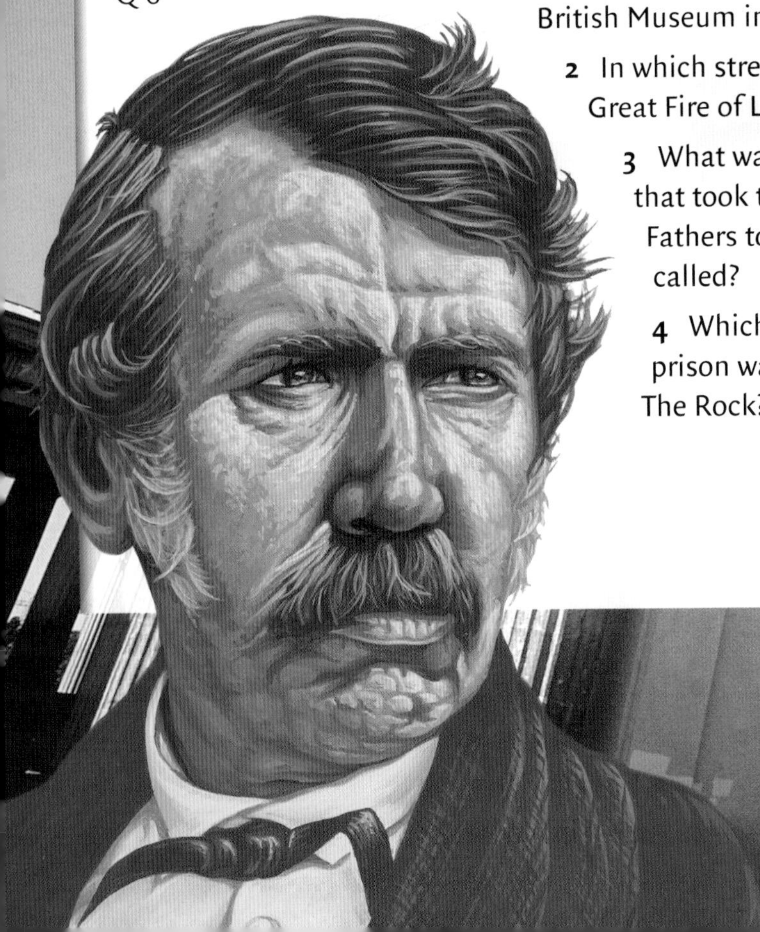

1 Which marbles were sold to the British Museum in 1816?

2 In which street did the Great Fire of London start?

3 What was the ship that took the first Pilgrim Fathers to America called?

4 Which San Francisco prison was known as The Rock?

5 How many men were commanded by a Roman centurion?

6 Who did Henry Morton Stanley meet in the African village of Ujiji?

7 During which war was the TV series *Blackadder Goes Forth* set?

8 Which Trojan beauty's face was said to have launched a thousand ships?

9 Which peak is the home of the ancient Greek gods?

10 Which European country was involved in a civil war from 1936 to 1939?

ANSWERS

1 The Elgin Marbles **2** Pudding Lane **3** The *Mayflower* **4** Alcatraz **5** 100 **6** Dr. Livingstone **7** World War I **8** Helen of Troy **9** Mount Olympus **10** Spain

Music Mania

1 Which 1990s Britpop band's hits included "Park Life"?

2 What is the surname of the brothers from Right Said Fred?

3 Which song from *The Lion King* earned Elton John an Oscar?

4 By what name is George O'Dowd better known?

5 Which duo had a Christmas No. 1 in 1982 with "Save Your Love"?

6 Which dance troupe made their *Top Of The Pops* debut in 1967?

7 Which song has been a hit for Norman Greenbaum, Dr. & The Medics and Gareth Gates?

8 Who wrote the words to "Candle in the Wind"?

9 Which band links the songs "Girls On Film" and "Wild Boys"?

10 Who won the Eurovision Song Contest for the U.K. singing "Love Shine a Light"?

Q 10

ANSWERS

1 Blur **2** Fairbrass **3** "Can You Feel The Love Tonight?" **4** Boy George **5** Renee and Renato **6** Pan's People **7** "Spirit In The Sky" **8** Bernie Taupin **9** Duran Duran **10** Katrina and the Waves

Fantastic Food

Can you identify these eight types of food?

1

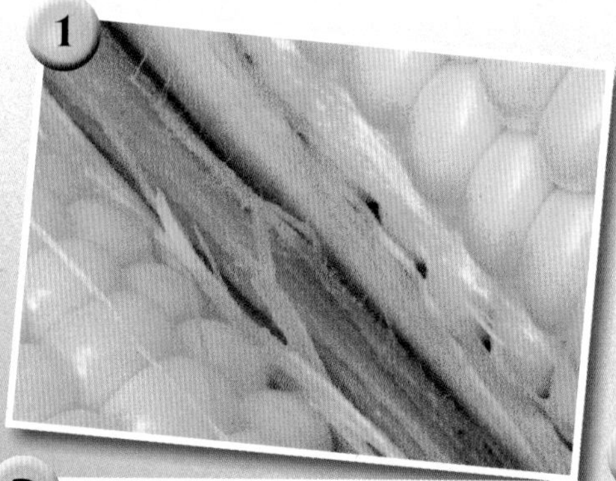

2

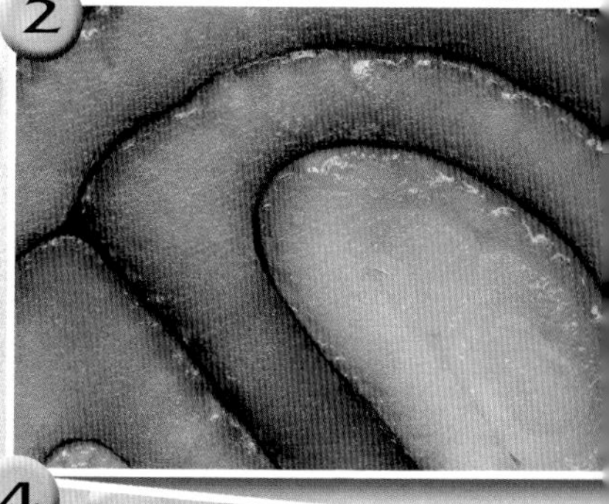

3

4

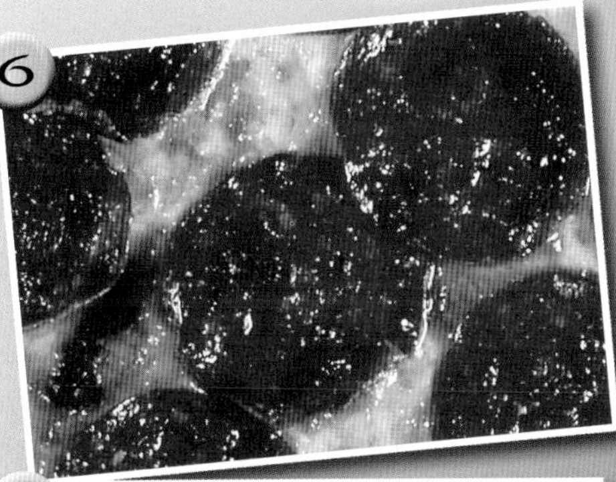

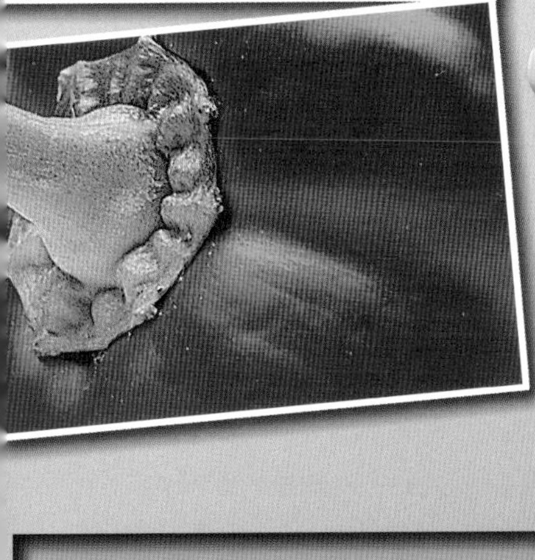

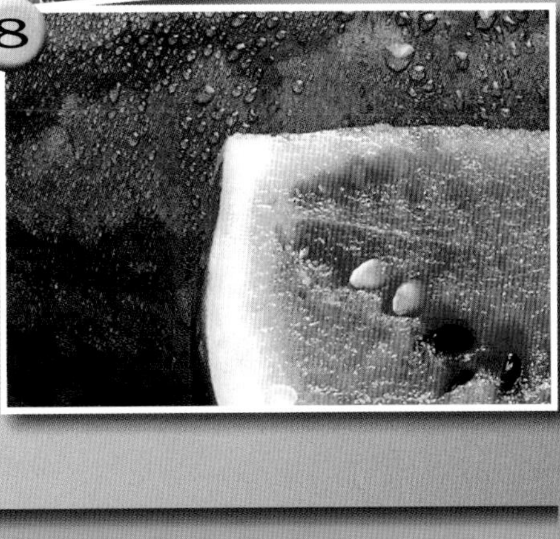

ANSWERS

1 Corn 2 Onion 3 Rasberry 4 Doughnut 5 Bread 6 Pizza 7 Pepper 8 Watermelon

Total Trivia

1 What is the Internet's largest online auction site called?

2 Which animal is the symbol of the U.S. Republican Party?

3 Which animal is the symbol of the U.S. Democratic Party?

4 *Knott's Landing* was a Californian spin-off of which popular U.S. TV soap?

5 Which religious group is known for leaving copies of the Bible in hotel rooms?

6 In 2001, 9 Downing Street became the official address of which government post?

7 Which of Jesus' disciples is the patron saint of fishermen?

8 What is the name of the central family in *The Sound of Music*?

BACKGROUND BONUS

What word is the Australian term for confectionary and a slang term for money?

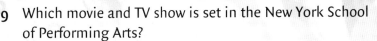

9 Which movie and TV show is set in the New York School of Performing Arts?

10 What did the Euro replace in Greece?

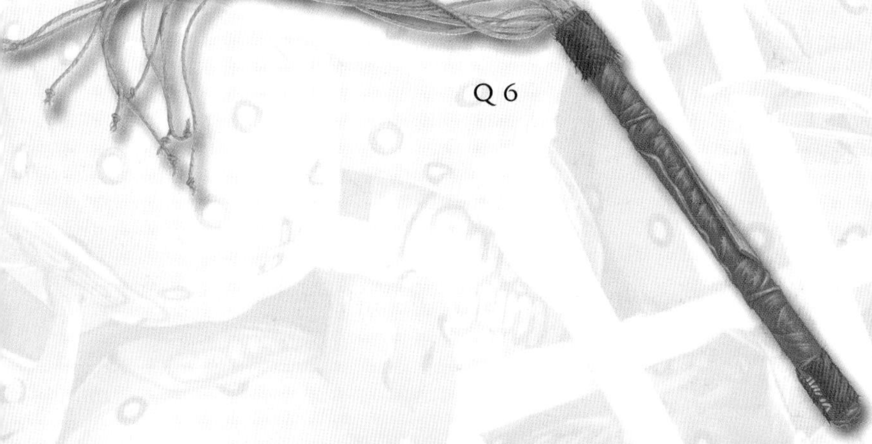

Q 6

ANSWERS

1 Ebay **2** Elephant **3** Donkey **4** Dallas **5** The Gideons **6** Government Chief Whip **7** St. Peter **8** The Von Trapp family **9** Fame **10** Drachma

Background Bonus Lolly

Global Matters

1. Which European country is divided into 26 areas called cantons?
2. Which is the largest Greek island?
3. In which African country is the Great Rift Valley?
4. Which U.S. state does the Arctic Circle pass through?
5. Is the Vatican flag yellow and white or white and blue?
6. Which building on Merseyside is known as Paddy's Wigwam?
7. Which river runs through the Grand Canyon?
8. What is the world's largest country with an X in its name?
9. Which state capital of West Virginia, United States, gave its name to a dance?
10. In which European country is the town of Spa, famed for its mineral springs?

LEVEL 2 · QUIZ 98

Q 8

ANSWERS

1 Switzerland **2** Crete **3** Kenya **4** Alaska **5** Yellow **6** Liverpool Cathedral **7** Colorado **8** Mexico **9** Charleston **10** Belgium

Scientifically Speaking

1 Which P is a table that lists the symbols of chemical elements and their atomic numbers?

2 What is the chemical symbol for silver?

3 Which F word is the soft spot on top of a baby's head?

Q 4

LEVEL 2 · QUIZ 99

4 Which planet gets its name from the Roman god of agriculture?

5 Which M is the layer of rock immediately under the Earth's surface?

6 By which four-letter name is the end of a magnet known?

7 What five-letter S word means "relating to the Sun"?

8 What is the chemical symbol for iron?

9 What would a doctor be testing with a small hammer called a plexor?

10 Which G is the main constituent of pencil lead?

ANSWERS

1 The Periodic Table **2** Ag **3** Fontanelle **4** Saturn **5** Mantle **6** Pole **7** Solar **8** Fe **9** A patient's reflexes **10** Graphite

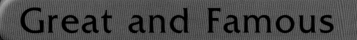

Great and Famous

1 Which star of E.T. penned an autobiography entitled *Little Girl Lost?*

2 Whom did Michael Howard replace as leader of the British Conservative Party in 2003?

Q 7

3 Which comedy duo had the first names of Bud and Lou?

4 Which music legend had a posthumous chart-topping song with "It Doesn't Matter Anymore"?

5 In which year did Elvis Presley and Marc Bolan both die?

6 Who links the movie *Calendar Girls* with the TV drama *Prime Suspect*?

7 Who announced his engagement to Heather Mills in 2001?

8 Which female soul singer holds the record for the most consecutive U.S. No. 1 singles?

9 Who split from David Guest, her fourth husband, in 2003?

10 Which Wild West marshal was played by Kurt Russell in *Tombstone*?

ANSWERS

1 Drew Barrymore 2 Iain Duncan Smith 3 Abbot and Costello 4 Buddy Holly 5 1977 6 Helen Mirren 7 Paul McCartney 8 Whitney Housten 9 Liza Minnelli 10 Wyatt Earp

Written Word

1 Which French word for dead-end literally means "bottom of the bag"?

2 Which L word is a horizontal beam over a doorway?

3 Which six-letter M word is a dealer in textile fabrics and fine cloth?

4 Which is the most used letter in the English language?

5 Which is the least used letter in the English language?

6 Which word can follow apple and family, and come before house and trunk?

7 Which name is given to the crossed-legged position in yoga?

8 What is the plural of ox?

9 Which O word can come after soap and before house?

10 In industry, which N is the opposite of privatization?

BACKGROUND BONUS

In *The Lion, the Witch and the Wardrobe* by C.S. Lewis, which season is linked to the White Witch?

ANSWERS

1 Cul-de-sac **2** Lintel **3** Mercer **4** E **5** Q **6** Tree **7** Lotus **8** Oxen **9** Opera **10** Nationalization

Background Bonus Winter

Sporting Chance

1 Which international soccer side was managed by Billy Bingham from 1980 to 1993?

2 Which sport featured in the Robert Redford movie *The Natural*?

3 In which country was the 2003 Rugby Union World Cup contested?

4 Who kept goal for England in the 1966 soccer World Cup?

Q 6

LEVEL 2 · QUIZ 102

5 Who won 102 soccer caps for Scotland and helped Liverpool FC to win three European cups?

6 Which three-letter word describes an unplayable serve in tennis?

7 Which American Football team is known as the 49ers?

8 Which nation did Brazil beat in the final of soccer's 2002 World Cup?

9 What is a cricket umpire trying to signal when extending both arms horizontally?

10 How many players in a rugby league team?

ANSWERS

1 Northern Ireland 2 Baseball 3 Australia 4 Gordon Banks 5 Kenny Dalglish 6 Ace 7 San Francisco 49ers 8 Germany 9 A wide 10 13

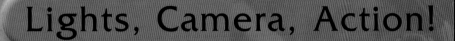

Lights, Camera, Action!

1 Who played the role of Captain Hook in the Steven Spielberg movie *Hook*?

2 In which TV series did George Clooney play the role of Dr. Douglas Ross?

3 In which decade was *Raiders of the Lost Ark* set?

4 Which 1974 disaster movie starred Paul Newman, Steve McQueen, Faye Dunaway and William Holden?

5 Who played the role of Hilda Ogden in *Coronation Street*?

6 "I Could Be So Good For You" is the theme song for which popular TV series?

7 In which TV series did Robson and Jerome play Dave and Paddy?

8 Which British TV show was screened in the United States under the title of *My Partner the Ghost*?

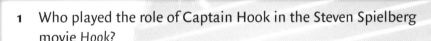

9 Who played the title role in *Master and Commander?*

10 What is the title of the theme song of the comedy drama MASH?

Q 2

ANSWERS

1 Dustin Hoffman **2** ER **3** The 1930s **4** The Towering Inferno **5** Jean Alexander **6** Minder **7** Soldier Soldier **8** Randall and Hopkirk Deceased **9** Russell Crowe **10** "Suicide Is Painless"

Natural Selection

1 Which animal's tears are said to be a sign of insincere grief?

2 Which M is the size of poodle between a standard and a toy?

3 Which tail-less breed of cat comes from the Isle of Man?

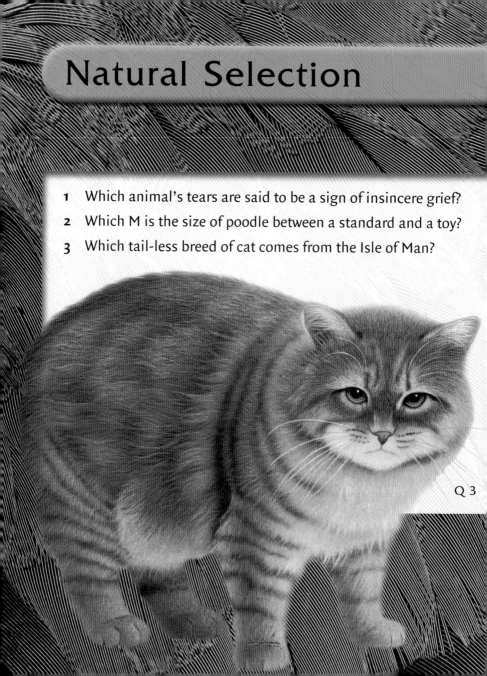

Q 3

4 Where are the withers on a horse's body?

5 Red Admiral and Postman are both species of what?

6 Which B is another name for the wood hyacinth?

7 What is an amphibian?

8 What can't the basenji dog and the dingo do that other dogs can?

9 Do apes have tails?

10 Which animal lives in a holt?

ANSWERS

1 Crocodile 2 Miniature 3 Manx 4 Between the shoulders 5 Butterfly 6 Bluebell 7 An animal that lives in water and on land 8 They cannot bark 9 No, only monkeys have tails 10 Otter

Written Word

1 Which nursery rhyme character found Lucy Locket's pocket?

2 Which of the seven dwarfs has a three-letter name?

3 Genesis, Exodus, Leviticus: what comes next?

4 Which character in *Gone with the Wind* was played in the movie by Clark Gable?

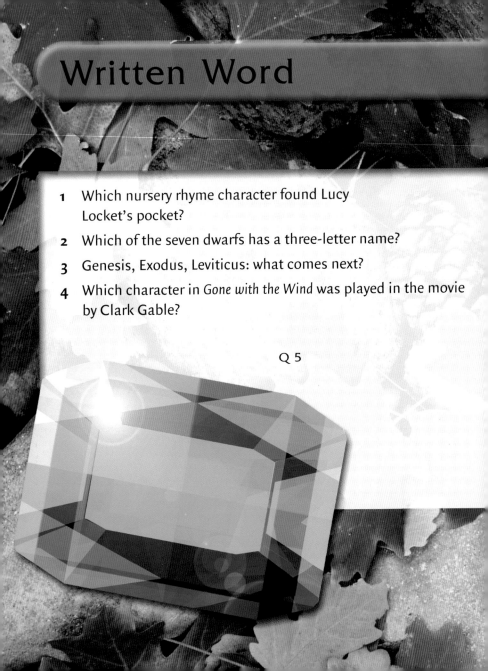

Q 5

LEVEL 2 • QUIZ 105

5 In which city does the Wizard of Oz live?

6 Which seabird was killed by the Ancient Mariner?

7 Which type of bird taught Dr. Doolittle to talk to the animals?

8 How many lines are in a sonnet?

9 Which movie star penned an autobiography entitled *Citizen Jane*?

10 Who created the *Mr. Men*?

BACKGROUND BONUS

Which season did John Keats describe as one of "mists and mellow fruitfulness"?

ANSWERS

1 Kitty Fisher **2** Doc **3** Numbers **4** Rhett Butler **5** The Emerald City **6** Albatross **7** Parrot **8** 14 **9** Jane Fonda **10** Roger Hargreaves

Background Bonus Autumn

Making History

1 Which wife of Louis XVI was guillotined in 1793?

2 Who was the first man to swim the English Channel?

3 Whom did Henry VIII divorce in 1533?

4 Which country did the Soviet Union invade in December 1979?

5 Who was elected president of South Africa in 1994?

6 What is Britain's oldest national daily newspaper?

7 Who was executed at Fotheringay Castle in 1587?

8 In which decade did the United States fight in the Korean War?

9 In which English city was Dick Turpin hanged in 1793?

10 At which 1913 English sporting event was suffragette Emily Davison killed?

LEVEL 2 • QUIZ 106

Q 6

ANSWERS

1 Marie Antoinette **2** Captain Matthew Webb **3** Catherine of Aragon **4** Afghanistan **5** Nelson Mandela **6** The Times **7** Mary Queen of Scots **8** The 1950s **9** York **10** The Epsom Derby

Music Mania

1 Which wood is traditionally used for making black piano keys?

2 Who recorded the best-selling album *Tubular Bells*?

3 Set in India, which Andrew Lloyd Webber musical opened in London in 2002?

4 Which girl group comprised Lewis, Blatt and the Appleton sisters?

Q 4

LEVEL 2 · QUIZ 107

5 Which religion is adhered to by the Osmonds?

6 Which colonel managed Elvis Presley?

7 What type of instrument is a balalaika?

8 Which country did Johnny Logan represent in the Eurovision Song Contest?

9 Three of the members of Abba were Swedish. What nationality was the fourth?

10 What is the name of Andrew Lloyd Webber's cellist brother?

ANSWERS

1 Ebony 2 Mike Oldfield 3 Bombay Nights 4 All Saints 5 Mormon 6 Tom Parker 7 A Russian guitar 8 The Republic of Ireland 9 Norwegian 10 Julian Lloyd Webber

Famous Faces

Can you identify these stars of music and cinema?

LEVEL 2 • QUIZ 108

6

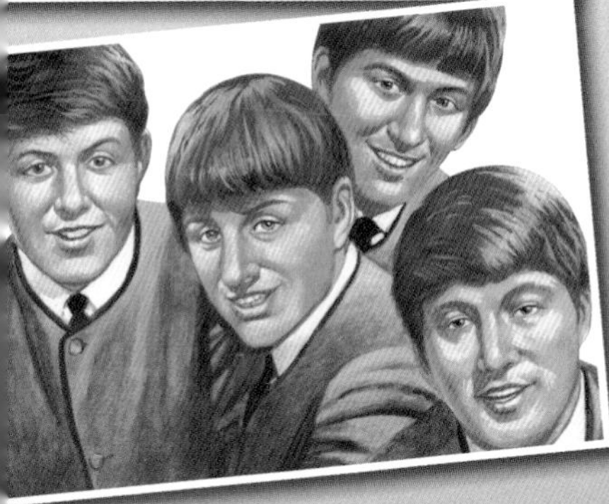

8

ANSWERS

1 Marilyn Monroe **2** Tom Cruise **3** Will Smith **4** Elizabeth Taylor **5** Luciano Pavarotti **6** Elvis Presley **7** The Beatles **8** Bob Marley

Total Trivia

1 Which oriental villain has been played in the movies by Christopher Lee, Boris Karloff and Peter Sellers?

2 What is the name of yeasted bread eaten with Indian food?

3 Which is the only month that represents a letter in the phonetic alphabet?

Q 6

BACKGROUND BONUS

Which plant provides a material that can be woven into soft, strong fabric?

4 Which animal represents a zoo on a British ordinance survey map?

5 In economics, what do the initials GDP stand for?

6 What is the name of the Flintstones' daughter?

7 Who wrote the novel *Robinson Crusoe?*

8 Which bird sat on the shoulder of Uncle Remus in the song "Zip-A-Dee-Doo-Dah"?

9 Which H is the part of a flag nearest to the pole?

10 In which U.S. state was the TV drama *Dr. Quinn Medicine Woman* set?

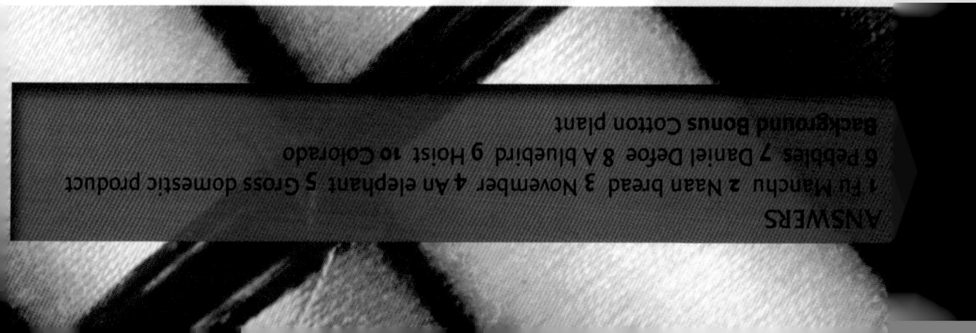

ANSWERS

1 Fu Manchu **2** Naan bread **3** November **4** An elephant **5** Gross domestic product **6** Pebbles **7** Daniel Defoe **8** A bluebird **9** Hoist **10** Colorado **Background Bonus** Cotton plant

Global Matters

Q 10

1 Is the city of Christchurch on New Zealand's North or South Island?

2 In which country is the city of Innsbruck?

3 Which is the largest castle in England?

4 Which Scottish city was the European City of Culture in 1990?

5 In which ocean does Sri Lanka lie?

6 Mont Blanc is the highest peak in which mountain range?

7 Which is the larger, the Black Sea or the Red Sea?

8 Which is the largest city that stands on the river Seine?

9 What is the name of New York City's stock exchange?

10 In which country did the lambada dance originate?

ANSWERS

1 South Island **2** Austria **3** Windsor castle **4** Glasgow **5** Indian Ocean **6** The Alps **7** The Black Sea **8** Paris **9** Dow Jones Index **10** Brazil

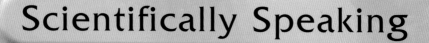

Scientifically Speaking

1 How many sides does a decagon have?
2 What is pyrophobia the fear of?
3 Which P is a pressure wave in a blood vessel that corresponds to the heart beat?
4 Which E is the outer most layer of the human skin?
5 What is the chemical symbol for tin?
6 Which N is a poisonous alkaloid present in tobacco?
7 Which H is a person who gains illegal entry into a computer?
8 What was the name of the first U.S. space station?
9 Which I word is the medical term for sleeplessness?
10 Which P is the most toxic element known?

LEVEL 2 • QUIZ 111

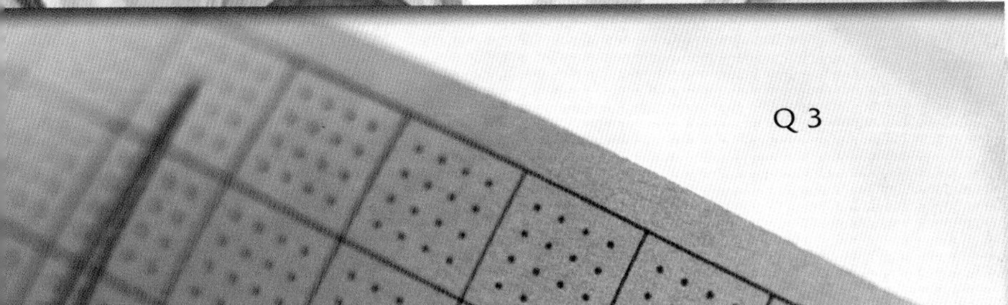

ANSWERS

1 10 **2** Fire **3** Pulse **4** Epidermis **5** Sn **6** Nicotine **7** Hacker **8** Skylab **9** Insomnia **10** Plutonium

Great and Famous

Q 2

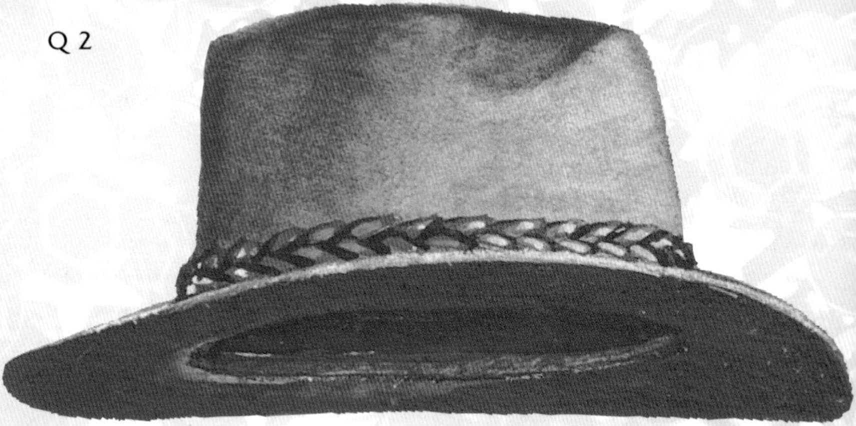

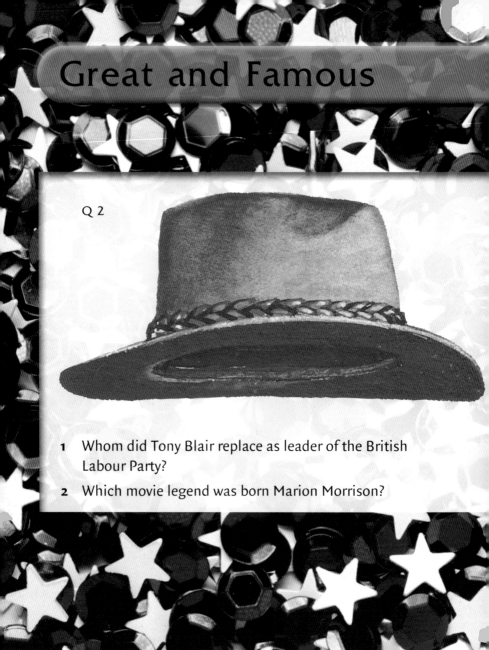

1 Whom did Tony Blair replace as leader of the British Labour Party?

2 Which movie legend was born Marion Morrison?

LEVEL 2 · QUIZ 112

3 Which player was presented with the 1966 soccer World Cup trophy by Queen Elizabeth II?

4 What name was given to Japanese pilots who performed suicide missions in World War II?

5 What was the last name of Bonnie Prince Charlie?

6 Who played the title role in the 1995 movie *Nixon*?

7 What nationality was the composer Richard Wagner?

8 Which peanut farmer went on to become president of the United States?

9 Alphabetically, who was the first of the Marx brothers?

10 Who connects the movies *Saturday Night Fever*, *Pulp Fiction* and *Look Who's Talking*?

ANSWERS

1 John Smith **2** John Wayne **3** Bobby Moore **4** Kamikaze **5** Stuart **6** Anthony Hopkins **7** German **8** Jimmy Carter **9** Chico **10** John Travolta

Sporting Chance

1. Which Ds are the indentations on a golf ball?
2. In which sport was Johnny Weissmuller an Olympic champion?
3. In tennis, which nation won the Davis Cup in 2003?
4. Soling, Tornado, and Finn are Olympic classes in which sport?
5. Who was Snooker World Champion from 1992 to 1996?
6. Which country, apart from Britain, has won rugby union's Six Nations championships?
7. What is a half nelson?
8. In which city were the 2002 Commonwealth Games held?
9. What does the Olympic motto *Citius, Altius, Fortius* mean?
10. In rugby union, which S is formed by eight forwards from each team?

BACKGROUND BONUS

Italy's Giuseppe Farina won the first world championship of which sport in 1950?

Q 10

ANSWERS

1 Dimples **2** Swimming **3** Australia **4** Yachting **5** Stephen Hendry **6** France **7** A wrestling hold **8** Manchester **9** Faster, higher, stronger **10** Scrum

Background Bonus Motor racing

Lights, Camera, Action!

Q 2

LEVEL 2 • QUIZ 114

1 Which 1997 movie sequel was sub-titled *The Lost World*?

2 In which 1984 movie did Daryl Hannah play a mermaid?

3 In *Star Trek*, what is the home planet of Mr. Spock's mother?

4 In which movie did Paul Newman and Robert Redford escape their pursuers by jumping into a river?

5 Which character is played by Peter Sellers in the *Pink Panther* movies?

6 Which role was played Diana Rigg in the TV show *The Avengers*?

7 What does the R stand for in J.R. Ewing?

8 Sweet Pea is the name of which cartoon character's baby?

9 Which British sitcom features the antics of Frank Spencer?

10 What was the first Australian soap to be screened on British television?

ANSWERS

1 *Jurassic Park* **2** *Splash* **3** Earth **4** *Butch Cassidy and the Sundance Kid* **5** Inspector Clouseau **6** Emma Peel **7** Ross **8** Olive Oyl **9** *Some Mothers Do 'ave 'em* **10** *The Sullivans*

Natural Selection

1 Which boy's name is also the name for a rabbit's home?
2 What is the term for the fossilized resin formed from the gum of conifer trees ?
3 Which sleepy mammal is also the name of one of the seven deadly sins?
4 Is an anchovy a flower, a fish or a fruit?
5 What is the collective noun for a group of crows?
6 Which species of fly is sometimes called a daddy-longlegs?
7 Which word can follow earth, glow and blood to give the names of three creatures?
8 Which flower has a name that means lion's tooth?
9 What does a pinniped have instead of feet?
10 Which is the fastest-growing member of the grass family?

LEVEL 2 • QUIZ 115

Q 9

ANSWERS
1 Warren **2** Amber **3** Sloth **4** A fish **5** A murder **6** Crane fly **7** Worm **8** Dandelion **9** Flippers **10** Bamboo

Making History

Q 8

LEVEL 2 · QUIZ 116

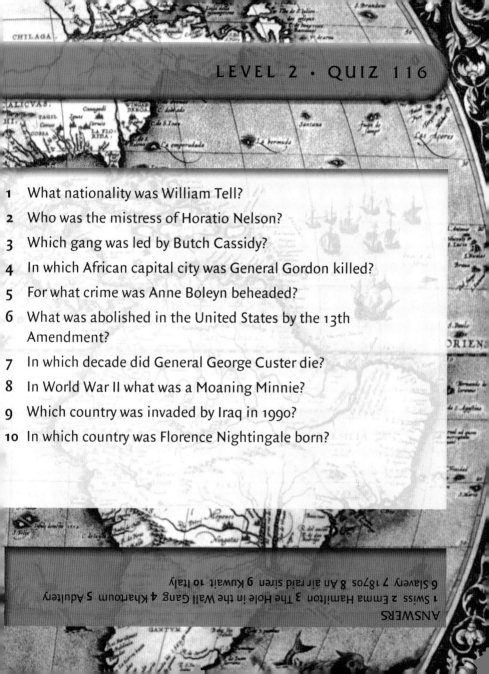

1 What nationality was William Tell?
2 Who was the mistress of Horatio Nelson?
3 Which gang was led by Butch Cassidy?
4 In which African capital city was General Gordon killed?
5 For what crime was Anne Boleyn beheaded?
6 What was abolished in the United States by the 13th Amendment?
7 In which decade did General George Custer die?
8 In World War II what was a Moaning Minnie?
9 Which country was invaded by Iraq in 1990?
10 In which country was Florence Nightingale born?

ANSWERS
1 Swiss **2** Emma Hamilton **3** The Hole in the Wall Gang **4** Khartoum **5** Adultery
6 Slavery **7** 1870s **8** An air raid siren **9** Kuwait **10** Italy

Music Mania

1 Whose life story was chronicled in the movie *Great Balls of Fire?*

2 In which movie did Clint Eastwood sing "I Talk To The Trees"?

3 In which country was the Elvis Presley movie *Fun in Acapulco* set?

4 Which movie won a Golden Globe for Best Musical in 2003?

5 Which song did Berlin perform in the movie *Top Gun?*

6 Who wrote the music for *The Sting?*

7 What was The Beatles' first movie called?

8 Which musical opens with the song "Oh What A Beautiful Morning"?

9 What was the first name of the character played by Julie Andrews in *The Sound of Music?*

10 *The Great Rock and Roll Swindle* featured the antics of which punk rock group?

BACKGROUND BONUS

Launched in the U.K in 1983, what can contain the equivalent of 500,000 A4 pages of information?

LEVEL 2 • QUIZ 117

Q 4

ANSWERS

1 Jerry Lee Lewis **2** *Paint Your Wagon* **3** Mexico **4** *Chicago* **5** "Take My Breath Away"
6 Scott Joplin **7** *A Hard Day's Night* **8** *Oklahoma* **9** Maria **10** The Sex Pistols
Background Bonus C.D.

Total Trivia

1 Which comedy series is associated with the phrase "And now for something completely different"?

2 Which horselike mythical creature is the official logo of *Reader's Digest* magazine?

3 Which saint's cross features on the Scottish flag?

4 What breed of dog is Snoopy?

5 In which British post did Andrew Motion replace Ted Hughes?

6 Who is married to Gomez in *The Addams Family*?

7 Phobos and Deimos are the moons of which planet?

8 What is the symbol for the star sign of Pisces?

9 What is the last letter of the Greek alphabet?

10 Which three-letter word can precede level, lion and sickness?

LEVEL 2 · QUIZ 118

Q 1

ANSWERS
1 Monty Python's Flying Circus 2 Pegasus 3 St. Andrew 4 A beagle 5 Poet Laureate
6 Morticia 7 Mars 8 Fish 9 Omega 10 Sea

Global Matters

1 What is the name of Scotland's largest loch?

2 Is the cross on the Norwegian flag red, white or blue?

3 Which is the world's second highest mountain?

4 In which U.S. city is the Golden Gate bridge?

5 In London, what was named after Benjamin Hall?

6 Which French palace, built for Louis XIV, contains the Hall of Mirrors?

7 What did the Boulder Dam change its name to in 1948?

8 Which country is home to the majority of Catalan speakers?

9 IA is the zip code of which U.S. state?

10 Tenerife and Lanzarote belong to which island group?

LEVEL 2 • QUIZ 119

ANSWERS

1 Loch Lomond **2** Blue **3** K2 **4** San Francisco **5** Big Ben **6** Palace of Versailles **7** Hoover Dam **8** Spain **9** Iowa **10** The Canaries

Creepy-Crawlies

Can you identify these creepy-crawly creatures?

1

2

3

4

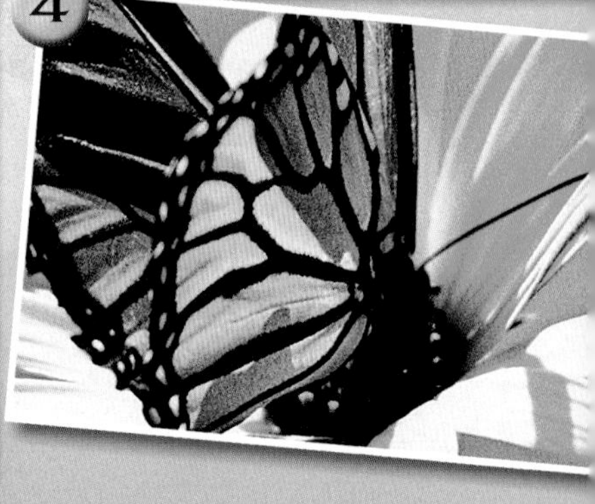

LEVEL 2 · QUIZ 120

6

8

ANSWERS
1 Bee **2** Ant **3** Woodlouse **4** Butterfly **5** Preying mantis **6** Dragonfly **7** Caterpillar **8** Scorpion

Lights, Camera, Action!

1 Who played the title role in the 1962 movie epic *Lawrence of Arabia?*

2 In which cult TV show did Patrick McGoohan declare "I am not a number, I am a man"?

3 Which comedy show is set in the village of Royston Vasey?

4 In which U.S. state is the Mafia drama *The Sopranos* set?

5 Which U.S. police TV show is associated with the quote "Let's be careful out there"?

6 Who plays the role of Bill in the Quentin Tarantino movie *Kill Bill?*

7 Who played the role of Detective Sergeant Bung in *Carry On Screaming?*

8 Which singer's life story was chronicled in the movie *Coal Miner's Daughter?*

BACKGROUND BONUS

Which 1976 movie starred Kris Kristofferson and Barbara Streisand?

9 Which former beauty queen went on to play Wonder Woman on TV?

10 Who was the leading lady in the Alfred Hitchcock thriller *The Birds?*

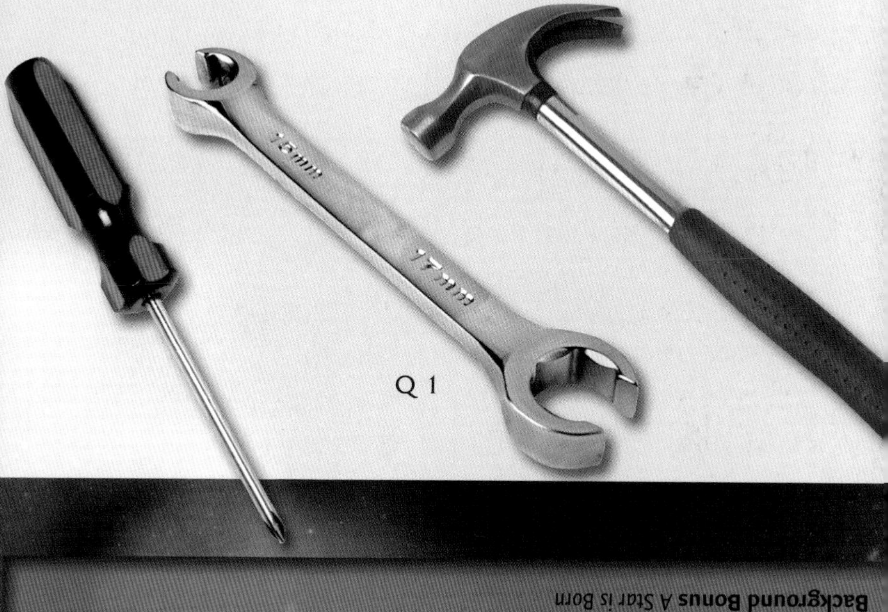

Q 1

ANSWERS

1 Peter O'Toole **2** *The Prisoner* **3** *The League Of Gentlemen* **4** New Jersey **5** *Hill St Blues* **6** David Carradine **7** Harry H. Corbett **8** Loretta Lynn **9** Linda Carter **10** Tippi Hedren

Background Bonus *A Star is Born*

Natural Selection

1 What other name for a pigeon hawk is shared by an Arthurian wizard?
2 By which name is a domesticated polecat also known?
3 Which six-letter S word means pertaining to apes?
4 From which plant is linen obtained?
5 Which breed of farm animal is a Gloucester Old Spot?
6 What was the first bird mentioned by name in the Bible?
7 Which breed of dog's name means badger hound?
8 Which bird lays the largest egg in proportion to the size of its body?
9 How many legs does a starfish have?
10 From which breed of goat is mohair obtained?

LEVEL 3 • QUIZ 122

ANSWERS

1 Merlin **2** Ferret **3** Simian **4** Flax **5** Pig **6** Raven **7** Daschund **8** Kiwi **9** Five **10** Angora

Written Word

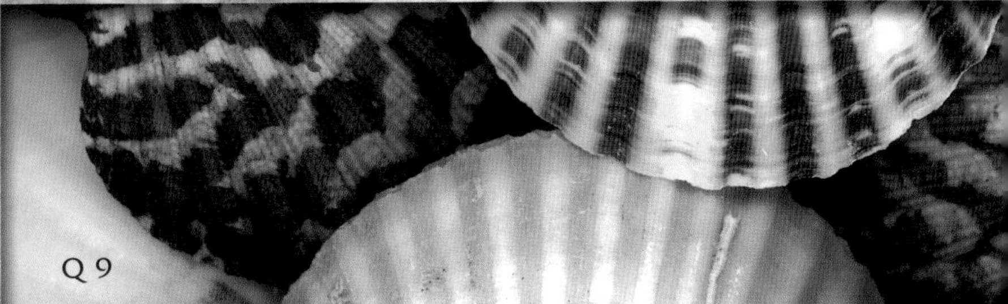

1 Who wrote the novel *The Lives and Loves of a She Devil*?

2 By which name is the literary character of Sir Percy Blakeney also known?

3 Who wrote the novel *The Bostonians*?

4 Which novel features an escaped convict called Magwitch?

5 Which novel by James Hilton is set at Brookfield School?

6 Which Shakespeare play features the character of Sir Toby Belch?

7 What type of bird is Fawkes in the *Harry Potter* stories?

8 Which author was portrayed by Nicole Kidman in *The Hours*?

9 Who penned the poem *Ode to the West Wind*?

10 Which novel features the character of Mrs. Do as you would be done by?

ANSWERS

1 Fay Weldon **2** *The Scarlet Pimpernel* **3** Henry James **4** *Great Expectations* **5** *Goodbye Mr. Chips* **6** *Twelfth Night* **7** A phoenix **8** Virginia Woolf **9** Percy Shelley **10** *The Water Babies*

Making History

1 Which king of England was known as Rufus due to his red hair?

2 Which lady was born in 1910 and won the Nobel Peace Prize 69 years later?

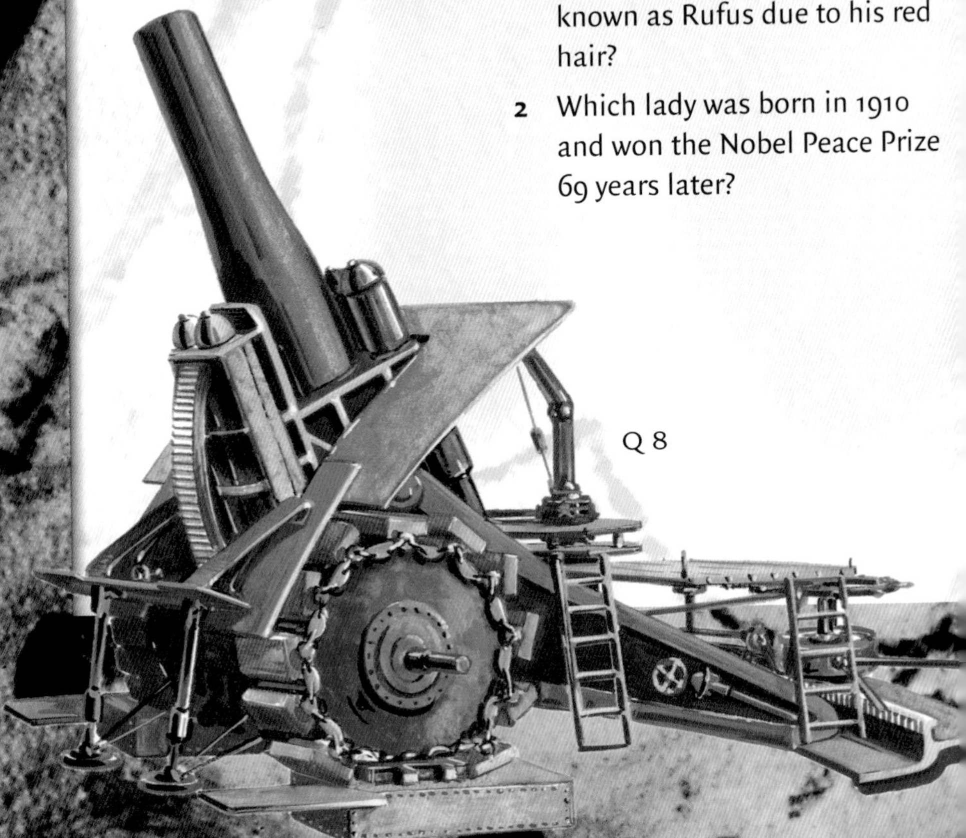

Q 8

LEVEL 3 · QUIZ 124

3 By which shorter name was Rodrigo Diaz de Vivar otherwise known?

4 What does the D stand for in Franklin D. Roosevelt?

5 Which media tycoon bought 20th Century Fox in 1985?

6 Which book of the Old Testament first lists the Ten Commandments?

7 In which U.S. city was the Quaker religion founded?

8 Which World War I weapon got its name from the wife of Gustav Krupp von Bohlen und Halbach?

9 Who was British prime minister at the end of World War I?

10 In which Italian town was Leonardo da Vinci born?

ANSWERS

1 William II **2** Mother Teresa **3** El Cid **4** Delano **5** Rupert Murdoch **6** Exodus **7** Philadelphia **8** Big Bertha **9** David Lloyd George **10** Vinci

Music Mania

1 Which Stephen Sondheim musical tells the story of a murderous barber?

2 Who was the first DJ to be heard on the BBC's Radio 1?

3 Which song written by Neil Diamond was a No. 1 hit for UB40?

4 Which SW is the former name of the English National Opera?

5 Which glam rock group was fronted by Marc Bolan?

6 According to the lyrics of the song, who is "the leader of the pack"?

7 Which American female singer died of a drug overdose in Los Angeles in 1970, aged 27?

8 What do the initials MOBO stand for with regard to music awards?

9 Which rock star recorded the album *The River*?

10 Which 1980s new-wave band was fronted by Clare Grogan?

BACKGROUND BONUS

Which Joni Mitchell album features the songs "Case Of You" and "River"?

LEVEL 3 · QUIZ 125

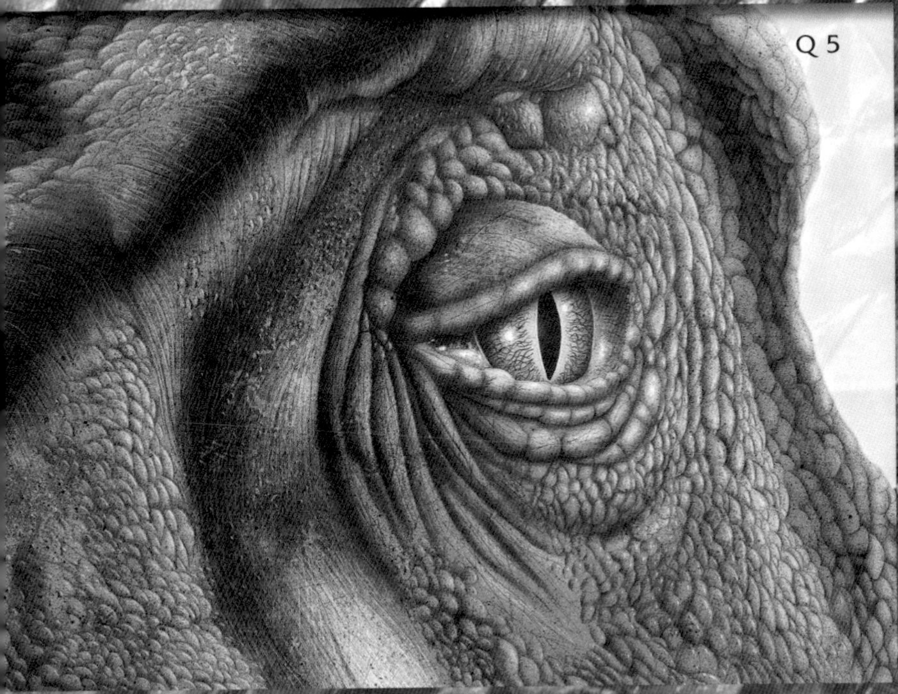
Q 5

ANSWERS

1 Sweeney Todd **2** Tony Blackburn **3** "Red Red Wine" **4** Sadlers Wells **5** T Rex **6** Jimmy **7** Janis Joplin **8** Music Of Black Origin **9** Bruce Springsteen **10** Altered Images

Background Bonus Blue

Total Trivia

Q 9

LEVEL 3 · QUIZ 126

1 Which three-letter word was removed from British coins in 1982?

2 Who directed the movie *A Passage to India*?

3 In which month does the star sign Leo begin?

4 Which nine-headed monster was slain by Hercules?

5 Ultramarine is a shade of which hue?

6 In which war did Joan of Arc fight against the English?

7 Which Texan city is known as the Alamo city?

8 Which is the highest mountain in North America?

9 Which Jedi has been played in the movies by Sir Alec Guinness and Ewan McGregor?

10 What is the heraldic name for black?

ANSWERS

1 New **2** David Lean **3** July **4** Hydra **5** Blue **6** The 100 Years War **7** San Antonio **8** Mount McKinley **9** Ben Kenobi **10** Sable

Global Matters

1 The Wolsey in Ipswich and The Whitworth in Manchester are names of what?

2 In which U.S. state is Anaheim, the home of a Disney theme park?

Q 1

3 Which country was called Kampuchea from 1976 to 1989?

4 Capitoline Hill is the tallest hill in which European capital city?

5 Which P is the capital of Kosovo?

6 Which English county is sometimes referred to as Constable Country?

7 Which German city has a name that means home of the monks?

8 The Bay of Pigs is on the coastline of which country?

9 Which group of Greek islands has a name that means twelve islands?

10 The Althing is the parliament of which European country?

ANSWERS

1 Art galleries 2 California 3 Cambodia 4 Rome 5 Pristina 6 Suffolk 7 Munich 8 Cuba 9 Dodecanese 10 Iceland

Scientifically Speaking

1 Which CO is the chemical name for quicklime?
2 Oil of vitriol is another name for which acid?
3 Which organs are affected by silicosis?
4 How many planets in our Solar System are larger than Earth?
5 An isohel is a line on a map showing areas of equal what?
6 Which brother of Marie won the Nobel Prize for Physics in 1903?
7 Which M is the name of the soft tissue in bone cavities?
8 An excess of which gas causes deep-sea divers to suffer from decompression sickness?
9 Which nerve carries signals from the retina to the brain?
10 Which acid is present in nettle and ant stings?

LEVEL 3 · QUIZ 128

Q 5

ANSWERS

1 Calcium oxide **2** Sulphuric acid **3** The lungs **4** Four **5** Sunshine **6** Pierre Curie **7** Marrow **8** Nitrogen **9** The optic nerve **10** Formic acid

Great and Famous

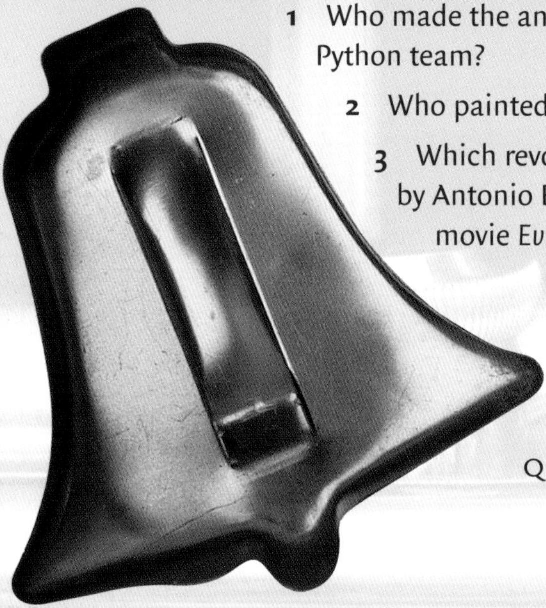

1 Who made the animations for the Monty Python team?

2 Who painted *The Blue Boy*?

3 Which revolutionary was portrayed by Antonio Banderas in the movie *Evita*?

Q 6

BACKGROUND BONUS

As well as the cornet, what other instrument did Louis Armstrong play whilst making the *Hot Five and Seven* recordings?

4 Who wears the Fisherman's Ring?

5 Who was best man at David Beckham and Victoria Adams' wedding?

6 Who played the title role in the movie *Billy Elliot*?

7 Which creator of *The Muppets* died in 1990?

8 In the Bible, who was the twin brother of Jacob?

9 Who was the mother of Liza Minnelli?

10 Who was assassinated by Nathuram Godse in 1948?

ANSWERS
1 Terry Gilliam **2** Thomas Gainsborough **3** Che Guevara **4** The Pope **5** Gary Neville **6** Jamie Bell **7** Jim Henson **8** Esau **9** Judy Garland **10** Mahatma Gandhi
Background Bonus Trumpet

Sporting Chance

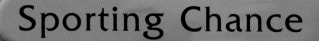

1 Which Spanish golfer is known as *El Niño*?

2 Who was the first cricketer to win 100 caps for England?

3 Who was the first cricketer to play in 100 Test Matches for Australia?

4 Which sport is governed by the ITTF?

Q 7

5 In which city is the 2008 Summer Olympics to be held?

6 What is the name of the stick in the game of lacrosse?

7 "Devil take the hindmost" is a type of race in which sport?

8 In which year was Alex Ferguson appointed soccer manager of Manchester United?

9 In the game of cricket, what is a dolly?

10 What is another name for the no. 10 iron in golf?

ANSWERS

1 Sergio Garcia **2** Colin Cowdrey **3** Allan Border **4** Table tennis **5** Beijing **6** Crosse **7** Cycling **8** 1986 **9** An easy catch **10** Wedge

Lights, Camera, Action!

1 Which TV show sees Kiefer Sutherland playing Agent Jack Bauer?

2 Which TV broadcaster presented the wildlife shows *Life on Earth* and *The Living Planet*?

Q 7

3 In the comedy show *The Royle Family*, what is the name of Jim Royle's wife?

4 In which city was the first *Terminator* movie set?

5 Who played the title role in *Schindler's List*?

6 On TV, who played the role of Sybil Fawlty?

7 In which Bond movie did Maud Adams play the title role?

8 Which movie earned Jodie Foster her first Best Actress Oscar?

9 Which TV comedy is set on Craggy Island?

10 In which Asian city is *The King and I* set?

ANSWERS

1 24 **2** David Attenborough **3** Barbara **4** Los Angeles **5** Liam Neeson **6** Prunella Scales **7** Octopussy **8** The Accused **9** Father Ted **10** Bangkok

Fabulous Flowers

Can you guess the names of these eight types of flower?

1

2

3

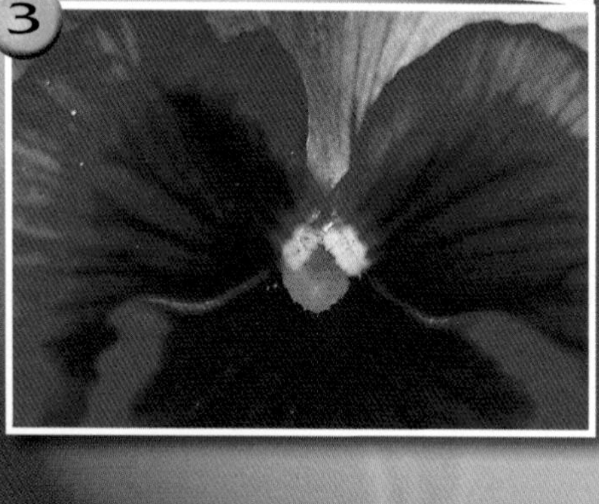

4

6

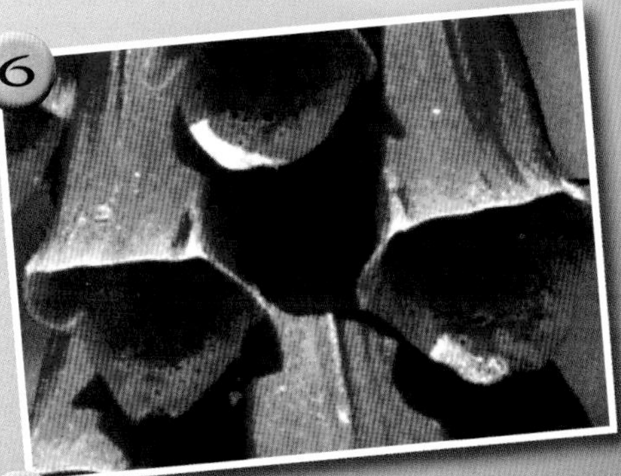

8

ANSWERS

1 Rhodedendron **2** Orchid **3** Pansy **4** Lily **5** Crocus **6** Foxglove **7** Bleeding heart **8** Water lily

Natural Selection

1 Which six-letter O word is another name for a painted leopard?

2 Which animal has species called mugger, marsh and Indian swamp?

3 In which park is London Zoo?

4 The British Wildlife Trust uses which animal as its symbol?

5 What is the term for the male reproductive organ of a plant?

6 Which disease was introduced into the U.K. in the 1950s to control the rabbit population?

7 Who is the Roman goddess of flowers?

8 What is a seal's young called?

9 Leatherback is the largest species of what?

10 What is the national flower of France?

BACKGROUND BONUS

Which type of fish has earned its common name through its habit of aggressively opening and closing its jaws?

LEVEL 3 • QUIZ 133

ANSWERS

1 Ocelot **2** Crocodile **3** Regent's Park **4** Badger **5** Stamen **6** Myxamatosis **7** Flora **8** Pup **9** Turtle **10** Fleur de Lys

Background Bonus Snapper

Making History

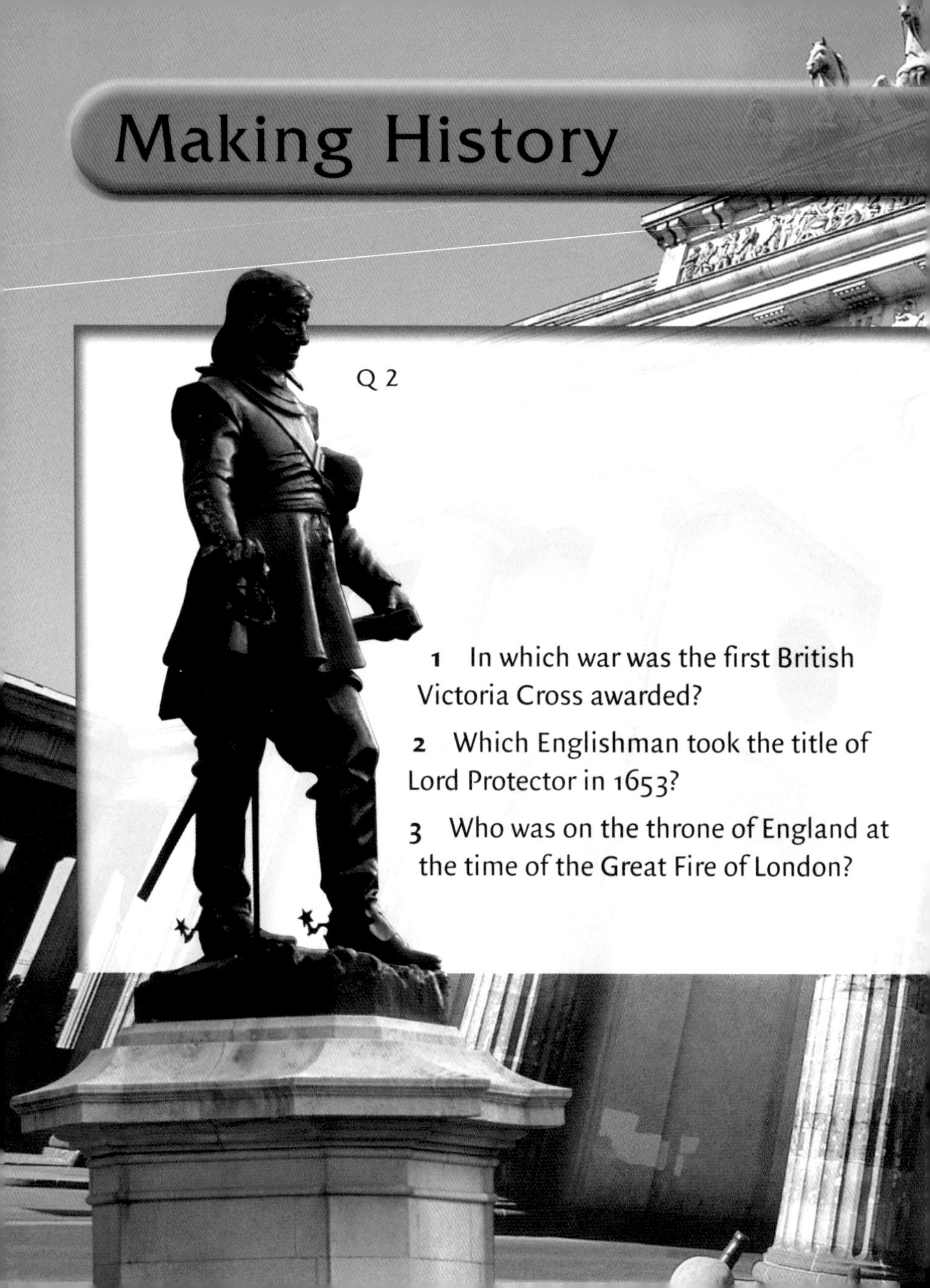

Q 2

1 In which war was the first British Victoria Cross awarded?

2 Which Englishman took the title of Lord Protector in 1653?

3 Who was on the throne of England at the time of the Great Fire of London?

4 In what decade was the Eiffel Tower opened to the public?

5 Which 20th-century conflict witnessed Operation Desert Storm?

6 Which U.S. city has hosted an annual marathon since 1897?

7 Who was the first U.S. president to win the Nobel Peace Prize?

8 To which of his wives did Henry VIII have the shortest marriage?

9 Which English king was known as Longshanks?

10 In which capital city was Leon Trotsky assassinated?

ANSWERS

1 The Crimean War 2 Oliver Cromwell 3 Charles II 4 1880s 5 The Gulf War 6 Boston 7 Theodore Roosevelt 8 Anne of Cleves 9 Edward I 10 Mexico City

Music Mania

1 The musical *Kiss Me Kate* was based on which Shakespeare play?

2 Which Motown classic opens with the line "I bet you wondered how I knew, about your plans to make me blue"?

3 What is the name of the villain in *The Threepenny Opera*?

4 Which song did Survivor record as the theme for *Rocky III*?

5 Which song did Don McLean record about the painter of irises?

6 What is the stage name of the rap artist Sean Coombs?

7 *Definitely Maybe* was the debut album of which group?

8 Which musical features the song "I Know Him So Well"?

9 Which Bee Gees hit contains the line "listen to the ground there is music all around"?

10 Donald, Barlow, Williams, Owen and Orange are the surnames of which defunct boy band?

LEVEL 3 · QUIZ 135

Q 1

ANSWERS

1 *The Taming of the Shrew* **2** "I Heard It Through The Grapevine" **3** Mack the Knife **4** "Eye Of The Tiger" **5** "Vincent" **6** Puff Daddy or P Diddy **7** Oasis **8** *Chess* **9** "Night Fever" **10** Take That

Total Trivia

1 What does a fletcher make?

2 Which oath begins with the words “I swear by Apollo the physician”?

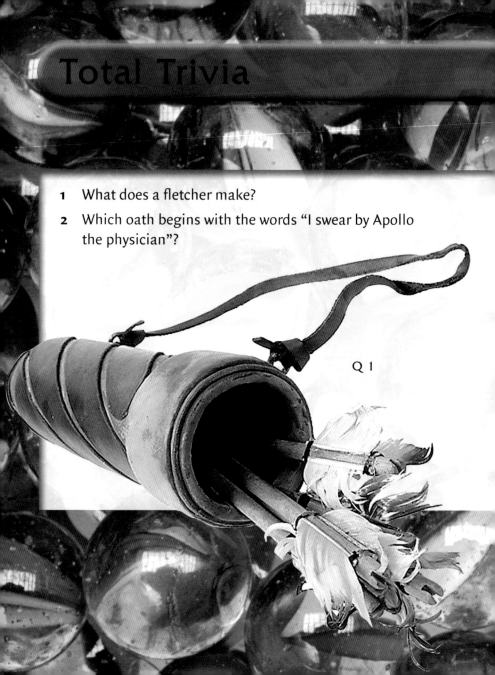

Q 1

3 Which theme park opened its doors to the public on April 12, 1992 in France?

4 Who wrote the poem *Song of Hiawatha*?

5 What nationality is the screen legend Greta Garbo?

6 What is the best-selling newspaper in the United States?

7 Which silver-haired comedy actor hosted the 2003 Oscar ceremonies?

8 Which Greek island did Shirley Valentine travel to?

9 Which 1988 movie saw Wesley Snipes playing a character that was half-human and half-vampire?

10 What does the acronym OPEC stand for?

ANSWERS
1 Arrows 2 Hippocratic Oath 3 Euro Disney 4 Henry Wadsworth Longfellow 5 Swedish 6 *The Wall Street Journal* 7 Steve Martin 8 Mykonos 9 Blade 10 Organization of Petroleum Exporting Countries

Global Matters

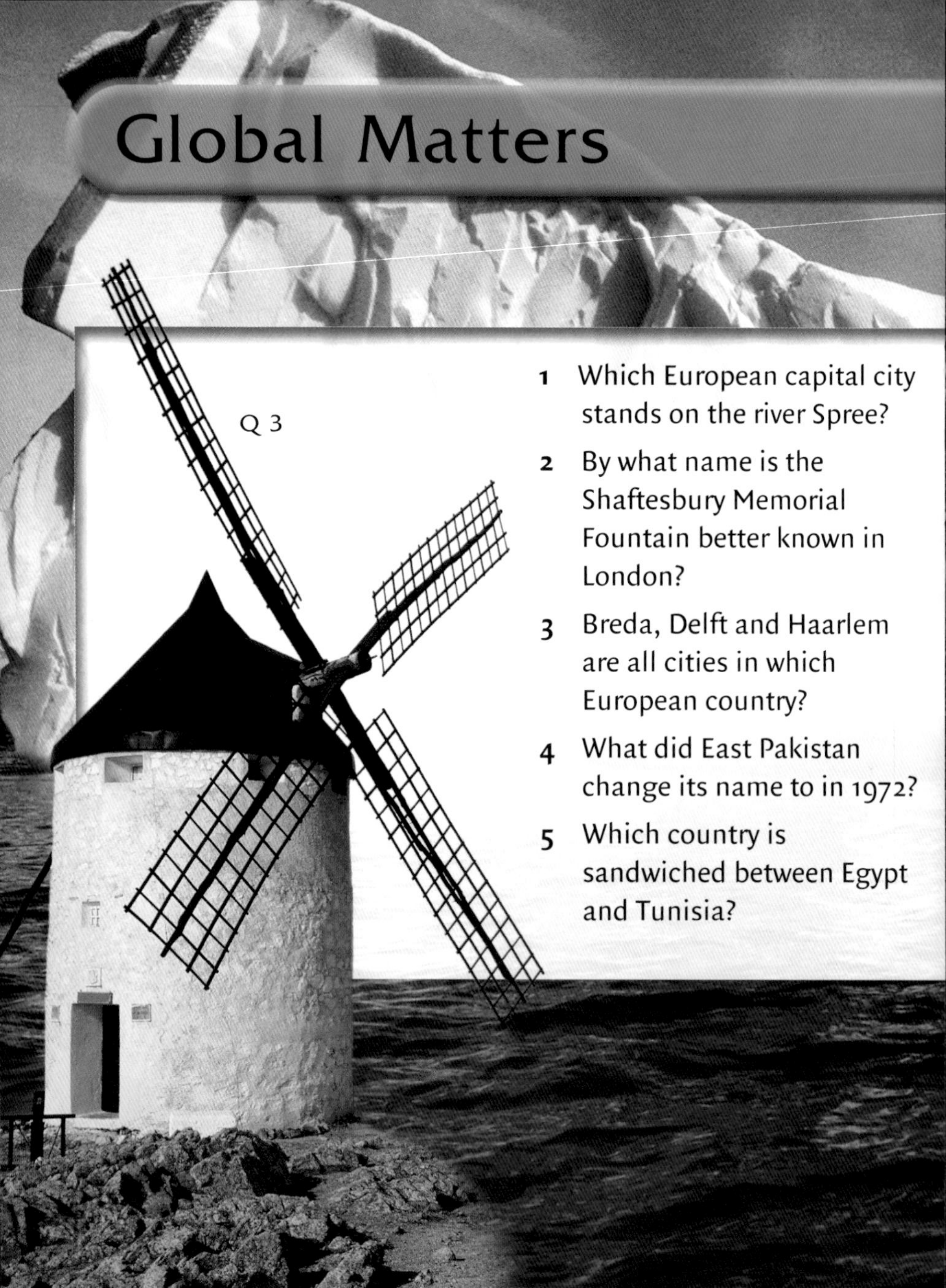

Q 3

1 Which European capital city stands on the river Spree?

2 By what name is the Shaftesbury Memorial Fountain better known in London?

3 Breda, Delft and Haarlem are all cities in which European country?

4 What did East Pakistan change its name to in 1972?

5 Which country is sandwiched between Egypt and Tunisia?

LEVEL 3 • QUIZ 137

6 Which British city is known as The Granite City?

7 On which river do the Victoria Falls lie?

8 Which is Alabama's largest city, also the name of a big English city?

9 In which African country is the port of Agadir?

10 Which inland sea is the world's largest lake?

BACKGROUND BONUS

Which is the coldest, windiest and driest of the continents, and is comprised of 98 percent ice and 2 percent rock?

ANSWERS

1 Berlin **2** Eros **3** Netherlands **4** Bangladesh **5** Libya **6** Aberdeen **7** Zambezi **8** Birmingham **9** Morocco **10** Caspian Sea

Background Bonus Antarctica

1 What is the disease Varicella commonly known as?

2 Toxicology is the study of what?

3 By which three letters is lysergic acid diethylamide also known?

4 What does a radiologist study?

5 What is the most common element in the Universe?

6 In rocket science, what is LOX short for?

7 Which Es are proteins in the body that act as biological catalysts?

8 Which part of the body contains a crown, a neck and a root?

9 Which hormone is responsible for a man's masculine appearance?

10 Who was the first British scientist to receive a knighthood?

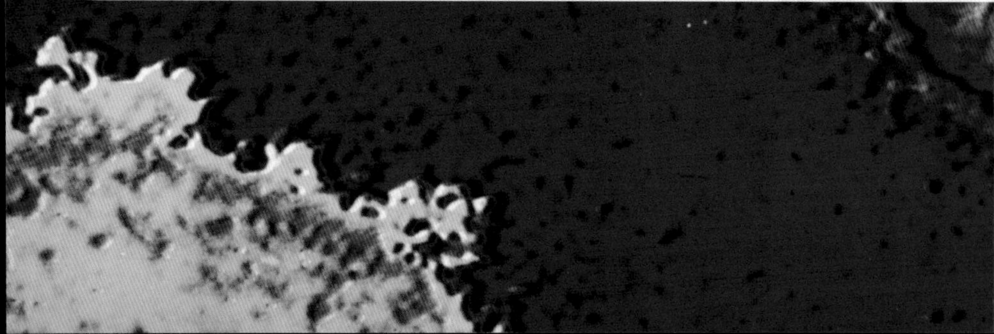

LEVEL 3 · QUIZ 138

Q 1

ANSWERS

1 Chickenpox **2** Poisons **3** LSD **4** X-rays **5** Hydrogen **6** Liquid oxygen **7** Enzymes **8** A tooth **9** Testosterone **10** Isaac Newton

Great and Famous

LEVEL 3 · QUIZ 139

1 Which husband of Marilyn Monroe penned the play *The Crucible?*

2 In which English county was Princess Diana born?

3 What is the name of the Pope's private army?

4 How were Paul and Linda McCartney and Denny Laine known in the world of pop music?

5 Who became senator for New York State in 2000?

6 Which disciple replaced Judas Iscariot?

7 Who played the title role in the movie *Miss Congeniality?*

8 By which one-word name is the Native American princess Rebecca Rolfe better known?

9 Which member of the Rat Pack was born Dino Crocetti?

10 Who provided the voice of Shrek in the animated movie?

ANSWERS

1 Arthur Miller 2 Norfolk 3 The Swiss Guard 4 Wings 5 Hilary Clinton 6 Matthias 7 Sandra Bullock 8 Pocahontas 9 Dean Martin 10 Mike Myers

Written Word

Q 5

LEVEL 3 · QUIZ 140

1 Which C word is the uppermost layer of a forest?
2 From which language does the word ombudsman derive?
3 Which word is the opposite of the nautical term “windward”?
4 What argument is a collective noun for a group of sparrows?
5 What does a numismatist collect?
6 What is the heraldic word for blue?
7 What do the initials ISBN stand for in a book?
8 Which three-letter word is Spanish for “gentleman”?
9 In tailoring, what does the word bespoke mean?
10 What is the only English anagram of the word alarming?

ANSWERS

1 Canopy 2 Swedish 3 Leeward 4 Quarrel 5 Coins or medals 6 Azure 7 International Standard Book Number 8 Don 9 Made to measure 10 Marginal

Sporting Chance

1 The St. Lawrence Ground is the home of which cricket club?

2 Who is the oldest soccer player to be capped for England?

3 In the game of baseball, what do the initials WP signify?

4 What title is given to the official who weighs jockeys and saddles before and after a horse race?

5 Which actor played Muhammed Ali in the 2001 movie *Ali*?

6 What nationality was the first Olympic gymnast to score a perfect 10?

7 Which sports company was founded by Adolph Dassler?

8 What is the name of the Melbourne stadium that hosts the Australian Open tennis championship?

9 Who captained America's Ryder Cup team in 1999?

10 In which city was Martina Navratilova born?

BACKGROUND BONUS

In which sport was Jim Redman six times world champion?

Q 4

ANSWERS

1 Kent **2** Stanley Matthews **3** Wild pitch **4** Clerk of the scales **5** Will Smith
6 Romanian **7** Adidas **8** Flinders Park **9** Ben Crenshaw **10** Prague

Background Bonus Motorcycle racing

Lights, Camera, Action!

1. Who played Cowley in *The Professionals* and Hudson in *Upstairs, Downstairs?*
2. What is Damian's surname in the *Omen* movies?
3. Which British royal family member founded a production company called Ardent Productions?
4. In which movies did Christopher Lloyd play the role of Dr. Brown?

Q 10

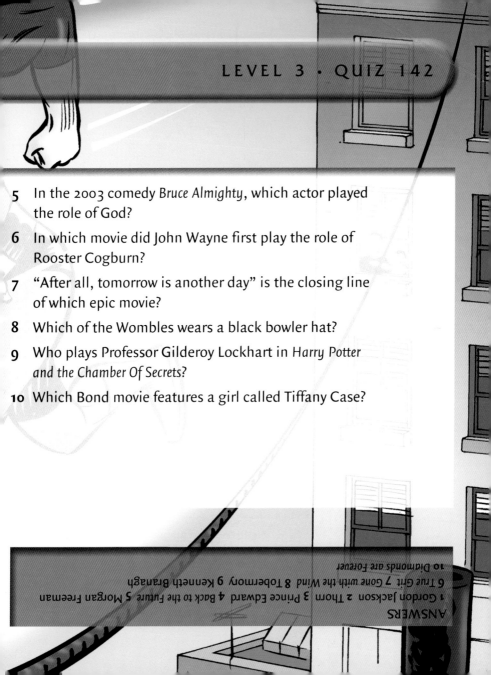

5 In the 2003 comedy *Bruce Almighty*, which actor played the role of God?

6 In which movie did John Wayne first play the role of Rooster Cogburn?

7 "After all, tomorrow is another day" is the closing line of which epic movie?

8 Which of the Wombles wears a black bowler hat?

9 Who plays Professor Gilderoy Lockhart in *Harry Potter and the Chamber Of Secrets?*

10 Which Bond movie features a girl called Tiffany Case?

ANSWERS

1 Gordon Jackson **2** Thorn **3** Prince Edward **4** Back to the Future **5** Morgan Freeman **6** True Grit **7** Gone with the Wind **8** Tobermory **9** Kenneth Branagh **10** Diamonds are Forever

Natural Selection

1 Which breed of terrier is named after the largest island in the Scottish Inner Hebrides?

2 What makes a hummingbird hum?

3 By which three letters is Mad Cow's Disease also known?

4 How many toes has an ostrich on each foot?

5 Welsh Mountain and Shetland are both breeds of what?

6 Which R word is an animal that chews cud?

7 Which has the drier skin, a frog or a toad?

8 Which bird, native to Australia, is known as the laughing jackass?

9 Whooper, trumpeter and mute are species of which bird?

10 Which P is the smallest species of bat native to Britain?

ANSWERS

1 Skye terrier **2** The beating of its wings **3** BSE **4** Two **5** Pony **6** Ruminant **7** A toad **8** Kookaburra **9** Swan **10** Pippistrelle

Amazing Architecture

Can you name these famous landmarks?

1

2

3

4

LEVEL 3 · QUIZ 144

6

8

ANSWERS

1 Taj Mahal **2** Parthenon **3** Notre Dame **4** Capitol building
5 Golden Gate Bridge **6** Tower of Pisa **7** St. Basil's Cathedral **8** Big Ben

Written Word

Q 9

BACKGROUND BONUS

Which novel by E.B. White features a pig called Wilbur?

1 Who penned the classic novel *Vanity Fair*?
2 Which book of the Bible first chronicles Moses' birth?
3 Which book of the Bible first chronicles Moses' death?
4 Which H.G. Wells novel is partly set in the year 802701AD?
5 What is Inspector Morse's first name?
6 Desdemona is the wife of which Shakespeare character?
7 Alphabetically, what is the first book of the Bible?
8 For what genre of novels are The Hugo Awards presented?
9 In the nursery rhyme, who killed Cock Robin?
10 What is the name of Miss Marple's home village?

ANSWERS

1 William Makepiece Thackeray **2** Exodus **3** Deuteronomy **4** The Time Machine **5** Endeavour **6** Othello **7** Acts **8** Sci-fi novels **9** The sparrow **10** St. Mary Mead

Background Bonus *Charlotte's Web*

Making History

1 In the 1970s, who were Britain's opponents in the Cod War?

2 In the Bible, who is the stepfather of Salome?

3 Who signed The Pact of Steel with Hitler in 1939?

4 In which year did the United States celebrate its bicentennial?

Q 3

5 In which South American country was the lost city of the Incas rediscovered in 1911?

6 What began in the United States in January 1920 and ended in December 1933?

7 Which wife of Henry VIII was the mother of Mary Tudor?

8 What was the name of Alfred the Great's kingdom?

9 At which battle was Richard III killed?

10 Who collaborated on The Communist Manifesto with Frederick Engels?

ANSWERS

1 Iceland **2** Herod **3** Benito Mussolini **4** 1976 **5** Peru **6** Prohibition **7** Catherine of Aragon **8** Wessex **9** The Battle of Bosworth Field **10** Karl Marx

Music Mania

1 Which hit record for The Bee Gees was covered by Steps in 1998?

2 What C is a musical instrument with a hexagonal bellow, metal reeds and finger studs?

3 Which rock guitarist is known as Slow Hand?

4 Which song written by Cat Stevens was a hit for both P.P. Arnold and Rod Stewart?

5 Where are the operas *Carmen* and *The Marriage of Figaro* set?

6 Who provided the lead vocals for the rock group Led Zeppelin?

7 Which musical was based on the H.G. Wells story *Kipps*?

8 Which song from *Butch Cassidy and the Sundance Kid* won a Best Song Oscar?

9 In The Beatles hit "Get Back", what is the home state of Jo Jo?

10 Where is the musical *Phantom of the Opera* set?

Q 6

ANSWERS

1 "Tragedy" **2** Concertina **3** Eric Clapton **4** "The First Cut Is The Deepest" **5** Seville **6** Robert Plant **7** *Half a Sixpence* **8** "Raindrops Keep Falling On My Head" **9** Arizona **10** Paris

Total Trivia

1 Which of the Teletubbies is yellow?

2 What is the Scottish equivalent of The Order of the Garter?

3 Which number is opposite 3 on a dice?

4 What is the name of the Lord Chancellor's seat in parliament?

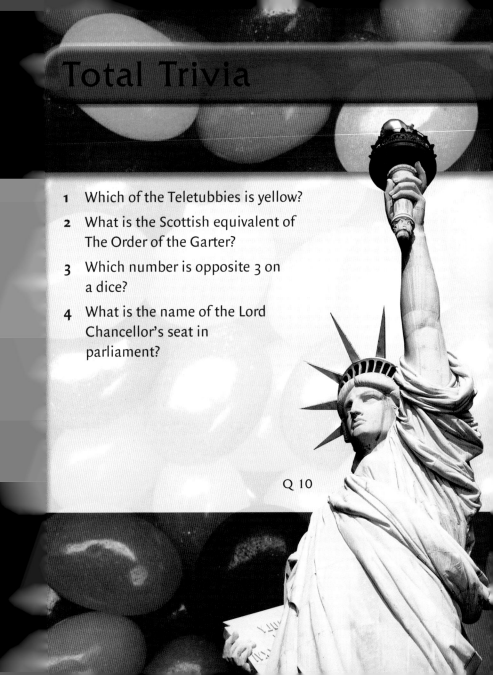

Q 10

LEVEL 3 · QUIZ 148

5 Which playing card is known as the black lady?

6 What does the I stand for in MI5?

7 Which bird is depicted on the Egyptian flag?

8 Which Belgian cartoon character celebrated his 70th birthday in 1999?

9 Who is the patron saint of lovers?

10 Gracie Mansion is the official residence of the mayor of which U.S. city?

ANSWERS

1 La La 2 The Order Of The Thistle 3 Four 4 The Woolsack 5 Queen of Spades 6 Intelligence 7 An eagle 8 Tin Tin 9 St. Valentine 10 New York

Global Matters

1 What is the name of the U.S. equivalent of Britain's SAS?

2 The Canadian city of Toronto stands on the shores of which lake?

3 What is the official language of Liechtenstein?

4 Which was the world's first city to have a population exceeding one million?

5 Which U.S. state is known as the Grand Canyon state?

6 Which sea separates Poland from the Scandinavian Peninsular?

7 In which Australian state does the city of Sydney lie?

8 Atlanta is the capital of which U.S. state?

9 What did Ceylon change its name to?

10 Which is the only U.S. state capital to end in X?

BACKGROUND BONUS

If it is summer in Buenos Aires, what season will it be in Oslo?

ANSWERS

1 The Delta Force **2** Lake Ontario **3** German **4** London **5** Arizona **6** The Baltic Sea **7** New South Wales **8** Georgia **9** Sri Lanka **10** Phoenix

Background Bonus Winter

Scientifically Speaking

1 What does the S stand for in the acronym SONAR?

2 Which hormone stimulates the nervous system and raises the heart rate?

3 Which is the only chemical element beginning with the letter U?

4 Which sex is a person with an XX chromosome?

5 What name is given to solid carbon dioxide?

6 Which is the only chemical element named after a U.S. state?

7 What is the highest point of a triangle called?

8 What is the square root of 121?

9 Which organ is affected by cirrhosis?

10 Which unit of pressure is represented by the symbol Pa?

Q 1

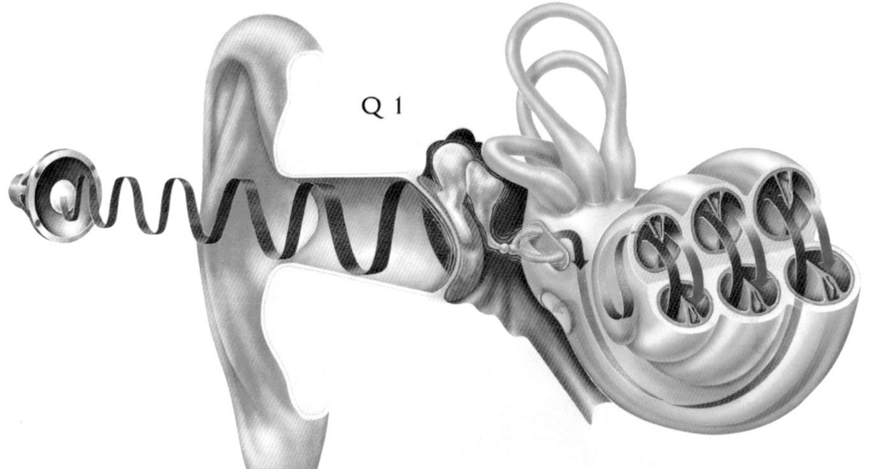

ANSWERS

1 Sound **2** Adrenalin **3** Uranium **4** Female **5** Dry ice **6** Californium **7** Apex **8** 11 **9** Liver **10** Pascal

Great and Famous

LEVEL 3 · QUIZ 151

1 In which year was Prince Charles born?
2 Whose portrait features on a U.S. $100 bill?
3 In which European capital was Harry Houdini born?
4 Eisenhower, Kennedy, Johnson, Nixon: who came next?
5 Who was born Jan Ludvik Hock and died at sea?
6 Which article of clothing got its name from a French trapeze artist born in 1830?
7 Which British prime minister was known as The Welsh Wizard?
8 Who is Charlie Sheen's actor brother?
9 Which star of the movie *Half a Sixpence* was born Thomas Hicks?
10 Who links the movies *Cleopatra*, *The Wild Geese* and *Where Eagles Dare?*

ANSWERS

1 1948 **2** Benjamin Franklin **3** Budapest **4** Ford **5** Robert Maxwell **6** Leotard after Jules Leotard **7** David Lloyd George **8** Emilio Estevez **9** Tommy Steele **10** Richard Burton

Sporting Chance

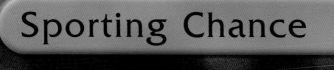

1 In which cricket stadium was the first FA Cup final played?

2 What is the area of an American Football gridiron called, where touchdowns are scored?

3 How many players in a Gaelic soccer team?

Q 8

4 Which snooker player wrote a book entitled *How to be Really Interesting*?

5 Do the Australian cricket team wear green or blue caps?

6 In 2003, who resigned as manager of Northern Ireland's soccer team?

7 Which city hosted the 2002 Winter Olympics?

8 In which country did the sport of kendo originate?

9 Which sport is played by Australia's Sydney City Roosters?

10 What do the initials HW stand for with regard to a cricket dismissal?

ANSWERS

1 The Oval **2** End zone **3** 15 **4** Steve Davis **5** Green **6** Sammy McIlroy **7** Salt Lake City **8** Japan **9** Rugby league **10** Hit wicket

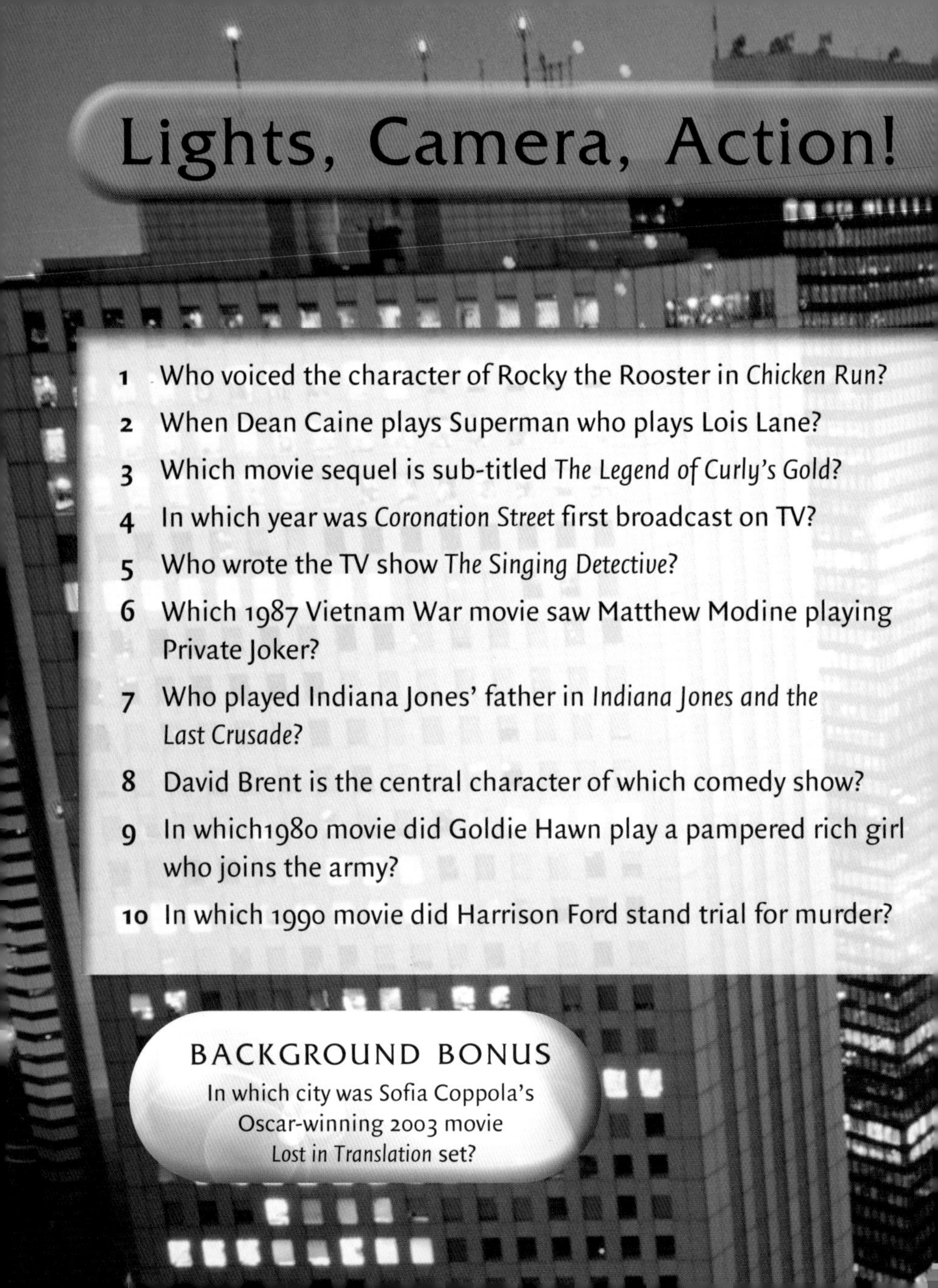

Lights, Camera, Action!

1. Who voiced the character of Rocky the Rooster in *Chicken Run?*
2. When Dean Caine plays Superman who plays Lois Lane?
3. Which movie sequel is sub-titled *The Legend of Curly's Gold?*
4. In which year was *Coronation Street* first broadcast on TV?
5. Who wrote the TV show *The Singing Detective?*
6. Which 1987 Vietnam War movie saw Matthew Modine playing Private Joker?
7. Who played Indiana Jones' father in *Indiana Jones and the Last Crusade?*
8. David Brent is the central character of which comedy show?
9. In which1980 movie did Goldie Hawn play a pampered rich girl who joins the army?
10. In which 1990 movie did Harrison Ford stand trial for murder?

BACKGROUND BONUS

In which city was Sofia Coppola's Oscar-winning 2003 movie *Lost in Translation* set?

Q 7

ANSWERS

1 Mel Gibson **2** Teri Hatcher **3** City Slickers II **4** 1960 **5** Dennis Potter **6** Full Metal Jacket **7** Sean Connery **8** *The Office* **9** Private Benjamin **10** Presumed Innocent

Background Bonus Tokyo

Natural Selection

1. In the U.S., what is the official bird of the smallest state?
2. In 1859, who published *On the Origin of Species*?
3. What is another name for the sea parrot?
4. Which is the world's heaviest snake?
5. Which three-letter word is another name for a wildebeest?
6. Which insects lives in a formicary?
7. Are polar bears native to the North Pole or the South Pole?
8. What is unusual about the birth process of armadillos?
9. Is an albacore a fish, a bird or a mammal?
10. Which is the only species of deer in which the female has antlers?

LEVEL 3 · QUIZ 154

Q 3

ANSWERS

1 Rhode Island Red **2** Charles Darwin **3** Puffin **4** Anaconda **5** Gnu **6** Ants **7** North Pole **8** They always give birth to identical twins **9** A fish **10** Caribou

Making History

Q 5

AMERICAE SIVE NOVI ORBIS, NOVA DESCRIPTIO.

LEVEL 3 · QUIZ 155

1 What was the Supreme Council of ancient Rome called?

2 Which seafarer was buried with a box of tobacco upon his death in 1618?

3 Who was the last monarch of the Stuart dynasty?

4 In 1863, who delivered an historic speech known as The Gettysburg Address?

5 In 1946, who claimed that an Iron Curtain had descended across of Europe?

6 Who deposed King Idris in 1969?

7 On which island was Napoleon Bonaparte born?

8 Which English king was known as The Unready?

9 Who succeeded Queen Victoria?

10 Which *Carry On* movie chronicled events of 1492?

ANSWERS

1 The Senate **2** Sir Walter Raleigh **3** Queen Anne **4** Abraham Lincoln **5** Winston Churchill **6** Colonel Gadaffi **7** Corsica **8** Ethelred the Unready **9** Edward VII **10** *Carry On Columbus*

Planets and Stars

Can you guess the names of these planets and constellations?

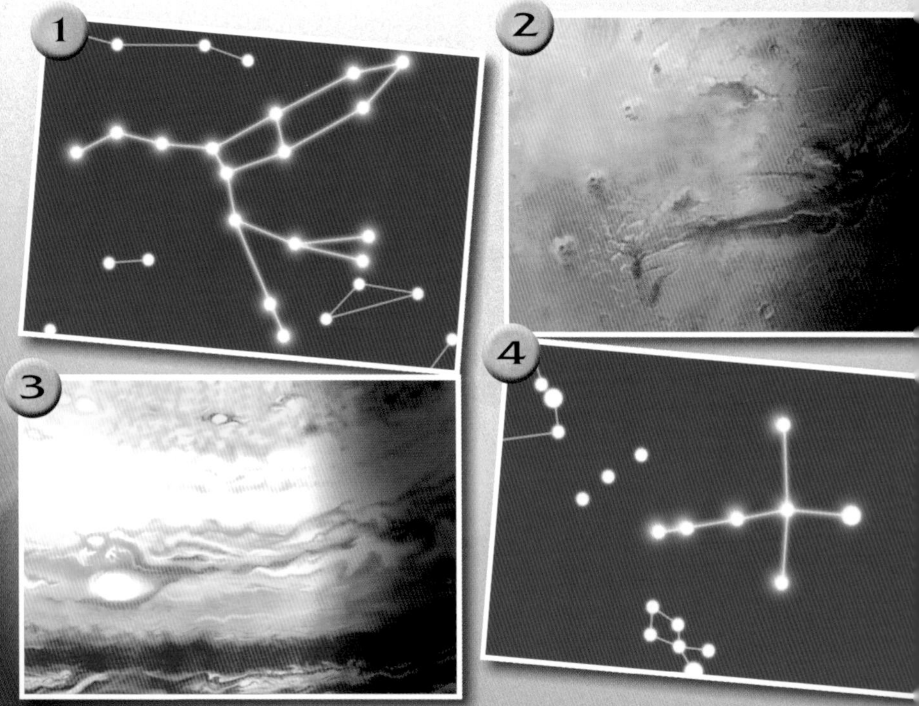

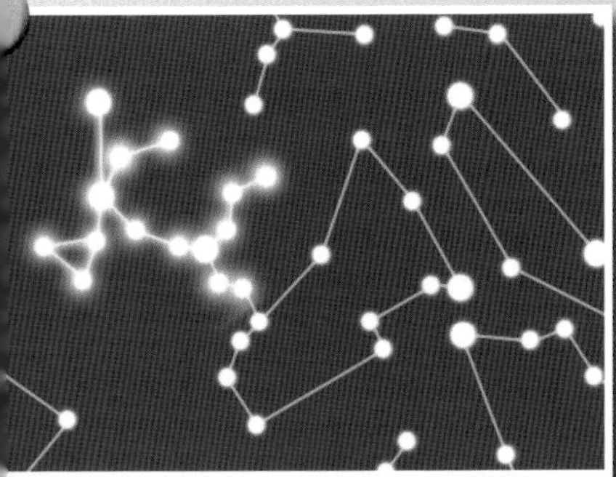

6

8

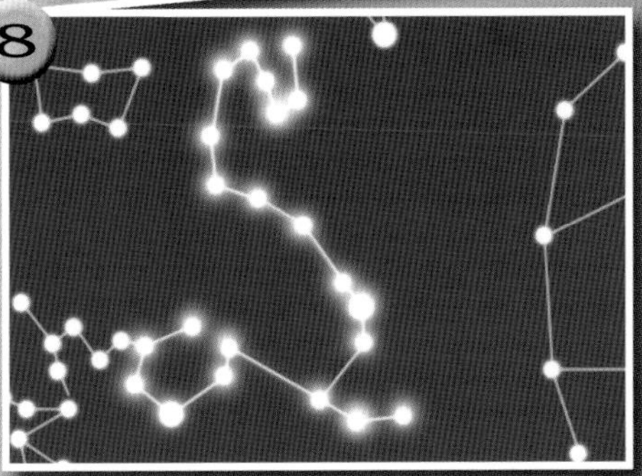

ANSWERS
1 The Great Bear **2** Mars **3** Jupiter **4** Cygnus **5** The Great Dog **6** Saturn **7** Uranus **8** The Scorpion

Music Mania

1 Which nation won the Eurovision Song Contest in 2003?

2 Which musical features the song "Anything You Can Do, I Can Do Better"?

3 What M is a device that marks time in music by means of an inverted pendulum?

4 Which opera heroine worked in a cigarette factory?

5 Who won the Eurovision Song Contest for the U.K. while singing in her bare feet?

Q 3

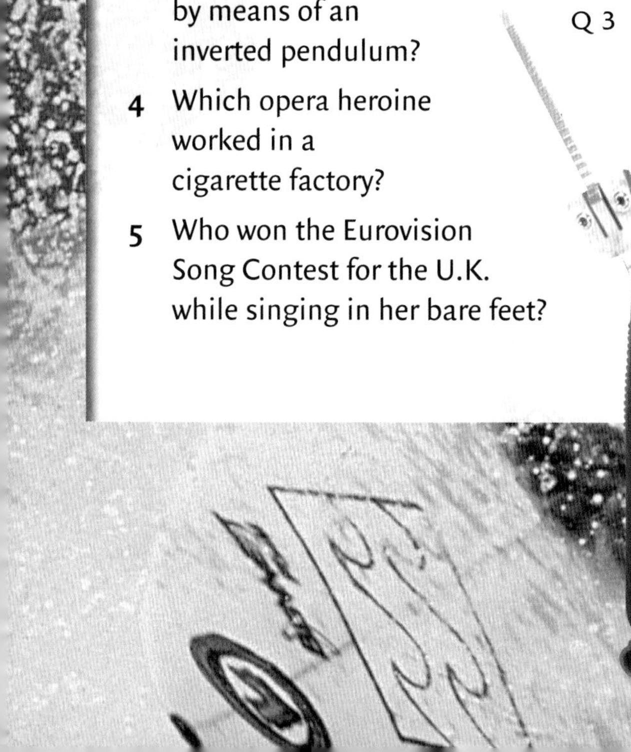

6 Which song ends with the line "God speed your love to me"?

7 Which song from the Disney movie *Aladdin* won a Best Song Oscar?

8 Which Beatles song is also the name of a street in Liverpool?

9 Which Abba hit contains the line "No more carefree laughter, silence ever after"?

10 Which musical tells the story of the Pontabee brothers and their search for suitable wives?

BACKGROUND BONUS

Which Beach Boys song begins with the line "If everybody had an ocean"?

ANSWERS

1 Turkey **2** *Annie get your Gun* **3** Metronome **4** Carmen **5** Sandie Shaw **6** "Unchained Melody" **7** "A Whole New World" **8** "Penny Lane" **9** "Knowing Me Knowing You" **10** *Seven Brides for Seven Brothers* **Background Bonus** "Surfin' USA"

Total Trivia

1 In 1999, Sean Connery campaigned on behalf of which U.K. political party?

2 How many years mark a sapphire wedding anniversary?

3 In which London borough was the Millennium Dome erected?

4 Which month of the year is named after the queen of the Roman gods?

5 In Arthurian legend, who is the father of Sir Galahad?

6 Which F word is land left unploughed for a year?

7 What is the cube root of one million?

8 Who sang the Bond theme for *Diamonds are Forever*?

9 Which P is a matador on horseback?

10 What is the name of Postman Pat's cat?

LEVEL 3 · QUIZ 158

ANSWERS

1 The Scottish Nationalist Party 2 45 years 3 Greenwich 4 June after Juno
5 Sir Lancelot 6 Fallow 7 100 8 Shirley Bassey 9 Picador 10 Jess

Global Matters

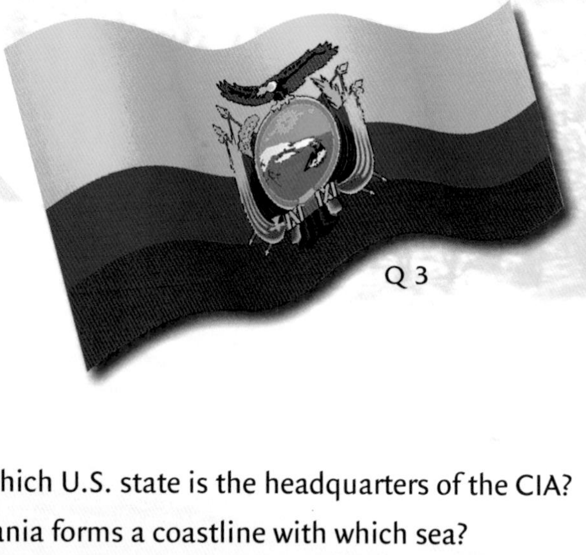

Q 3

1 In which U.S. state is the headquarters of the CIA?

2 Albania forms a coastline with which sea?

LEVEL 3 · QUIZ 159

3 Which country do the Galapagos Islands belong to?

4 Which capital city is home to the Little Mermaid statue?

5 Which is the oldest university in the United States?

6 The city of Tokyo is located on which Japanese island?

7 Which Asian city is home to the Taj Mahal?

8 What was the capital city of England before London?

9 What is the name of the famous tower in Chicago?

10 What did Saigon change its name to?

ANSWERS

1 Virginia **2** Adriatic Sea **3** Ecuador **4** Copenhagen **5** Harvard University **6** Honshu **7** Agra **8** Winchester **9** The Sears Tower **10** Ho Chi Minh City

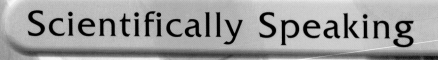

Scientifically Speaking

1 C is the chemical symbol for which element?

2 What do the initials CNS stand for with regard to the human body?

3 The moons of which planet are all named after Shakespearean characters?

4 Is sulphur green or yellow?

5 What is another name for the third molars?

Q 3

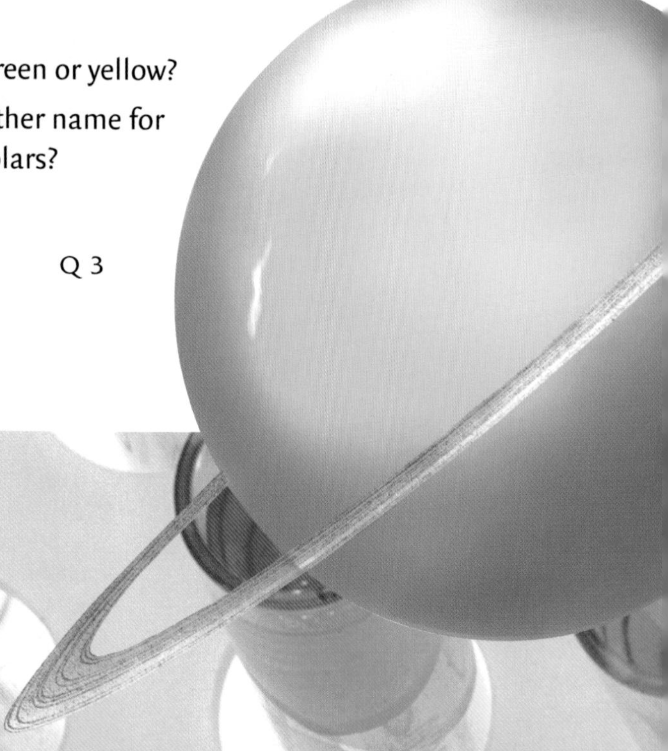

6 What do the initials CPU stand for in computing?

7 What name is given to an angle of less than 90 degrees?

8 What measures 12 on the Beaufort Scale?

9 What is the liquid part of the blood called?

10 Which vitamin is also known as ascorbic acid?

ANSWERS

1 Carbon **2** Central Nervous System **3** Uranus **4** Yellow **5** Wisdom teeth **6** Central Processing Unit **7** Acute angle **8** Hurricane **9** Plasma **10** Vitamin C

Great and Famous

1 What does the C stand for in Arthur C. Clarke?

2 On TV, who has played a timelord and a scarecrow?

3 Which member of Laurel and Hardy was born in Britain?

4 Who has presented the TV programme *The Sky at Night* for over 40 years?

5 Who performed his *River Dance* for the first time in Dublin in 1994?

6 Which singer was named Man of the Year in 1985 after organizing the Live Aid concert?

7 Which fashion designer introduced the New Look in 1947?

8 In 2000, which golfer wrote a controversial book entitled *Into the Bear Pit?*

9 In 1990, who became the first female president of the Irish Republic?

10 Which U.S. state was named after Queen Henrietta Maria?

BACKGROUND BONUS

Which post-impressionist painter attempted to take the life of fellow-artist Paul Gaugin before taking his own?

ANSWERS

1 Charles 2 Jon Pertwee 3 Stan Laurel 4 Patrick Moore 5 Michael Flatley 6 Bob Geldof 7 Christian Dior 8 Mark James 9 Mary Robinson 10 Maryland

Background Bonus Vincent Van Gogh

Written Word

Q 2

LEVEL 3 · QUIZ 162

1 According to the proverb, what can't you get from a sow's ear?

2 What is the board game of draughts known as in the United States?

3 Which H is Spanish for "man"?

4 What is the superlative of the word funny?

5 Which instrument has a name derived from the Hawaiian for "jumping flea"?

6 If a person's face is described as rugose, is it red, wrinkled or freckled?

7 What does the prefix neo denote?

8 Which R is an official language of Switzerland?

9 According to the proverb, what is cleanliness next to?

10 Which T is the art of shaping hedges into ornamental figures?

ANSWERS

1 A silk purse **2** Checkers **3** Hombre **4** Funniest **5** Ukulele **6** Wrinkled **7** New **8** Romansch **9** Godliness **10** Topiary

Sporting Chance

1 In which sport is a Canadian pairs race contested?
2 How many players are there in a baseball team?
3 Which Parisian stadium hosts the French Open tennis championships?
4 Which South African golfer was known as The Man in Black?

Q 7

5 Which sport is played on an area measuring 2.7 m (9 ft) by 1.5 m (5 ft)?

6 What sport is played by the London Towers?

7 Which British driver was the first teenager to score championship points in Formula One motor racing?

8 In skiing, does green or blue indicate a beginners' slope?

9 Which Q is the player that throws the ball in American football?

10 On which piece of sporting equipment is a *tsukahara* performed?

ANSWERS

1 Canoeing 2 Nine 3 Roland Garros 4 Gary Player 5 Table tennis 6 Basketball 7 Jensen Button 8 Green 9 Quarterback 10 A vaulting horse

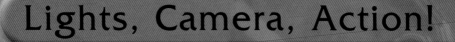

Lights, Camera, Action!

1 In which movie did Burt Lancaster play the convict Robert F. Stroud?

2 Who played the roles of both Michael and Dorothy in *Tootsie*?

3 In which 1986 movie did Paul Hogan leave Walkabout Creek to travel to New York City?

4 In which sitcom do Sharon and Tracey share a house in Chigwell?

5 Which "creepy" TV family live in the town of Cemetery Ridge?

6 In which movie did Jim Carrey play a character suffering from schizophrenia?

7 Who played Paris in the TV show *Mission Impossible*, but was better known for his role as an alien?

8 Which actor was coming to dinner in *Guess who's Coming to Dinner?*

9 Which actress was portrayed in *Mommie Dearest*?

10 In which comedy movie did Robert DeNiro subject Ben Stiller to a lie-detector test?

Q 4

ANSWERS

1 *Birdman of Alcatraz* **2** Dustin Hoffman **3** *Crocodile Dundee* **4** *Birds of A Feather* **5** *The Addams Family* **6** *Me, Myself and Irene* **7** Leonard Nimoy **8** Sidney Poitier **9** Joan Crawford **10** *Meet the Parents*

Natural Selection

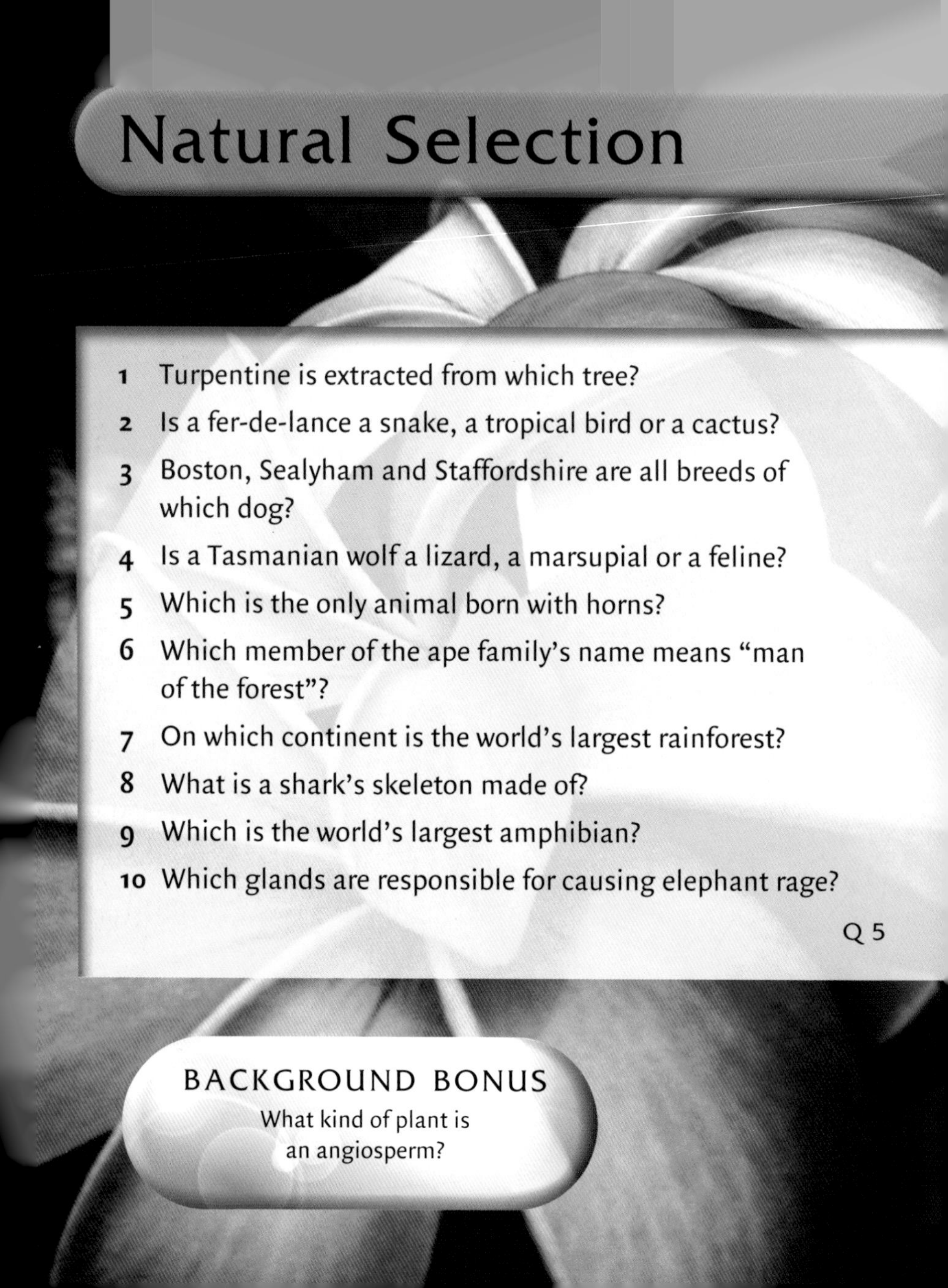

1 Turpentine is extracted from which tree?
2 Is a fer-de-lance a snake, a tropical bird or a cactus?
3 Boston, Sealyham and Staffordshire are all breeds of which dog?
4 Is a Tasmanian wolf a lizard, a marsupial or a feline?
5 Which is the only animal born with horns?
6 Which member of the ape family's name means "man of the forest"?
7 On which continent is the world's largest rainforest?
8 What is a shark's skeleton made of?
9 Which is the world's largest amphibian?
10 Which glands are responsible for causing elephant rage?

Q 5

BACKGROUND BONUS

What kind of plant is an angiosperm?

ANSWERS

1 Pine tree **2** Snake **3** Terrier **4** Marsupial **5** Giraffe **6** Orang-utan **7** South America **8** Cartilage **9** Giant salamander **10** Musth glands

Background Bonus A flowering plant

Written Word

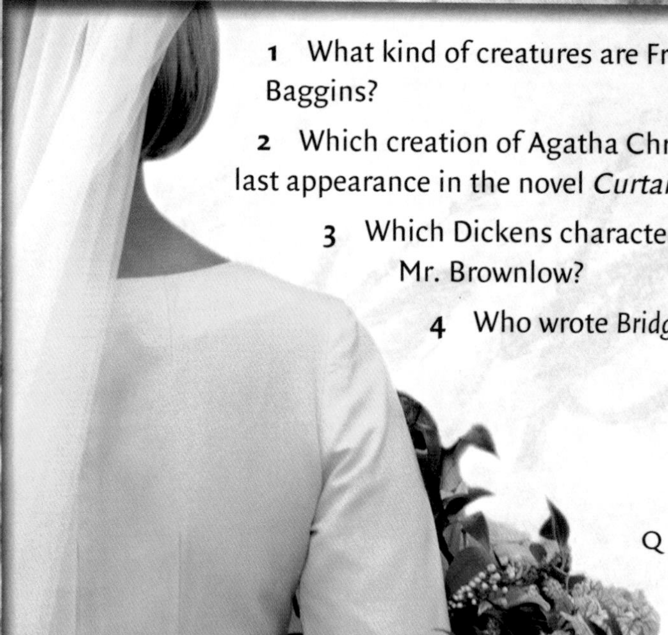

1 What kind of creatures are Frodo and Bilbo Baggins?

2 Which creation of Agatha Christie made his last appearance in the novel *Curtain*?

3 Which Dickens character was adopted by Mr. Brownlow?

4 Who wrote *Bridget Jones's Diary*?

Q 5

5 Captain Charles Ryder is the central character in which novel?

6 What is the name of the factory owner in *Charlie and the Chocolate Factory*?

7 Who created the characters of Lucy Van Pelt and Charlie Brown?

8 Who wrote the book *The Female Eunuch*?

9 In the nursery rhyme, who put pussy in the well?

10 Which Daniel Defoe literary creation was born in Newgate Prison?

ANSWERS

1 Hobbits **2** Hercule Poirot **3** Oliver Twist **4** Helen Fielding **5** Brideshead Revisited **6** Willy Wonka **7** Charles Schultz **8** Germaine Greer **9** Little Johnny Green **10** Moll Flanders

Making History

1 Which king did Guy Fawkes and his co-conspirators attempt to assassinate in the Gunpowder Plot?

2 Which Shakespeare character became king of Scotland in 1040?

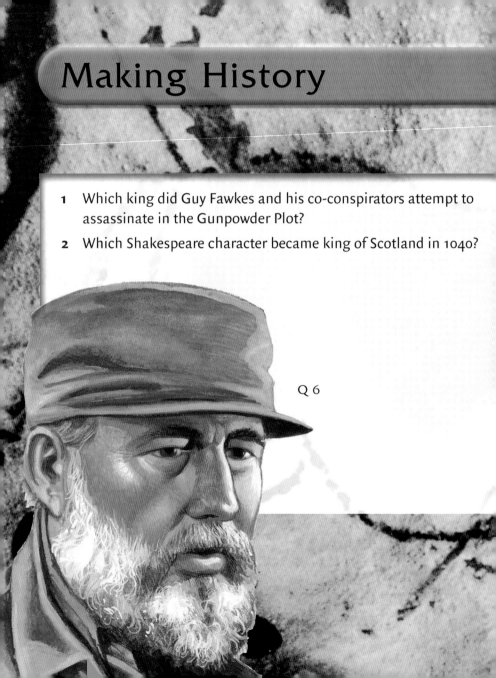

Q 6

LEVEL 3 • QUIZ 167

3 Which state did Russia sell to the United States in 1867?

4 Which British TV sitcom was based on the activities of World War II's Home Guard?

5 What was the capital of Scotland prior to 1437?

6 Who became leader of Cuba in 1959?

7 Which British nurse was executed in Belgium in 1915?

8 Were Theodore Roosevelt and Franklin D. Roosevelt related?

9 In which English town was the Magna Carta signed?

10 Who led the slaves of Rome in rebellion in 73BC?

ANSWERS

1 James I **2** Macbeth **3** Alaska **4** *Dad's Army* **5** Perth **6** Fidel Castro **7** Edith Cavell **8** Yes, they were cousins **9** Runnymede **10** Spartacus

Animal Antics

Can you guess the names of these animals from their beaks and mouths?

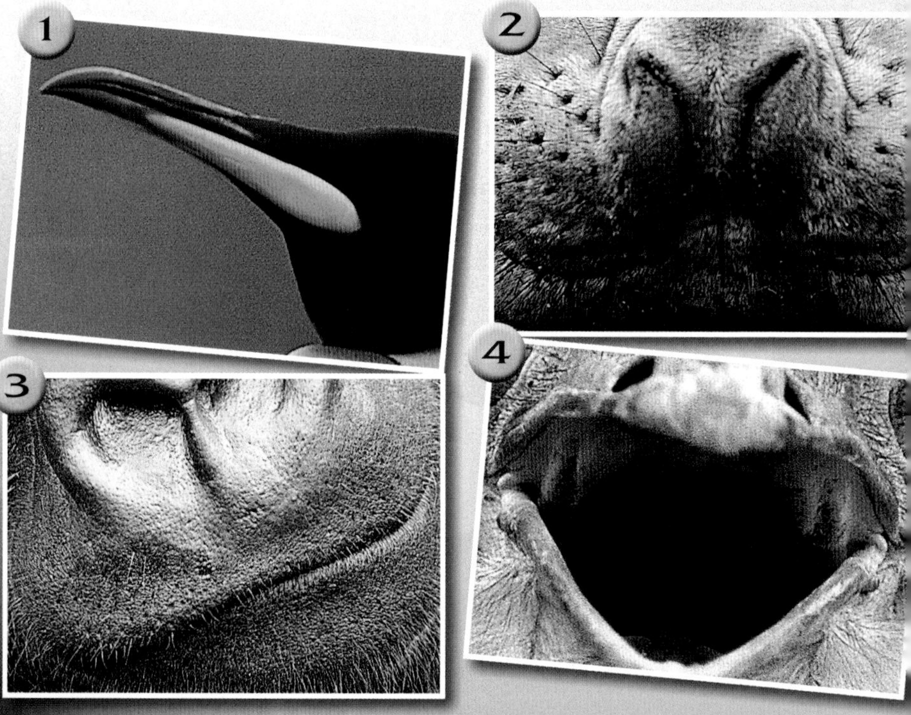

LEVEL 3 · QUIZ 168

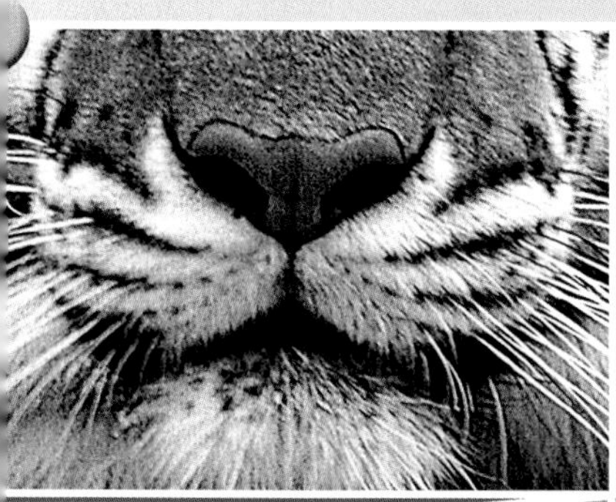

6

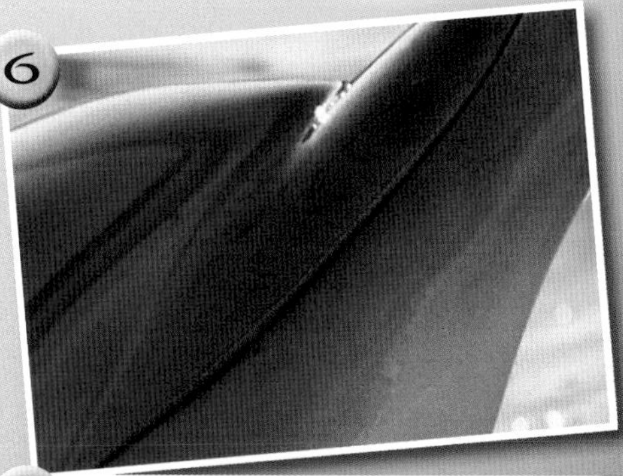

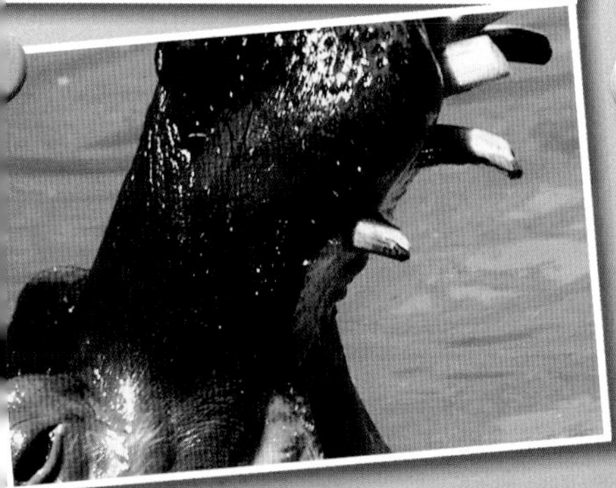

8

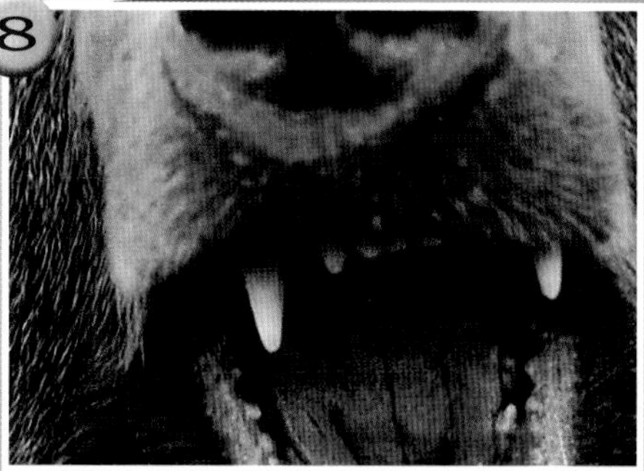

ANSWERS
1 Penguin 2 Seal 3 Gorilla 4 Ostrich 5 Tiger 6 Dolphin 7 Hippopotamus
8 Grizzly Bear

Music Mania

1 How many quavers are there in a semibreve?

2 Which singer was born George Ivan?

3 Which country did Celine Dion represent at the Eurovision Song Contest?

4 How is Marvin Lee Aday better known?

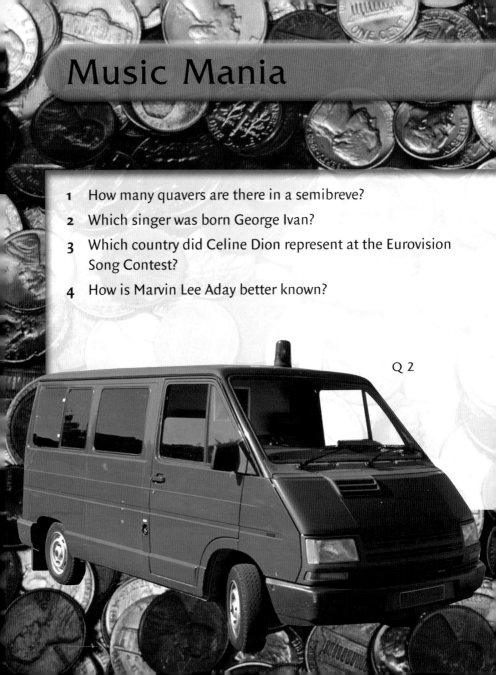

Q 2

5 In the song "Three Steps To Heaven", what is step three?

6 Who left the Spice Girls in May 1998?

7 What do the initials EMI stand for with regard to the record label?

8 Who provided lead vocals for Wet Wet Wet?

9 Which rock legend was played by Val Kilmer in the 1991 movie *The Doors*?

10 The rock group Uriah Heep took its name from a character in which Dickens' novel?

BACKGROUND BONUS

Which Pink Floyd song begins with the sound of cash registers opening?

ANSWERS

1 Eight **2** Van Morrison **3** Switzerland **4** Meat Loaf **5** "You kiss and hold her tightly" **6** Geri Halliwell **7** Electric And Music Industries **8** Marti Pellow **9** Jim Morrison **10** *David Copperfield* **Background Bonus** "Money"

Total Trivia

1 What is German for two?
2 From which card game did the term Grand Slam originate?
3 Which fabric gets its name from the city of Damascus?
4 Which Australian bridge is nicknamed The Coat Hanger?
5 Are the leather seats in the House of Commons red or green?
6 In which TV show did the character Kermit the frog first appear?
7 Which is the oldest university in France?
8 Which Bond villain has the first name of Auric?
9 "Elliot" was the first spoken word of which extraterrestrial character?
10 Which pantomime features the character of Idiot Jack?

LEVEL 3 · QUIZ 170

Q 2

ANSWERS
1 *Zwei* **2** Bridge **3** Damask **4** Sydney Harbour Bridge **5** Green **6** *Sesame Street* **7** The Sorbonne **8** *Goldfinger* **9** *E.T.* **10** Dick Whittington

Global Matters

1 Which U.S. state's flag depicts the Union Jack in the top left-hand corner?

2 Which U.S. city gets its name from the capital of ancient Egypt?

3 Which mountain range separates Europe and Asia?

4 In which Middle Eastern city is the Dome of the Rock?

Q 6

LEVEL 3 · QUIZ 171

5 In which country is Casablanca?
6 The Great Barrier Reef lies off the coast of which Australian state?
7 Mount Eiger lies in which European country?
8 What is the official language of San Marino?
9 Which U.S. city is known as Mile High City?
10 What does the Statue of Liberty wear on her feet?

ANSWERS
1 Hawaii **2** Memphis **3** The Urals **4** Jerusalem **5** Morocco **6** Queensland **7** Switzerland **8** Italian **9** Denver **10** Sandals

Scientifically Speaking

1 Where is the gluteus maximus muscle located?

2 What does an electrocardiograph record?

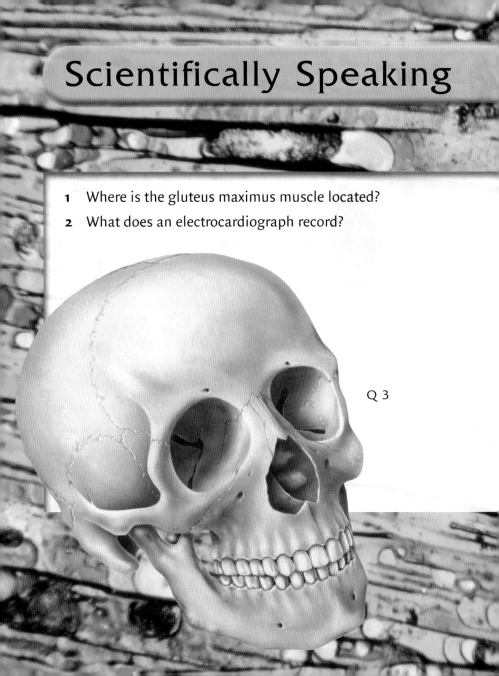

Q 3

LEVEL 3 · QUIZ 172

3 Which is the hardest bone in the human body?
4 What can be true, false or floating?
5 Which P is the science of making artificial limbs?
6 An otoscope is used for looking inside what?
7 Which BT is the common name for the hallux?
8 Which is the rational side of the brain, the left or the right?
9 Which F is a sheath from which a hair grows?
10 What is the philtrum?

ANSWERS
1 The buttocks 2 Heart beat 3 Jaw bone 4 Ribs 5 Prosthetics 6 The ear 7 Big toe 8 Left side 9 Follicle 10 The groove between the top lip and nose

Great and Famous

1 Who links the movies *Casino Royale*, *Bananas* and *Annie Hall*?

2 Who founded the Body Shop?

3 Which dictator was arrested in a London clinic in October 1998?

4 In the Bible, who is the father of Ham, Shem and Japeth?

5 On TV, which actor has played Ironside and Perry Mason?

6 Which Russian exhibited his imperial Easter eggs at the Paris Exhibition in 1900?

7 In 1993, who shared the Nobel Peace Prize with Nelson Mandela?

8 Which first did Valentina Tereshkova achieve in 1963?

9 Which Native American chief led the victorious forces at the Battle of the Little Big Horn?

10 Which U.S. president was assassinated in 1901?

BACKGROUND BONUS

Which novel by Victor Hugo contains one of the most famous acts of revenge in world literature?

LEVEL 3 • QUIZ 173

ANSWERS

1 Woody Allen **2** Anita Roddick **3** General Pinochet **4** Noah **5** Raymond Burr **6** Carl Fabergé **7** F.W. de Klerk **8** The first woman in space **9** Chief Sitting Bull **10** William McKinley **Background Bonus** *The Hunchback of Notre Dame*

Sporting Chance

Q 1

LEVEL 3 · QUIZ 174

1 Which sport is played by the Barcelona Dragons?

2 In which sport do competitors “soop the ice”?

3 Which trophy is presented to rugby union World Cup winners?

4 Which Liverpool striker was voted BBC Sports Personality of the Year in 1998?

5 On a golf course, what do the initials GUR signify?

6 Which S is a skier’s quilt trousers, held up by shoulder straps?

7 Which Grand National winner of the 1980s shares its name with a mountain?

8 Which former manager of the England soccer team died in April 1999?

9 Which cricketer was the first player to take 300 Test wickets?

10 What is the pet name of Australia’s rugby union team?

ANSWERS

1 American football **2** Curling **3** William Webb Ellis Trophy **4** Michael Owen **5** Ground under repair **6** Salopettes **7** Ben Nevis **8** Alf Ramsey **9** Fred Trueman **10** The Wallabies

Lights, Camera, Action!

1 Who connects the movies *Little Women*, *Beetlejuice* and *Edward Scissorhands*?

2 Who plays Trigger in *Only Fools and Horses*?

3 Who plays Sarah Connor in the *Terminator* movies?

4 Which British sitcom ended with the marriage of Richard De Vere and Audrey Forbes Hamilton?

5 In which movie did Sylvester Stallone make his debut as Rambo?

6 Which silent movie star's statue stands in Leicester Square, London?

7 In which TV show does John Nettles play the role of DCI Barnaby?

8 Which actor links the *The Magnificent Seven*, *Westworld* and *The King and I*?

9 Who played Miss Jones in the sitcom *Rising Damp?*

10 Who played Gary Cooper's wife in *High Noon?*

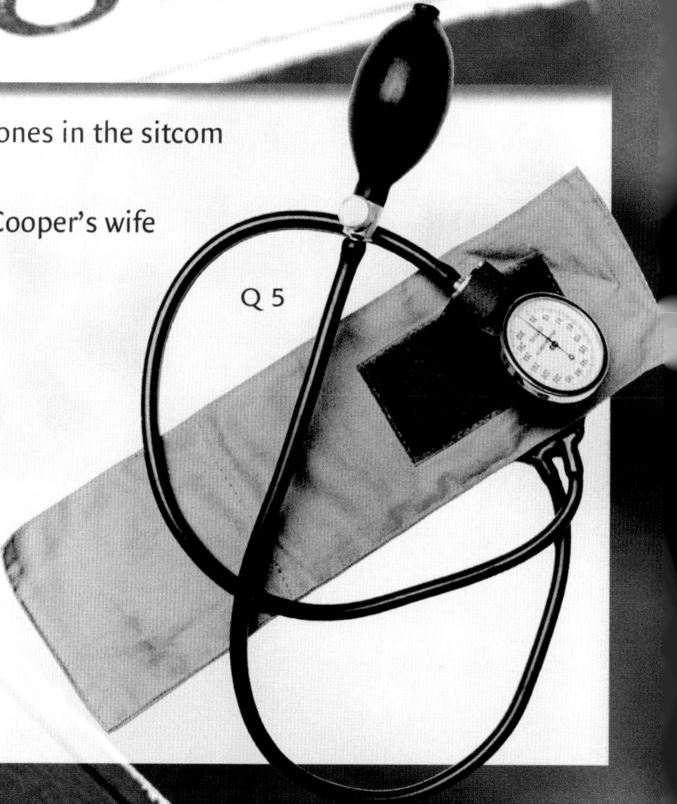

Q 5

ANSWERS

1 Winona Ryder **2** Roger Lloyd Pack **3** Linda Hamilton **4** To The Manor Born **5** *First Blood* **6** Charlie Chaplin **7** *Midsomer Murders* **8** Yul Brynner **9** Frances De La Tour **10** Grace Kelly

Natural Selection

1. Sandwich, Arctic, little and common are all species of which bird?
2. What is another name for a German shepherd dog?
3. After humans, which land mammal has the longest life expectancy?
4. Toulouse and Embden are both breeds of which farm bird?
5. Which species of whale possesses an ivory tusk?
6. In which country did budgerigars originate?
7. Which plant is named after the Greek goddess of the rainbow?
8. Which bird has the longest wingspan?
9. Is a sea cucumber a plant or an animal?
10. Which planet is also the name for a fox's home?

LEVEL 3 · QUIZ 176

Q 7

ANSWERS

1 Tern **2** Alsatian **3** Elephant **4** Goose **5** Narwhal **6** Australia **7** Iris **8** Albatross **9** An animal **10** Earth

Making History

1 Who was married to Edward Borough, Thomas Seymour and Henry VIII?

2 Who was Britain's longest reigning king?

3 In which decade was the National Health Service founded in the U.K.?

4 Which British general led the victorious troops at the Battle of El Alamein?

5 Who was the last tsar of Russia?

Q 2

6 In which European country was the monarchy abolished by a 1946 referendum?

7 In which war was the Battle of Balaklava fought?

8 Who was the leader of the conspirators involved in the Gunpowder Plot?

9 Who was the first Plantaganet monarch?

10 Who led the Peasant's Revolt in 1301?

BACKGROUND BONUS

In 1952, which London bridge began to rise with traffic still on it, forcing a bus to leap from one bascule to the other?

ANSWERS

1 Catherine Parr 2 George III 3 1940s 4 General Montgomery 5 Nicholas II 6 Italy 7 The Crimean War 8 Robert Catesby 9 Henry II 10 Wat Tyler

Background Bonus Tower Bridge

Music Mania

1 Which record producer was known as the fifth Beatle?

2 Which song opens with the line “Isn’t it rich, aren’t we a pair”?

3 Henry Steinway is associated with the manufacture of which instrument?

4 Which A is a solo song in an opera?

5 Who were the first British group to have a No. 1 hit in the United States?

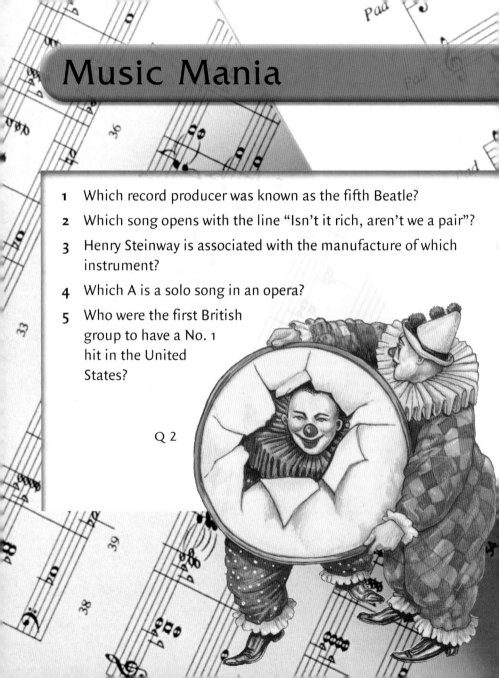

Q 2

6 How many times did the U.K. win the Eurovision Song Contest in the 20th century?

7 The Miracles backed which Motown legend?

8 Which musical features the song "It Ain't Necessarily So"?

9 Which opera was written to commemorate the opening of the Suez Canal?

10 Which Gilbert and Sullivan operetta is set in Japan?

ANSWERS

1 George Martin **2** "Send In The Clowns" **3** Pianos **4** Aria **5** The Tornados **6** Five times **7** Smokey Robinson **8** Porgy and Bess **9** Aida **10** The Mikado

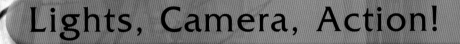

Lights, Camera, Action!

1 Who played the title role in the 1984 movie *Supergirl*?

2 When Kevin Costner played Robin Hood, who played the Sheriff of Nottingham?

3 In which U.S. city are the headquarters of CNN Television?

4 Which star of the sitcom *Happy Days* became an Oscar-winning director?

5 For which 2001 movie did Julia Roberts win a Best Actress Oscar?

6 What is the name of the Daleks' home planet?

7 Who played Ashley Pitt in the 1960s movie *The Great Escape*?

8 In which *Carry On* movie did Sid James play the Rumpo Kid?

9 Who played the pigeon lady in the movie *Home Alone 2*?

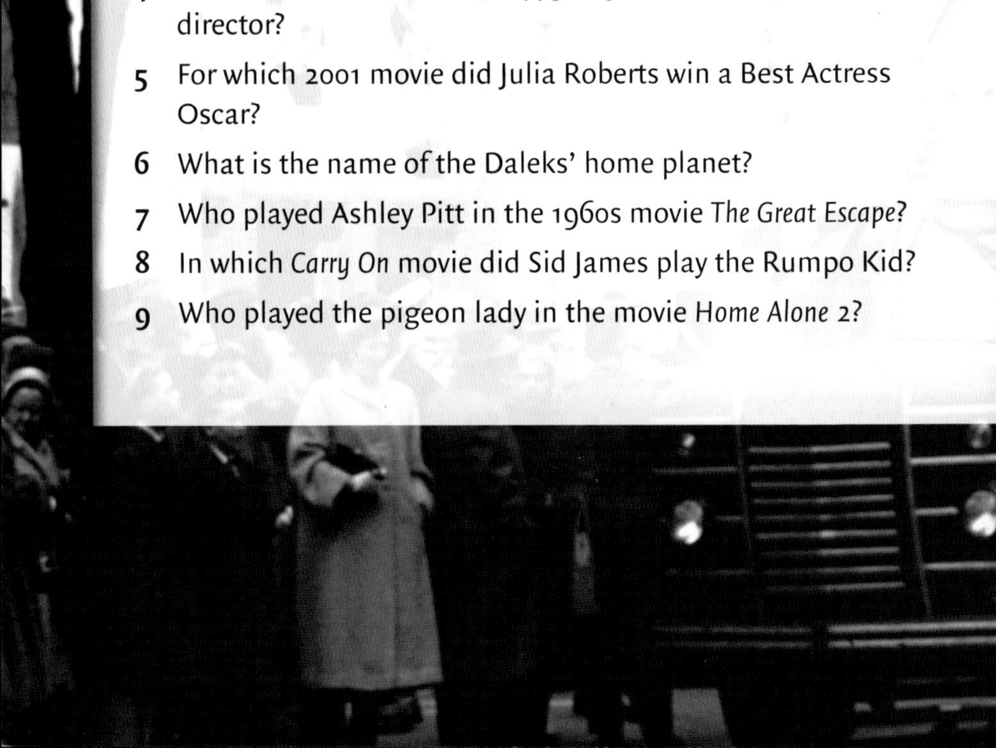

10 Who married Steven Spielberg after being directed by him in *Indiana Jones and the Temple Of Doom?*

Q 8

ANSWERS

1 Helen Slater **2** Alan Rickman **3** Atlanta **4** Ron Howard **5** *Erin Brockovich* **6** Skaro **7** David McCallum **8** *Carry On Cowboy* **9** Brenda Fricker **10** Kate Capshaw

Amazing Art

Can you identify eight famous artists from these paintings?

1

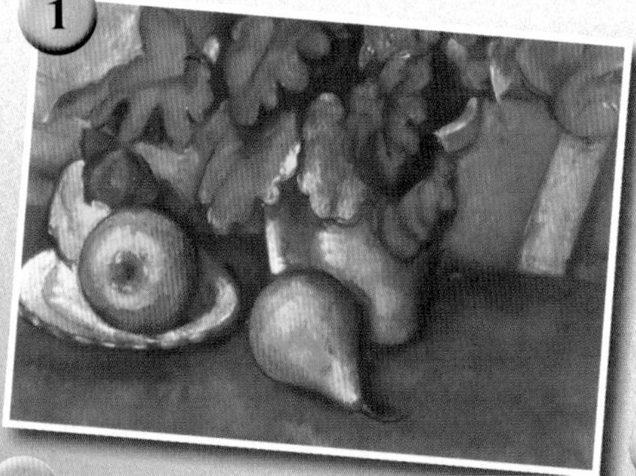

2

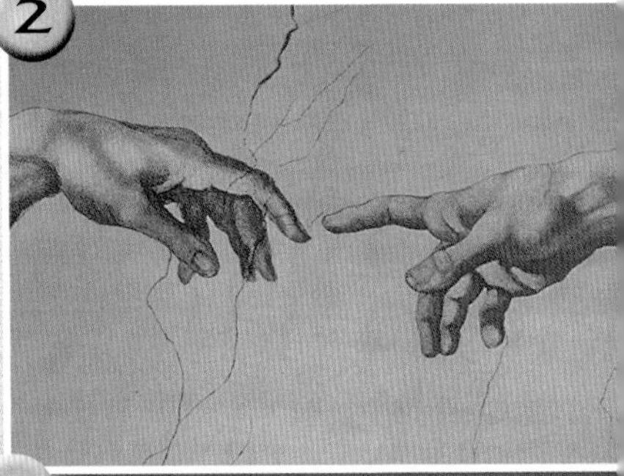

3

4

5

6

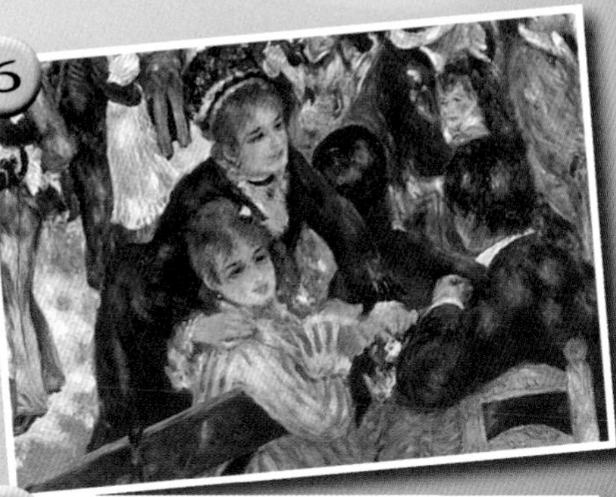

7

8

ANSWERS
1 Cézanne 2 Michelangelo 3 Van Gogh 4 Constable 5 Turner 6 Renoir 7 Monet 8 Gauguin

Natural Selection

1 Which land mammal has the longest eye lashes?
2 Which W is a young otter?
3 Which S is another name for a butcherbird?
4 Which type of grasshopper gets its name from the sound made by males rubbing their wings together?
5 Which animal family does the panda belong to?
6 Which word is the collective noun for a group of toads?
7 Which S is another name for the great maple?
8 Which A contains a flower's pollen?
9 In the plant world, what is the common name for the *Helianthus*?
10 Is a neap tide a low or a high tide?

BACKGROUND BONUS

Which species of duck feeds by "dabbling"?

Q 5

ANSWERS

1 Camel **2** Whelp **3** Shrike **4** Katydid **5** Raccoon **6** A knot of toads **7** Sycamore **8** Anther **9** Sunflower **10** Low tide

Background Bonus Mallard

Written Word

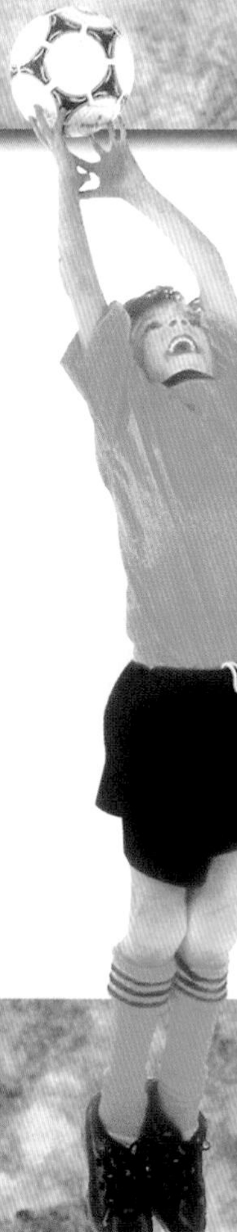

1 Name any year in which Robert Burns was alive.

2 Which Shakespeare play ended with Benedict marrying Beatrice?

3 In which country were the parents of Roald Dahl born?

4 John Ridd was the hero of which classic novel?

5 Which detective novel opens with the murder of Miles Archer?

Q 9

6 Who created the literary character of Father Brown?

7 *The Reluctant Jester* is the autobiography of which Goon member?

8 According to the *Harry Potter* novels, in which year was Harry born?

9 Which novel by Joseph Heller features the character of Captain Yossarian?

10 The title character of which novel married Mr. Rochester?

ANSWERS

1 1759 to 1796 **2** *Much Ado about Nothing* **3** Norway **4** *Lorna Doone* **5** *The Maltese Falcon* **6** G.K. Chesterton **7** Michael Bentine **8** 1981 **9** *Catch 22* **10** *Jane Eyre*

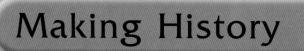

Making History

1. How many children did Queen Victoria bear?
2. Who is the only prime minister to appear on a British bank note?
3. Which scientist became Master of the Royal Mint in 1699?
4. During World War II, what was the name of the Japanese counterpart to Lord Haw Haw?
5. What is the last name of the legendary King Arthur?
6. Who was dismissed as Archbishop of Canterbury in 1556 and burnt at the stake?
7. Name any year in which Genghis Khan was alive.
8. The poem *Casabianca*, which features the line " The boy stood on the burning deck", is an account of which battle?
9. In the Bible, who was King Ahab's wife?
10. Which Florentine artist painted *The Adoration Of The Magi?*

LEVEL 4 · QUIZ 183

Q 4

ANSWERS

1 Nine **2** The Duke of Wellington **3** Sir Isaac Newton **4** Tokyo Rose **5** Pendragon **6** Thomas Cranmer **7** 1162 to 1227 **8** The Battle of the Nile **9** Jezebel **10** Sandro Botticelli

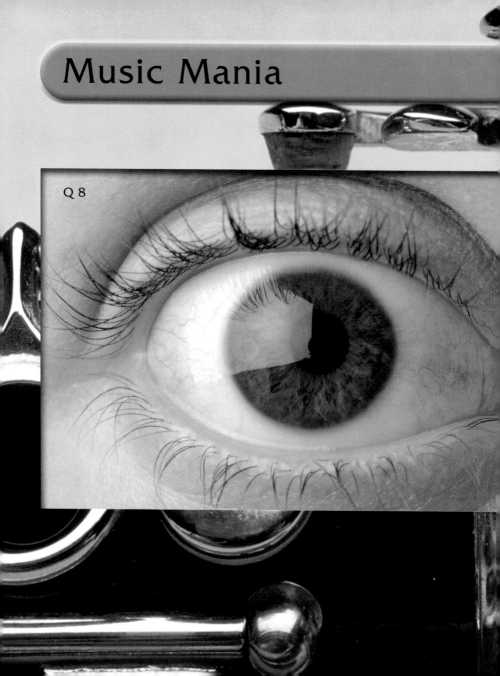

Music Mania

Q 8

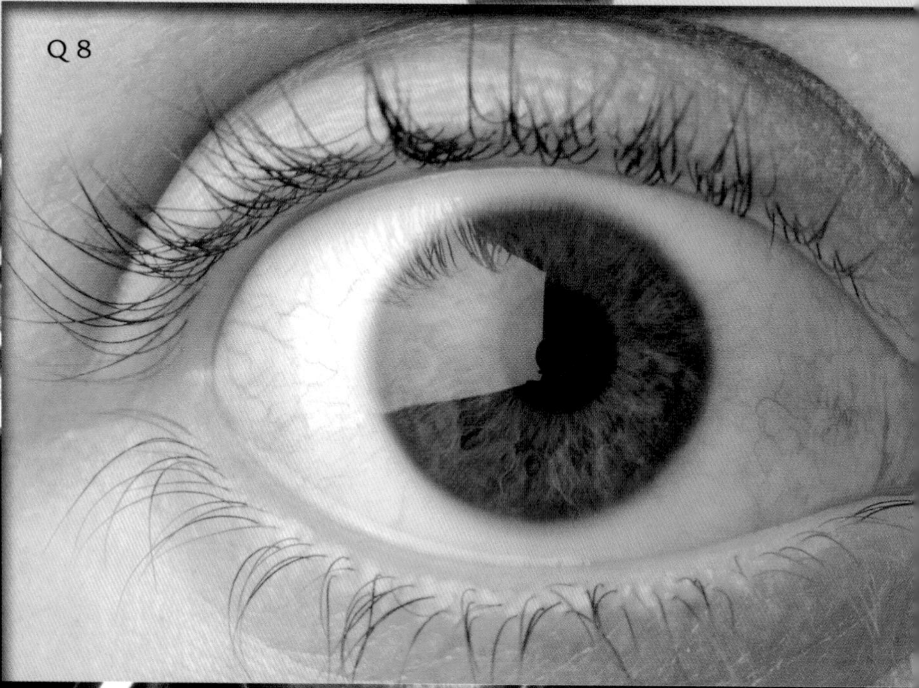

LEVEL 4 · QUIZ 184

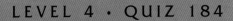

1 Which 1979 No. 1 hit has the line "It's cold outside and the paint's peeling off my wall"?

2 Which pop star was ordained as Mother Bernadette Maria?

3 In which South American country was Chris de Burgh born?

4 Which 1960s band topped the charts with the Lennon and McCartney composition "Michelle"?

5 Who sang with Cliff Richard on the 1986 hit "All I Ask Of You"?

6 Which song was a No. 1 hit for Elvis Presley, 25 years after his death?

7 Which duo began performing under the name of Tom and Jerry?

8 Who recorded the best-selling album *Automatic For The People*?

9 Who provided lead vocals for The Pretenders?

10 Which 1960s pop star was born Terence Nelhams?

ANSWERS

1 "Are Friends Electric" 2 Sinead O'Connor 3 Argentina 4 The Overlanders 5 Sarah Brightman 6 "A Little Less Conversation" 7 Simon and Garfunkel 8 REM 9 Chrissie Hynde 10 Adam Faith

Total Trivia

1 By which five-letter name is the fictional character of Don Diego de la Vega better known?

2 What does a deltiologist collect?

3 Which Oscar-winning movie saw Dustin Hoffman and Tom Cruise gambling in Las Vegas?

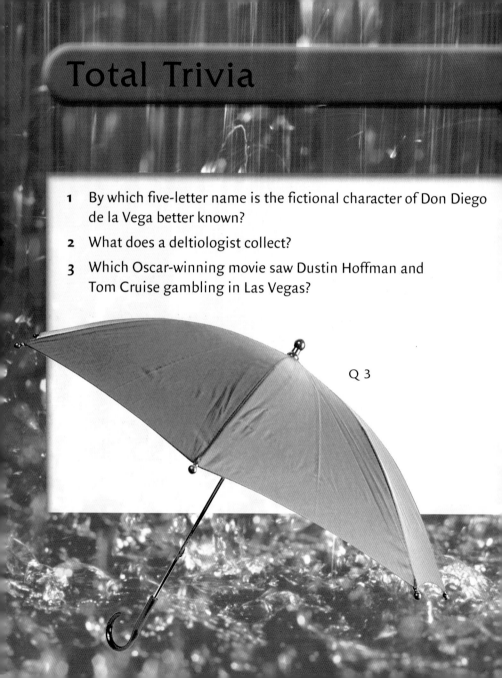

Q 3

4 What do the letters KG indicate after a person's name?

5 Which I is the Japanese art of flower arranging?

6 Which S is another name for variola?

7 Which Hollywood legend links *Whatever Happened to Baby Jane?* and *All about Eve?*

8 Who, according to Shakespeare, was the Queen of the Fairies?

9 In 1989, which electronics company bought Columbia Pictures?

10 What is the highest civil decoration in France?

BACKGROUND BONUS

Which Gene Kelly musical did Jackie Chan parody during a fight scene in his movie *Shanghai Knights?*

ANSWERS

1 Zorro **2** Postcards **3** Rain Man **4** Knight of the Garter **5** Ikebana **6** Smallpox **7** Bette Davis **8** Titania **9** Sony **10** The Legion of Honour

Background Bonus *Singin' in the Rain*

Global Matters

1 What is Europe's highest capital city?

2 What is the largest island in the world beginning with the letter S?

3 Princeton University lies in which U.S. state?

4 In which mountain range is Ben Nevis?

5 What is the country of origin of Aldi supermarkets?

6 The Oscar-winning movie *The Pianist* is set mainly in which city?

7 Which French city has a name that means by the waters?

8 After Rome and Milan, which is Italy's biggest city?

9 Which U.S. state is known as the Show Me State?

10 Which is the oldest U.S. state?

LEVEL 4 • QUIZ 186

Q8

ANSWERS
1 Madrid **2** Sumatra **3** New Jersey **4** The Grampians **5** Germany **6** Warsaw **7** Bordeaux **8** Naples **9** Missouri **10** Delaware

Q 7

LEVEL 4 · QUIZ 187

1 By which name is the drug MDMA commonly known?

2 Which disease derived its name from the Greek for coal?

3 What is made by the sublingual and the submaxillary glands?

4 Which viral infection is caused by the Epstein-Barr virus?

5 Cot death is also known by the acronym SIDS. What do these initials stand for?

6 What process, introduced in 1856, made the mass production of steel possible?

7 What is the opposite of estivation?

8 By which six-letter name is Diamorphine Hydrochloride better known?

9 Which disease is derived from the Italian for "bad air"?

10 What shape is the duodenum?

ANSWERS

1 Ecstasy 2 Anthrax 3 Saliva 4 Glandular fever 5 Sudden Infant Death Syndrome 6 The Bessemer process 7 Hibernation 8 Heroin 9 Malaria 10 Shaped like a horseshoe

Great and Famous

1 In which year did the reggae legend Bob Marley die?

2 What is boxer Lennox Lewis' middle name, which he shares with a former Roman emperor?

3 Who played the title role in the 2002 movie *The Pianist*?

4 Which pop star was born Stuart Goddard?

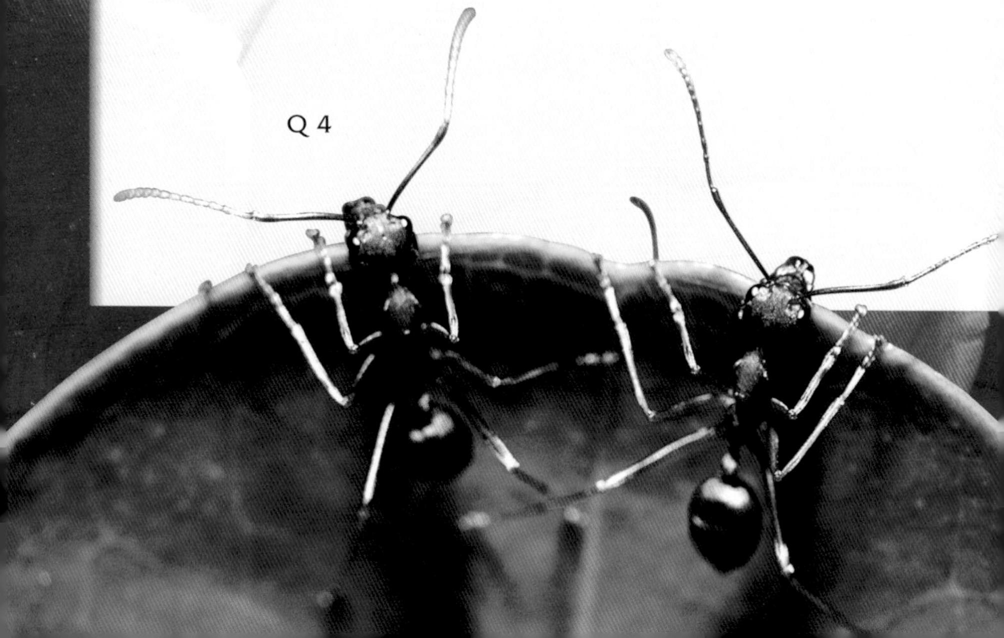

Q 4

5 Which former President of France died in 1996 aged 79?

6 Who painted *The Laughing Cavalier*?

7 In which city did Adolf Hitler refuse to shake the hand of Jesse Owen?

8 Who was Bill Clinton's vice president?

9 Who directed the multi-Oscar winning movie *Titanic*?

10 Whose epitaph in Westminster Abbey, London, reads "A talent to amuse"?

ANSWERS

1 1981 **2** Claudius **3** Adrien Brody **4** Adam Ant **5** François Mitterand **6** Franz Hals **7** Berlin **8** Al Gore **9** James Cameron **10** Noel Coward

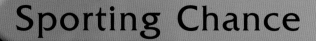

Sporting Chance

1 Who was the first boxer to gain a heavyweight world title?

2 Which was the only Belgian city to host the Summer Olympics in the 20th century?

3 What does the WG stand for in the name of W.G. Grace?

4 In which sport has Victor Barna won several world titles?

Q 4

LEVEL 4 · QUIZ 189

5 Which U.S. city is home to the American football team The Bengals?

6 To which town did Wimbledon FC move their base in 2003?

7 Sofia Gardens was the home ground of which county cricket club?

8 Which football club are nicknamed The Canaries?

9 Who was manager of Liverpool FC when they won the European Cup in 1984?

10 In 1991, who broke Bob Beamon's 23-year-old long jump world record?

BACKGROUND BONUS

In the 11th century, which popular sport began as a form of handball played by French and Italian monks?

ANSWERS

1 Floyd Patterson **2** Antwerp **3** William Gilbert **4** Table tennis **5** Cincinnati **6** Milton Keynes **7** Glamorgan **8** Norwich City **9** Joe Fagin **10** Mike Powell

Background Bonus Tennis

Lights, Camera, Action!

1 Which Gerry Anderson TV show featured the characters of Commander Shore and Marina?

2 On whose novel was the TV drama *The Jewel in the Crown* based?

3 Who played Edward in the historical TV drama *Edward and Mrs. Simpson?*

4 In which 1988 movie did Bob Hoskins play a private eye called Eddie Valiant?

5 In which movie was Dustin Hoffman seduced by Mrs. Robinson?

6 Who played Clint Eastwood's female partner in the movie *The Enforcer?*

7 Which villain was played by Arnold Schwarzenegger in the movie *Batman and Robin?*

8 In *Only Fools and Horses*, what is the middle name of Rodney Trotter?

9 Which actor replaced Martin Sheen as the U.S. President in the political TV drama *The West Wing*?

10 Which Oscar-winning movie features a dog called Two Socks?

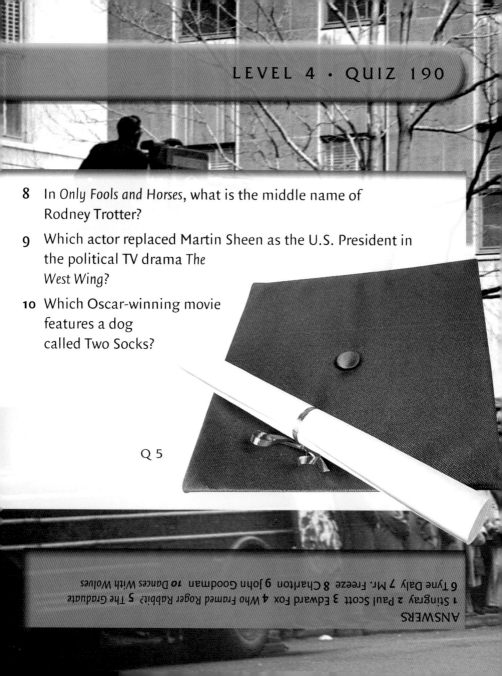

Q 5

ANSWERS

1 Stingray **2** Paul Scott **3** Edward Fox **4** *Who Framed Roger Rabbit?* **5** *The Graduate* **6** Tyne Daly **7** Mr. Freeze **8** Charlton **9** John Goodman **10** *Dances With Wolves*

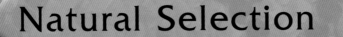

Natural Selection

1 Which G is the more common name for the cranesbill?
2 The Sargasso Sea was named after a type of what?
3 What is the world's smallest primate?
4 Which RS is the alternative name for a dogfish?
5 An exaltation is the collective noun for which bird?
6 Which WL is the national flower of Bangladesh?
7 What is a leafminer?
8 Which N is the name for a young grasshopper?
9 What island was home to the now extinct dodo?
10 What family of birds does the robin belong to?

LEVEL 4 · QUIZ 191

Q 6

ANSWERS

1 Geranium **2** Seaweed **3** Mouse lemur **4** Rock salmon **5** Lark **6** Water lily **7** A species of fly **8** Nymph **9** Mauritius **10** Thrush

Beautiful Birds

Can you identify these birds?

LEVEL 4 · QUIZ 192

5

6

7

8

ANSWERS

1 Golden eagle **2** Flamingo **3** Puffin **4** Great horned owl **5** Peacock **6** Bald eagle **7** Macaw **8** Snowy owl

Making History

1 Which U.S. city witnessed major earthquakes in 1906 and 1989?

2 How old was Britain's youngest prime minister, William Pitt the Younger, when he took office?

3 Which model of plane was used by the Dambusters in World War II?

4 Who led the Dambusters raid in World War II?

5 Which year of the 1960s witnessed the Great Train Robbery?

6 In which palace was Queen Elizabeth I born?

7 Who killed Billy the Kid?

8 Eboracum was the Roman name for which English city?

9 In which country was Che Guevara born?

10 Which English King reigned for ten years but spent only six months in England?

BACKGROUND BONUS

Hieratic and demotic are forms of which ancient script?

Q 10

ANSWERS

1 San Francisco **2** 24 years old **3** Lancaster **4** Guy Gibson **5** 1963 **6** Greenwich Palace **7** Sheriff Pat Garrett **8** York **9** Argentina **10** Richard the Lionheart

Background Bonus Hieroglyphs

Music Mania

1 Which Barry Manilow hit was covered by Take That?

2 What is the title of the national anthem of Australia?

3 Which No. 1 hit for Blondie featured on the soundtrack of the movie *American Gigolo*?

4 Which song from the movie *The Sound of Music* was a chart hit for Shirley Bassey?

LEVEL 4 · QUIZ 194

5 Which classical composer was nicknamed The Poet of the Piano?

6 At the 1996 Grammy Awards, who received a posthumous Lifetime Achievement Award, 12 years after his death?

7 Under what name did the 60s pop trio Yarrow, Stookey and Travers record?

8 Who composed the TV theme for Miami Vice?

9 Which N is a piece of music that describes a night scene?

10 Which chart-topping duo originally performed under the name of Caesar and Cleo?

ANSWERS

1 "Could It Be Magic" 2 "Advance Australia Fair" 3 "Call Me" 4 "Climb Every Mountain" 5 Chopin 6 Marvin Gaye 7 Peter, Paul and Mary 8 Jan Hammer 9 Nocturne 10 Sonny and Cher

Total Trivia

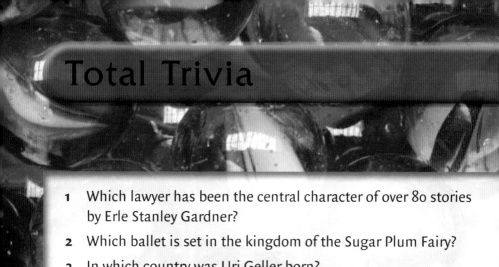

1 Which lawyer has been the central character of over 80 stories by Erle Stanley Gardner?

2 Which ballet is set in the kingdom of the Sugar Plum Fairy?

3 In which country was Uri Geller born?

4 What collective name is given to the eight oldest universities in the United States?

5 Which movie legend was born Arthur Stanley Jefferson?

6 In which city was Christopher Columbus born?

7 The adjective murine refers to which animal?

8 In which city was the movie *Cabaret* set?

9 In which board game can players "hit a blot"?

10 Which C is the name given to an assembly of cardinals?

Q 2

ANSWERS

1 Perry Mason 2 *The Nutcracker Suite* 3 Israel 4 The Ivy League 5 Stan Laurel 6 Genoa 7 Mouse 8 Berlin 9 Backgammon 10 Conclave

Global Matters

1 What is the capital of the island of Madeira?

2 In which country is the world's highest waterfall?

3 Hoy, Flotta and Westray are all members of which island group?

4 In which commonwealth country is Dominion Day celebrated in July?

5 The Bahamas lie off the coast of which U.S. state?

6 Which African country has the highest population?

7 Which group of islands was once known as the Fortunate Islands?

8 Which U.S. state is nicknamed the Equality State?

9 From which country did Iceland achieve independence in 1944?

10 Mount Cook is the highest peak in which country?

Q

LEVEL 4 · QUIZ 196

ANSWERS

1 Funchal **2** Venezuela **3** The Orkneys **4** Canada **5** Florida **6** Nigeria **7** Canaries **8** Wyoming **9** Denmark **10** New Zealand

Scientifically Speaking

1 Where on the human body is the skin the thinnest?

2 Which planet was called Phosphorous by the ancient Greeks?

3 The majority of the world's population are dextral. What does this mean?

4 What is the name of the flap of cartilage that prevents food from entering the windpipe?

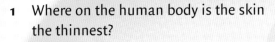

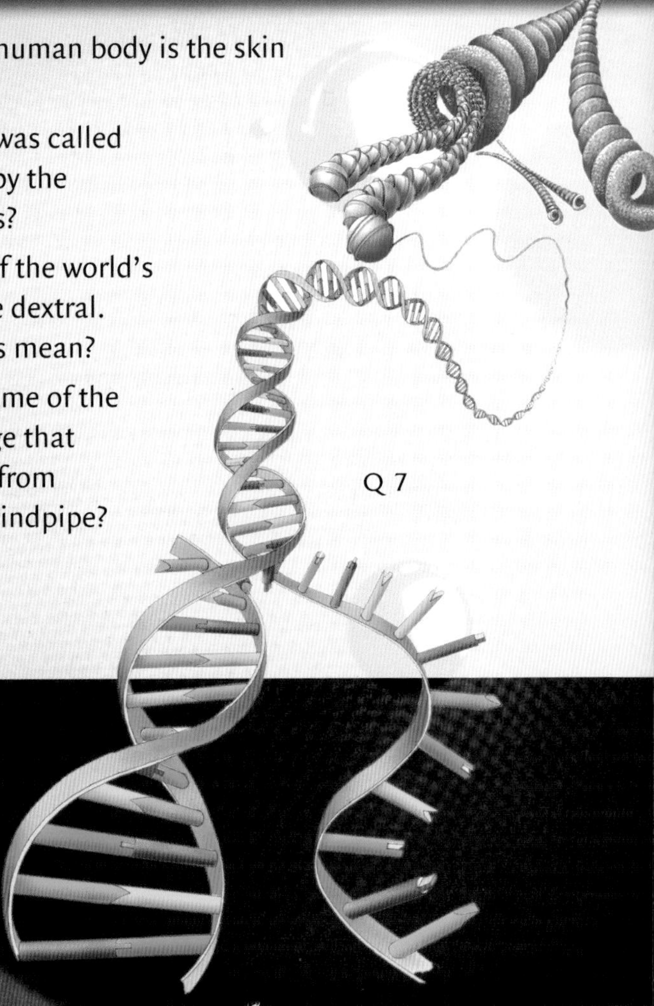

Q 7

LEVEL 4 · QUIZ 197

5 In Morse Code, what letter is denoted by a single dot?

6 In which century did the scientist Sir Isaac Newton die?

7 Crick and Watson received a Nobel Prize for the discovery of what?

8 Which bitter fluid is secreted by the liver and stored in the gall bladder?

9 What part of the body is affected by glossitis?

10 Which E describes a disease that is always present in a population?

BACKGROUND BONUS

Which metal gave rise to the phrase "mad as a hatter" and is so dense that lead will float in it?

ANSWERS

1 The eyelids **2** Venus **3** Right-handed **4** Epiglottis **5** E **6** 18th century **7** DNA **8** Bile **9** The tongue **10** Endemic

Background Bonus Mercury

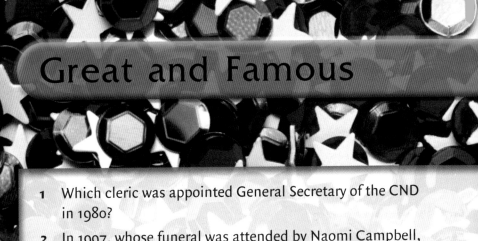

Great and Famous

1 Which cleric was appointed General Secretary of the CND in 1980?

2 In 1997, whose funeral was attended by Naomi Campbell, Elton John and Princess Diana?

3 What nationality is Marie Tussaud, the founder of the famed waxwork museum?

4 In the Bible, who married Sarah and Keturah?

5 Who wrote the song “Every Time We Say Goodbye”?

6 On which Greek Island was Prince Philip born?

7 The 1968 Oscar ceremonies were postponed for two days due to whose assassination?

8 Who was the last inmate of Spandau Prison?

9 In the Bible, who performed the dance of the seven veils?

10 Who played the role of Mary in the movie *There's Something about Mary*?

Q 5

ANSWERS

1 Bruce Kent **2** Gianni Versace **3** Swiss **4** Abraham **5** Cole Porter **6** Corfu **7** Martin Luther King **8** Rudolph Hess **9** Salome **10** Cameron Diaz

Written Word

1 The 1995 movie *Clueless* starring Alicia Silverstone, was based on which Jane Austen novel?

2 What type of bird dug the grave in the nursery rhyme "Who Killed Cock Robin"?

3 In which novel did a ship called *The Demeter* sail to Whitby?

4 Which adventure novel was originally entitled *The Chronic Argonauts?*

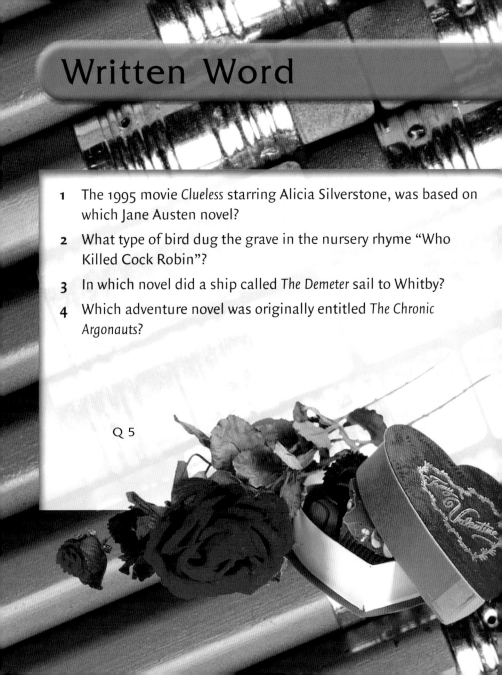

Q 5

5 Which play by Willie Russell was adapted into a movie starring Pauline Collins?

6 Which character, created by Dashiel Hammett, went in search of the Maltese Falcon?

7 Which famous novel has an opening chapter entitled *A Long Expected Party*?

8 What is the surname of the author who has a park in Moscow named after him?

9 Michael Henchard is the mayor of which fictional town?

10 Which literary character married Sophia Western?

ANSWERS

1 Emma 2 Owl 3 *Dracula* 4 *The Time Machine* 5 *Shirley Valentine* 6 Sam Spade 7 *Lord of the Rings* 8 Gorky 9 Casterbridge 10 Tom Jones

Sporting Chance

Q 10

1 The name of which sport is derived from the French word for shepherd's crook?

2 At which sports stadium are the Jack Hobbs Gates?

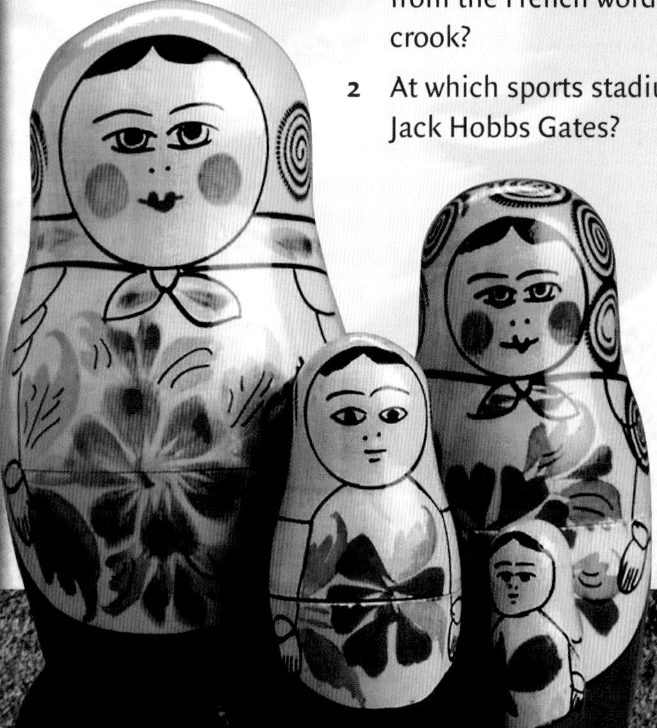

LEVEL 4 · QUIZ 200

3 Which ground did Manchester City leave for the City of Manchester Stadium?

4 Who beat Phil Taylor in the final of the 2003 World Darts Championships?

5 Who captained the victorious European team in the 1995 Ryder Cup?

6 Which Scottish golf course staged the inaugural British Open?

7 In which sport do competitors use a tab, a bracer and a chest guard?

8 Which Canadian was crowned snooker World Champion in 1980?

9 Who was the first British Formula One World Champion?

10 Which city hosted the 1980 Summer Olympics?

ANSWERS

1 Hockey **2** The Oval **3** Maine Road **4** John Part **5** Bernard Gallagher **6** Prestwick **7** Archery **8** Cliff Thorburn **9** Mike Hawthorn **10** Moscow

Lights, Camera, Action!

1 Who played Batgirl in the 1997 movie *Batman and Robin?*

2 Which film studios were founded in Buckinghamshire in 1936?

3 Who co-starred in 15 movies with his wife Jill Ireland?

4 In which 1985 movie thriller did Glen Close shoot dead Jeff Bridges?

5 Which cartoon crime fighter is assisted by a cat called Spot?

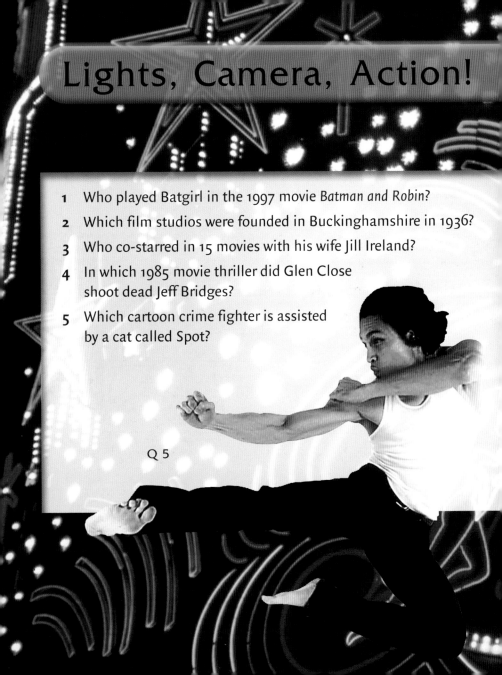

Q 5

6 Who did Mork report to at the end of each episode of *Mork and Mindy?*

7 In which TV series did David Jason play Pop Larkin?

8 Who piloted Thunderbird 1?

9 Who played Gregory in the movie *Gregory's Girl?*

10 Who co-starred with his then wife Ali McGraw in the movie *The Getaway?*

BACKGROUND BONUS

In which 1995 movie did Nicholas Cage star as a former movie executive trying to drink himself to death?

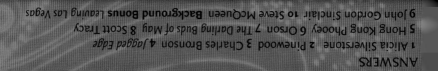

ANSWERS

1 Alicia Silverstone **2** Pinewood **3** Charles Bronson **4** *Jagged Edge* **5** Hong Kong Phooey **6** Orson **7** *The Darling Buds of May* **8** Scott Tracy **9** John Gordon Sinclair **10** Steve McQueen **Background Bonus** *Leaving Las Vegas*

Natural Selection

1 Which country are lemurs native to?

2 Which J is the national flower of Indonesia?

3 Sockeye, pink and Chinook are all species of which fish?

4 Which P is the alternative name for a scaly anteater?

5 What is the alternative name for the mountain ash?

6 What does it mean if an animal is described as oviparous?

7 In which country did the Lhasa Apso breed of dog originate?

8 Taurophobia is a fear of which animal?

9 Ramshorn, wandering and marsh are all species of what?

10 In the plant world, what is the more common name for the galanthus?

ANSWERS

1 Madagascar **2** Jasmine **3** Salmon **4** Pangolin **5** Rowan **6** It lays eggs **7** Tibet **8** Bulls **9** Snail **10** Snowdrop

Written Word

1 Who is Shakespeare's Moor of Venice?

2 Which author created the private detective Philip Marlowe?

3 What does the H stand for in the name of D.H. Lawrence?

4 In which story did Sherlock Holmes investigate a case at Grimpen Mire?

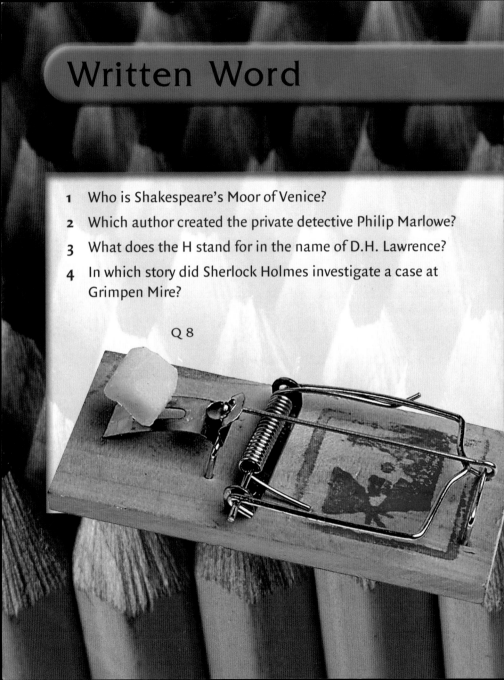

Q 8

LEVEL 4 · QUIZ 203

5 Which classic novel is narrated by a lawyer called Jonathan Harker?

6 Which novel is sub-titled *A Romance in Exmoor*?

7 Who is the only author to have a station named after him on the French Metro?

8 Which play features the characters of Christopher Wren, Mrs. Boyle and Sergeant Trotter?

9 What is the name of the farm in *Animal Farm*?

10 Which literary ecologists were created by Elizabeth Beresford?

ANSWERS

1 Othello 2 Raymond Chandler 3 Herbert 4 *The Hound of the Baskervilles*
5 *Dracula* 6 *Lorna Doone* 7 Victor Hugo 8 *The Mousetrap* 9 Manor Farm
10 The Wombles

Music Icons

Can you identify these eight famous musicians?

1

2

3

4

6

8

ANSWERS
1 Jimi Hendrix **2** Debbie Harry **3** Joni Mitchell **4** Bruce Springsteen
5 Frank Sinatra **6** Chrissie Hynde **7** Kurt Cobain **8** Miles Davis

Making History

1 What type of weapon was a culverin?

2 Which war gave Britain control of Hong Kong?

3 In 1980, which world-famous musician was shot dead outside his Manhattan apartment?

4 In what year did Queen Elizabeth II and Prince Philip celebrate their silver wedding anniversary?

5 In World War II, which country was invaded by the Allies in Operation Avalanche?

6 Which British king's son was nicknamed The Black Prince?

7 Who died in World War I after penning the poem *The Soldier*?

8 Prior to 1810, where was all British coinage minted?

9 In which Scottish valley did the Campbell's massacre the MacDonald's in 1692?

BACKGROUND BONUS

Which art form links Edward Burne-Jones, Henry Holiday and William Morris?

ANSWERS

1 A cannon **2** The Opium War **3** John Lennon **4** 1972 **5** Italy **6** Edward III **7** Rupert Brooke **8** The Tower of London **9** Glencoe **10** Crimean War

Background Bonus They were all stained-glass artists

Music Mania

1 In which country did The Bee Gees have their first No. 1 hit?

2 Which song has been a hit for Brian Hyland and Jason Donovan?

3 Who famously set fire to his guitar at the 1967 Monterrey pop festival?

4 Which 1967 musical is based on a novel entitled *The Once and Future King*?

5 Which musical instrument is affectionately known as "the gentleman of the woodwinds"?

6 Which No. 1 hit opens with the line "I thought love was only true in fairytales"?

7 Which Gilbert and Sullivan operetta is set in the Tower of London?

8 Which former member of The Rolling Stones died in a swimming pool?

9 What does the musical instruction "adagio" indicate?

10 Which P is a piece of music that imitates the style of another composer?

Q 1

ANSWERS

1 Australia 2 "Sealed With A Kiss" 3 Jimi Hendrix 4 Camelot 5 Bassoon 6 "I'm A Believer" 7 Yeoman of the Guard 8 Brian Jones 9 Slowly 10 Pastiche

Total Trivia

1 On what date in December is St. Stephen's Day celebrated?

2 Which movie introduced the character of Indiana Jones?

3 Who is the Greek god of sleep?

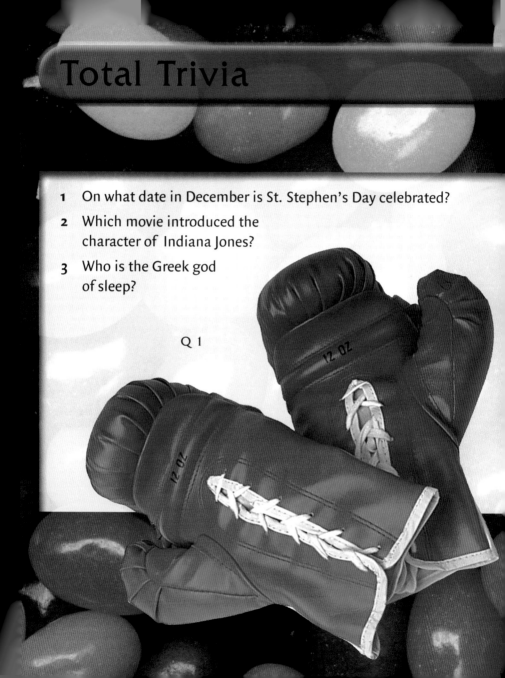

Q 1

4 What is the nickname of Bournemouth FC?

5 What is the wife of a Sultan called?

6 Which U.S. state is nicknamed The Cotton State?

7 How many squares are on a Scrabble board?

8 The name of which legendary place means “isle of apples”?

9 What did the Euro replace in Austria?

10 LGW is the code for which airport?

ANSWERS

1 December 26 - Boxing Day **2** *Raiders of the Lost Ark* **3** Hypnos **4** The Cherries
5 Sultana **6** Alabama **7** 225 **8** Avalon **9** Schilling **10** Gatwick

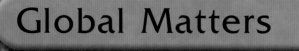

Global Matters

1 What is the capital of Belarus?

2 Which straits separate Sicily from the mainland of Italy?

3 Tahiti is the largest island in which island group?

Q 6

4 In which city is Sing Sing Prison?

5 Brazil forms its longest land border with which country?

6 What is the largest county in the Republic of Ireland?

7 What is the capital of the United Arab Emirates?

8 Brisbane is the state capital of which Australian state?

9 Which trench is the deepest point of the Pacific Ocean?

10 Which South American city is the most highly populated Portuguese-speaking city in the world?

ANSWERS

1 Minsk 2 The Straits of Messina 3 The Society Islands 4 New York 5 Paraguay 6 Cork 7 Abu Dhabi 8 Queensland 9 Marianas Trench 10 Sao Paulo

Scientifically Speaking

1 Which G is a boy's name and also the unit of magnetic force?
2 What is the more common name for the thyroid cartilage?
3 What I is the name given to a whole or natural number?
4 In which decade was insulin first used to treat diabetes?
5 What part of the body is inflamed by encephalitis?
6 Which S is studied by a pedologist?
7 What is the more popular name for a bird's furculum?
8 Which gas is the chief cause of acid rain?
9 Pyrosis is the technical term for which common ailment?
10 Which planet has craters called Goya, Raphael and Monet?

BACKGROUND BONUS

Andromeda, Triangulum Spiral and the M87 are all names of what?

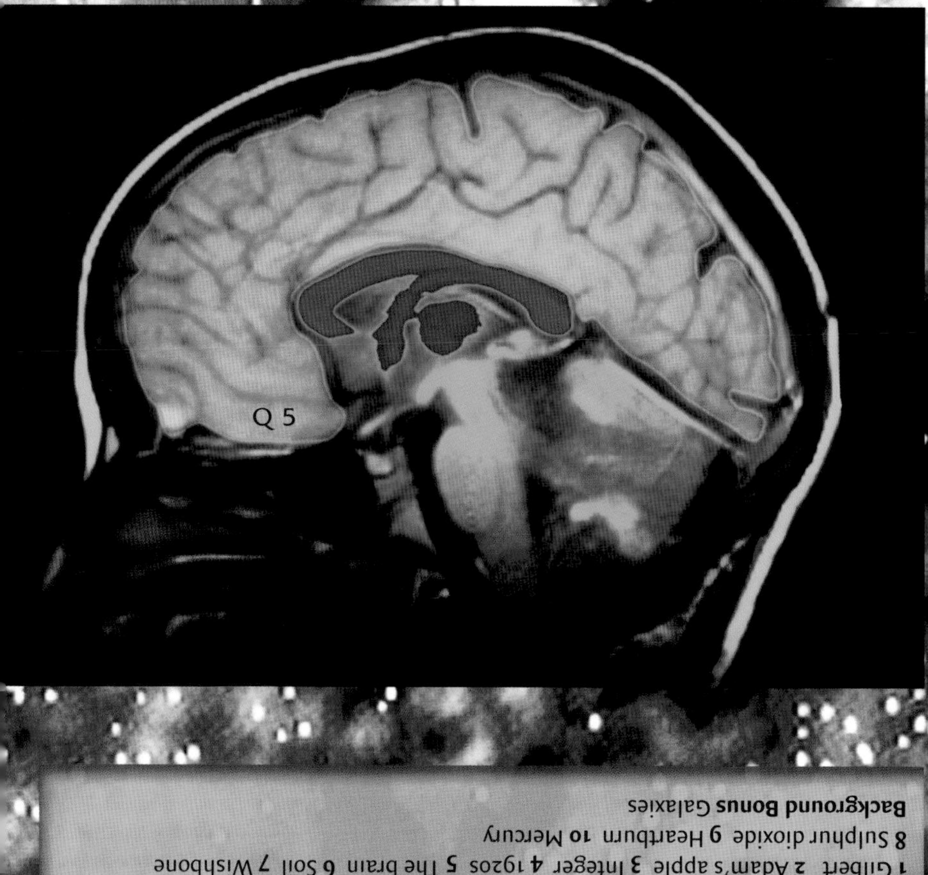

ANSWERS

1 Gilbert **2** Adam's apple **3** Integer **4** 1920s **5** The brain **6** Soil **7** Wishbone **8** Sulphur dioxide **9** Heartburn **10** Mercury

Background Bonus Galaxies

Great and Famous

1 How old was Marilyn Monroe when she died?

2 Who was the Vice President of Jimmy Carter?

3 Which entertainer was born Michael Dumble-Smith?

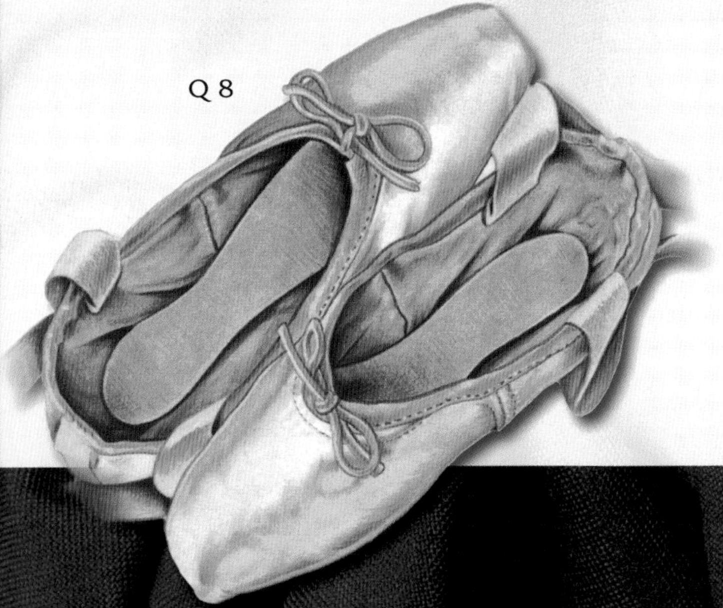

Q 8

4 Which movie star was the first wife of Ronald Reagan?

5 Who wrote the novel *Peyton Place*?

6 Umberto II was the last king of which European nation?

7 Who was the first boxer to defeat Muhammed Ali?

8 *Eastenders*' star Martin Kemp was the bassist in which 80s New Romantic band?

9 Who was Britain's first Prime Minister?

10 What was the first name of Eva Peron's husband?

ANSWERS

1 36 2 Walter Mondale 3 Michael Crawford 4 Jane Wyman 5 Grace Metalious 6 Italy 7 Joe Frazier 8 Spandau Ballet 9 Robert Walpole 10 Juan

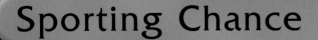

Sporting Chance

1. In which Scottish city does St. Johnstone FC play their home matches?
2. In which sport do competitors wear a loincloth called a mawashi?
3. Which athletic event is named from the Greek words for ten and contest?
4. What sport is played by the Seattle Supersonics?
5. Which Italian footballer scored the only goal in the 2000 FA Cup final?
6. In which decade was the FA Cup final first contested at Wembley?
7. In which sport is the Vince Lombardi Trophy awarded?
8. Which football club was the first install an artificial pitch?

LEVEL 4 • QUIZ 211

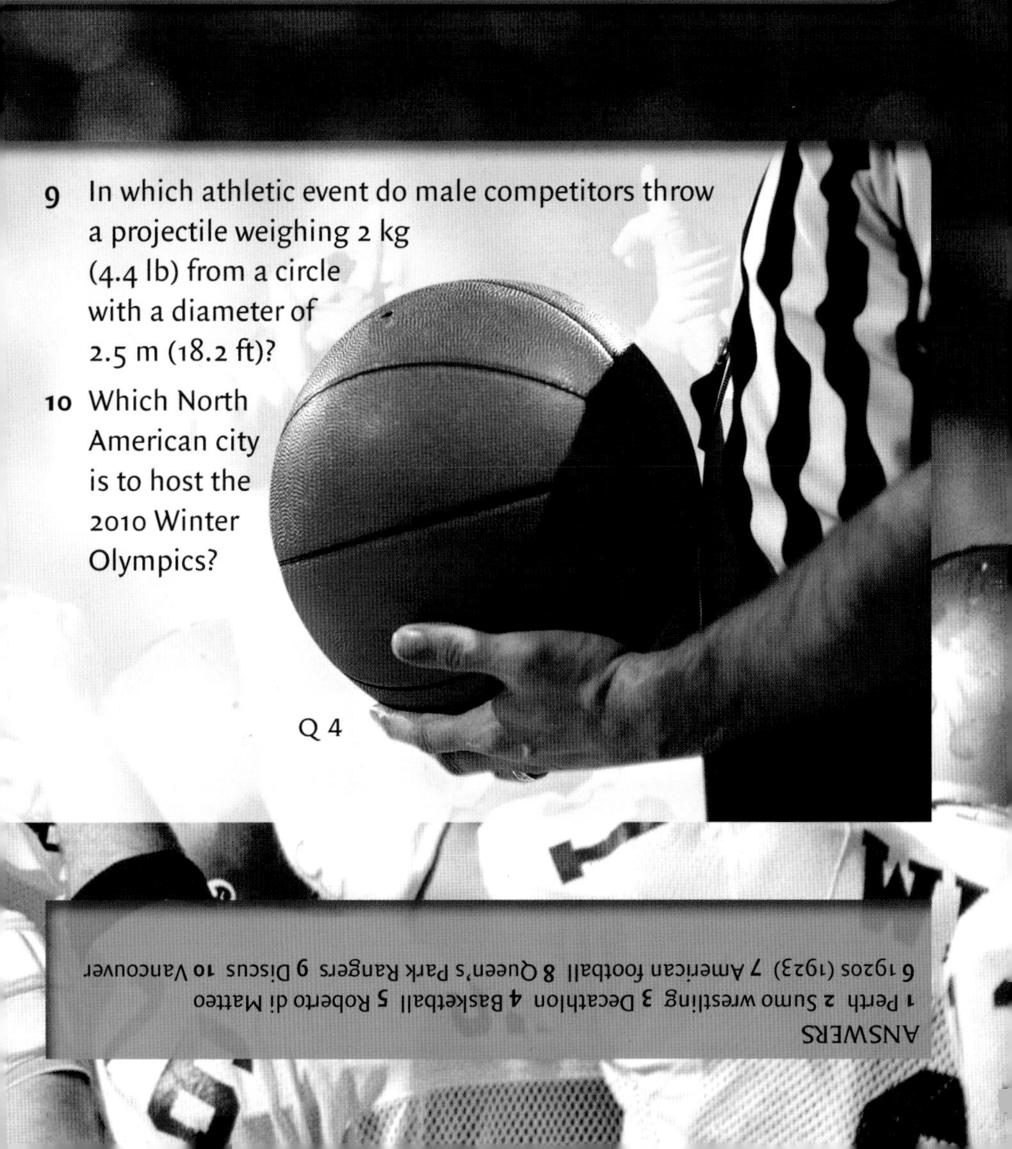

9 In which athletic event do male competitors throw a projectile weighing 2 kg (4.4 lb) from a circle with a diameter of 2.5 m (18.2 ft)?

10 Which North American city is to host the 2010 Winter Olympics?

Q 4

ANSWERS

1 Perth 2 Sumo wrestling 3 Decathlon 4 Basketball 5 Roberto di Matteo 6 1920s (1923) 7 American football 8 Queen's Park Rangers 9 Discus 10 Vancouver

Lights, Camera, Action!

1 Which musical features two rival gangs called the Jets and the Sharks?

2 Who played Sabrina Duncan in the TV show Charlie's Angels?

3 Which murderer was chillingly portrayed by Richard Attenborough in 10, *Rillington Place*?

4 In which popular US comedy show did Kirstie Alley replace Shelley Long?

5 Who played the role of Archie Leach in the movie *A Fish Called Wanda*?

6 Who played the secret agent Napoleon Solo in *The Man from UNCLE*?

7 Which children's TV show celebrated its 40th anniversary in 1998?

8 In which movie did Mel Gibson play the role of Colonel Benjamin Martin?

9 What is the name of Rodney Trotter's wife in *Only Fools and Horses?*

10 Who played Brad Pitt's wife in the movie *Seven?*

ANSWERS

1 *West Side Story* **2** Kate Jackson **3** John Christie **4** *Cheers* **5** John Cleese **6** Robert Vaughn **7** *Blue Peter* **8** *The Patriot* **9** Cassandra **10** Gwyneth Paltrow

Natural Selection

1 Aspirin was originally obtained from the bark of which tree?

2 King, emperor and rockhopper are all species of which bird?

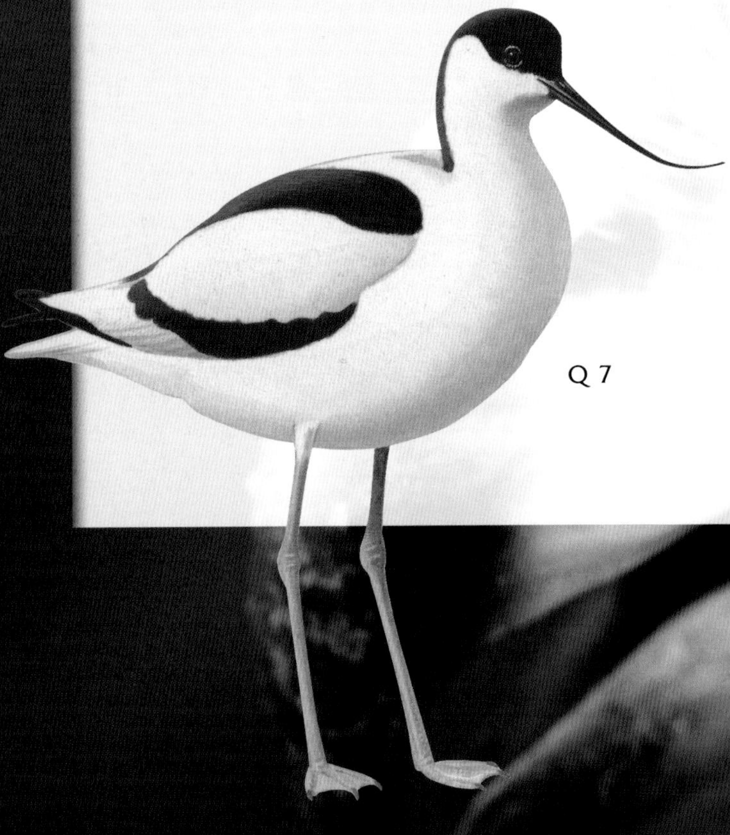

Q 7

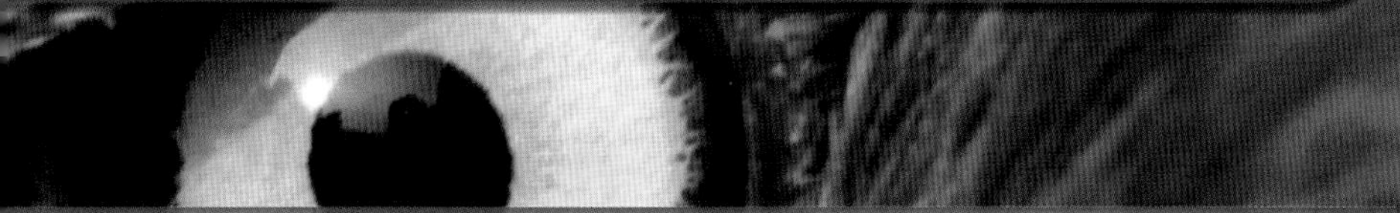

3 What D is the national flower of Mexico?

4 Which five-letter S word is the name for a young hog?

5 In the plant world, which G is the alternative name for baby's breath?

6 What tree has types called green, white, blue and black?

7 What bird is the symbol of the RSPB?

8 Which P describes plants that live for many years?

9 Broad-breasted bronze is a breed of which farm bird?

10 What animal has white, black Indian and Sumatran varieties?

BACKGROUND BONUS

Which bird can spot its prey from up to 3.2 km (2 mi) away and has the Latin name *Aquila Chrysaetos?*

ANSWERS

1 Willow **2** Penguin **3** Dahlia **4** Shoat **5** Gypsophylia **6** Ash **7** Avocet **8** Perennial **9** Turkey **10** Rhinoceros

Background Bonus Golden eagle

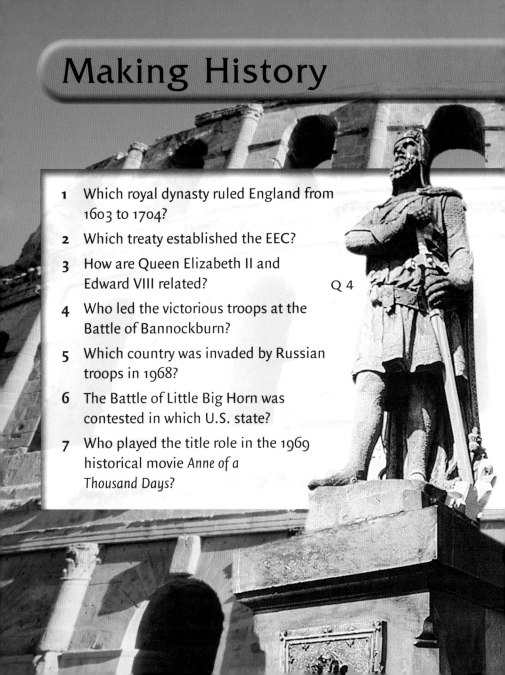

Making History

1 Which royal dynasty ruled England from 1603 to 1704?

2 Which treaty established the EEC?

3 How are Queen Elizabeth II and Edward VIII related?

4 Who led the victorious troops at the Battle of Bannockburn?

5 Which country was invaded by Russian troops in 1968?

6 The Battle of Little Big Horn was contested in which U.S. state?

7 Who played the title role in the 1969 historical movie *Anne of a Thousand Days*?

Q 4

8 Which former British Prime Minister had the first names of William Ewart?

9 In October 1983, which island did armed forces take control of under the command of General Austin?

10 Who resigned as Secretary of State for War in the British government in 1963?

ANSWERS

1 The Stuarts **2** The Treaty of Rome **3** Niece and uncle **4** Robert the Bruce **5** Czechoslovakia **6** Montana **7** Genevieve Bujold **8** W.E. Gladstone **9** Grenada **10** John Profumo

Music Mania

1 Which song contains the line "Linger on the sidewalk where the neon signs are pretty"?

2 The operetta *HMS Pinafore* is set in which coastal town?

3 Of which instrument is Ravi Shankar a virtuoso?

4 Under what name did Bill Medley and Bobby Hatfield top the music charts?

5 What surname did Gary Numan and Cliff Richard both share?

6 In 1999, which rock star announced a reunion tour with the E Street Band?

7 Which song was a hit for both Abba and Westlife ?

8 What is the title of Beethoven's only opera?

9 Who wrote the song "Take Me Home Country Roads"?

10 David Van Day and Theresa Bazaar were better known as what?

LEVEL 1 • QUIZ 215

Q 5

ANSWERS

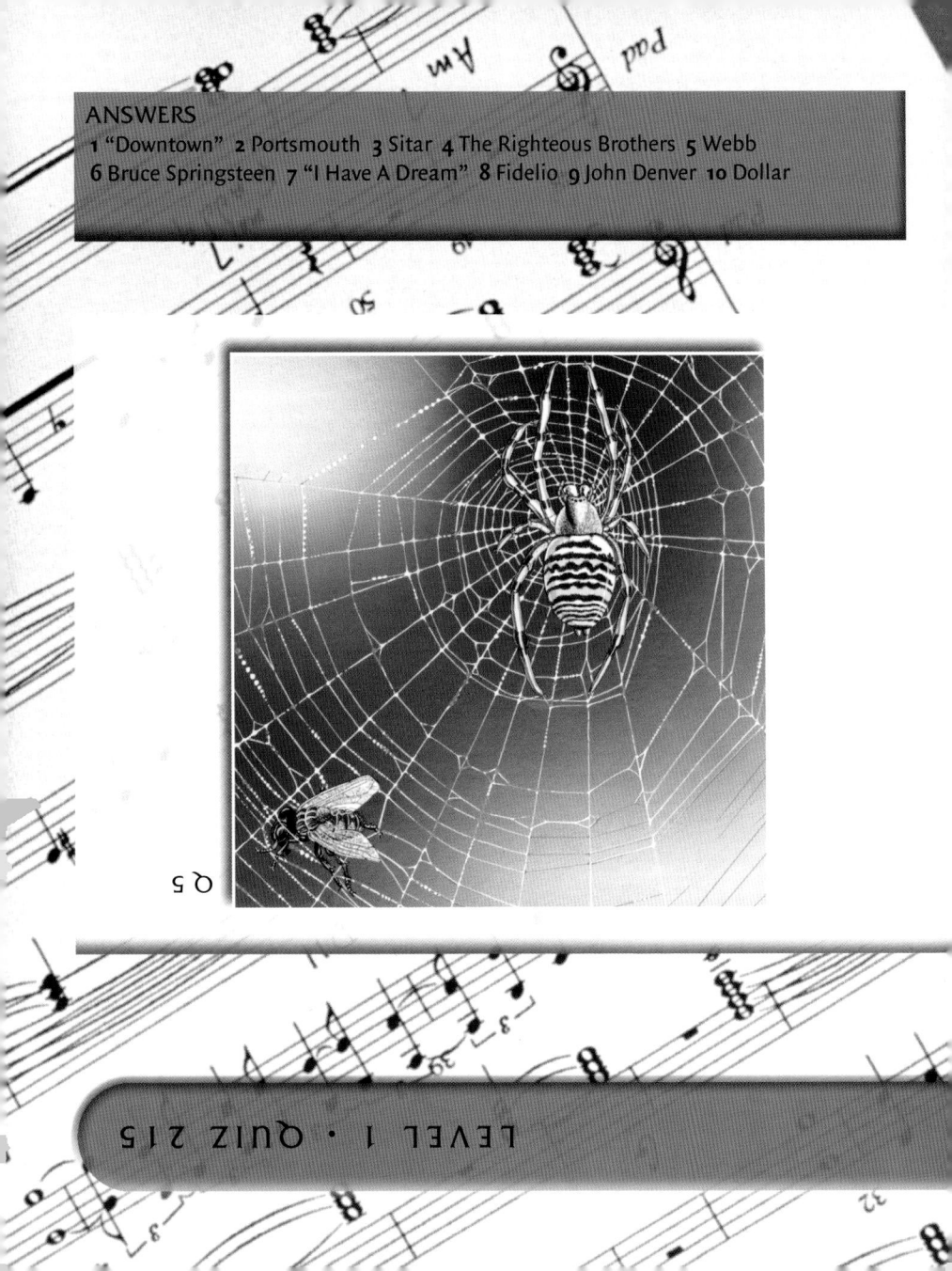

1 "Downtown" **2** Portsmouth **3** Sitar **4** The Righteous Brothers **5** Webb **6** Bruce Springsteen **7** "I Have A Dream" **8** Fidelio **9** John Denver **10** Dollar

Country Links

These pictures are all associated with particular countries. Can you guess the country names?

1

2

3

4

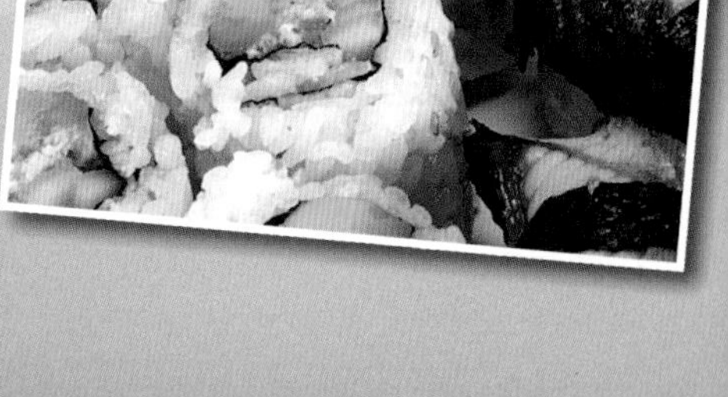

LEVEL 4 · QUIZ 216

5

6

7

8

ANSWERS

1 England **2** Brazil **3** Australia **4** Japan **5** Canada **6** North America **7** China **8** Holland

Total Trivia

1 What is a Kerry Blue?
2 On whose novel was the movie *The Godfather* based?
3 The Kalahari Desert lies chiefly in which country?
4 Which Hollywood star was born Bernard Schwartz?
5 Cape Farewell lies at the southern tip of which country?

Q 5

6 In the Church of England, what rank of clergy is directly below a bishop?

7 Who played the title role in the TV show *Father Ted*?

8 What is the world's most northerly desert?

9 What was the name of the cat that lived at 10, Downing Street until 1997?

10 Which SS is the name given to the longest day of the year?

BACKGROUND BONUS

What did the scientist William Gilbert discover about the Earth in 1600?

ANSWERS

1 A breed of terrier dog **2** Mario Puzo **3** Botswana **4** Tony Curtis **5** Greenland **6** Archdeacon **7** Dermot Morgan **8** The Gobi Desert **9** Humphrey **10** Summer Solstice

Background Bonus That it was magnetic

Global Matters

Q 5

LEVEL 4 · QUIZ 218

1 In which London borough is the Royal Albert Hall?

2 Which currency unit is shared by Libya, Tunisia and Jordan?

3 In which U.S. state does Mount Rushmore lie?

4 At which African capital city does the White Nile converge with the Blue Nile?

5 Which republic occupies the eastern part of the island of Hispaniola?

6 What is the most westerly capital city on mainland Europe?

7 Which U.S. state is known as the Keystone State?

8 Which African country has a name that means Lion Mountains?

9 What is the chief town on the island of Guernsey?

10 What is the official language of Surinam?

ANSWERS

1 Kensington **2** Dinar **3** South Dakota **4** Khartoum **5** Dominican Republic **6** Lisbon **7** Pennsylvania **8** Sierra Leone **9** St. Peter Port **10** Dutch

Scientifically Speaking

1 What is the more common name for otalgia?

2 Which halogen gas is represented by the symbol of F?

3 From which metal is the ore dolomite obtained?

4 Ti is the chemical symbol of which element?

5 What is the middle shade of a rainbow?

6 What is the cube root of 512?

7 What is the non-technical name for a dactylogram?

8 What does the P stand for in the Internet abbreviation http?

9 What C is an element that derives its name from the Greek for green?

10 What does the R stand for with regard to the MMR vaccine?

LEVEL 4 · QUIZ 219

Q9

ANSWERS

1 Ear ache **2** Fluorine **3** Magnesium **4** Titanium **5** Green **6** Eight **7** A fingerprint **8** Protocol **9** Chlorine **10** Rubella

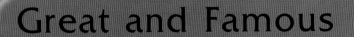

Great and Famous

1 In which capital city was Marie Curie born?

2 Who was Prime Minister of Australia from 1991 to 1996?

3 Who designed the Volkswagen Beetle?

4 Which composer's reputed last words were "I shall hear in heaven"?

5 Whose circus claimed to be "The greatest show on Earth"?

6 Who is the mother of actress Carrie Fisher?

7 Who wrote the novel *First Among Equals*?

8 Who played the role of Keith Partridge in the TV show *The Partridge Family*?

9 Who was the first American to be crowned World Chess Champion?

10 Montezuma II was the last king of which ancient civilization?

ANSWERS

1 Warsaw **2** Paul Keating **3** Ferdinand Porsche **4** Beethoven **5** Barnum & Bailey's Circus **6** Debbie Reynolds **7** Jeffrey Archer **8** David Cassidy **9** Bobby Fischer **10** The Aztecs

Written Word

1 What does the foreign phrase "al fresco" mean?

2 In computer jargon, what is the word "bit" short for?

3 Which three words complete the proverb "Marry in haste and ..."?

4 In a church, what is contained in a stoup?

5 What is a pangram?

6 What is the more common name for the sport of pugilism?

7 How does the word cenotaph translate into English?

8 What F is the official language of Iran?

9 Who are in charge in a theocracy?

10 What does a multicavous object have a lot of?

BACKGROUND BONUS

Which novel by Ernest Hemingway led to his reciept of the Noble Prize for literature in 1954?

Q 9

ANSWERS

1 In the open air **2** Binary digit **3** Repent at leisure **4** Holy water **5** A sentence that contains all the letters of the alphabet **6** Boxing **7** Empty tomb **8** Farsi **9** Priests or the clergy **10** Holes **Background Bonus** *The Old Man and the Sea*

Sporting Chance

Q 2

1 Which team won the Superbowl in 2002?

2 Which African nation won the opening game of the 2002 soccer World Cup finals?

3 By what name is the horse racing venue Prestbury Park better known?

4 Which Dutch club was managed by Bobby Robson after he vacated the England job?

5 What do the initials MCC stand for?

6 Which article of clothing is presented to the winner of golf's U.S. Masters?

7 Which is the oldest of Britain's horse racing classics?

8 What is the name of the Cambridge reserve crew in the Oxford and Cambridge boat race?

9 Which combat sport has a name that means the "gentle way"?

10 Which Olympic gold medallist was elected MP for Falmouth and Cambourne in 1992?

ANSWERS

1 New England Patriots 2 Senegal 3 Cheltenham 4 PSV Eindhoven 5 Marylebone Cricket Club 6 Green jacket 7 St. Leger 8 Goldie 9 Judo 10 Sebastian Coe

Lights, Camera, Action!

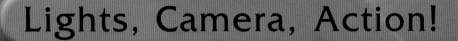

1 In which movie was Jim Carrey a lawyer called Fletcher Reed?

2 In which city is the TV show *Frasier* set?

3 When Robin Williams played Popeye, who played Olive Oyl?

4 Which 60s TV show, featured the characters of Darren, Samantha and Tabitha?

5 What is the name of Homer Simpson's eldest child?

Q 4

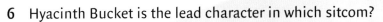

6 Hyacinth Bucket is the lead character in which sitcom?

7 Who played the title role in the 1999 movie *The Talented Mr. Ripley?*

8 What is the first name of the TV detective Kojak?

9 How are Steve Martin, Chevy Chase and Martin Short collectively known in the title of a 1986 movie?

10 Which classic movie was adapted from a play entitled *Everybody Comes to Rick's?*

ANSWERS

1 *Liar Liar* **2** Seattle **3** Shelley Duvall **4** *Bewitched* **5** Bart **6** *Keeping Up Appearances* **7** Matt Damon **8** Theo **9** *The Three Amigos* **10** *Casablanca*

Natural Selection

LEVEL 4 · QUIZ 224

1 Where do demersal creatures live?

2 On the body of a horse, where is the frog?

3 What game is played with the fruit of a horse chestnut?

4 What breed of dog was named after a character in the Walter Scott novel *Guy Mannering*?

5 In the plant world, which G is the alternative name for a sword lily?

6 The oil of which spice is a traditional cure for toothache?

7 Which mountain range is the natural habitat of the llama?

8 Do gramnivorous creatures eat insects, grass or fruit?

9 What is a quahog?

10 Which U.S. state gives its name to a species of beetle that is known for attacking potato crops?

ANSWERS

1 On the seabed 2 In the hooves 3 Conkers 4 Dandy Dinmont 5 Gladioli 6 Cloves 7 The Andes 8 Grass 9 A marine clam 10 Colorado

Written Word

1 In which decade did H.G. Wells die?
2 Which seafaring novel opens with the line "Call me Ishmael"?
3 Who wrote the novel *A Town Like Alice?*
4 The musical *The Boys From Syracuse* is based on which Shakespeare play?
5 In which English town is the Royal Shakespeare Theatre?
6 Which nursery rhyme character threw an old man down the stairs because he wouldn't say his prayers?
7 Who penned a trilogy of novels entitled *Lark Rise to Candleford?*
8 Flora Poste is the lead character in which novel?
9 Who wrote *Rich Man, Poor Man?*
10 Which author created the character of Gunga Din?

BACKGROUND BONUS

Which novel contains the line "I was exceeding surpris'd with the print of a man's naked foot on the shore..."

Q 2

ANSWERS

1 1940s **2** Moby Dick **3** Nevil Shute **4** A Comedy Of Errors **5** Stratford Upon Avon **6** Goosey Goosey Gander **7** Flora Thompson **8** Cold Comfort Farm **9** Irwin Shaw **10** Rudyard Kipling **Background Bonus** Robinson Crusoe

Making History

Q 9

LEVEL 4 · QUIZ 226

1 What connects the deaths of Harold II, Richard I and William Rufus?

2 What surname is shared by the 9th and 23rd Presidents of the United States?

3 Which naval battle is also known as The Battle of Aboukir Bay?

4 In which country was the French Foreign Legion founded?

5 In which square was Pope John Paul II shot in 1981?

6 Which country were England's opponents in the War of Jenkins Ear?

7 Which Asian leader died in 1989 after 62 years in power?

8 Who was President of Yugoslavia from 1953 to 1980?

9 In which country was Cleopatra born?

10 At which 1690 battle did William III defeat James II?

ANSWERS

1 They were all killed by arrows 2 Harrison 3 Battle of the Nile 4 Algeria 5 St. Peter's Square 6 Spain 7 Emperor Hirohito 8 Marshall Tito 9 Greece 10 Battle of the Boyne

Music Mania

1 The Commotions provided the backing for which pop star?

2 Which rock group recorded the bestselling album *The Joshua Tree?*

Q 3

3 Under what name did Steven Georgiou record several hit records?

4 Who topped the pop charts in 1999 with the song "Mambo No 5"?

5 In which country was the singer Kiri te Kanawa born?

6 Which song contains the line "Why do birds suddenly appear, every time you are near"?

7 Who did the Spice Girls sack as their manager in 1998 as a demonstration of "girl power"?

8 Who wrote the song "Love Is All Around"?

9 How old was Buddy Holly when he died?

10 Which musical features the song "Send In The Clowns"?

ANSWERS

1 Lloyd Cole 2 U2 3 Cat Stevens 4 Lou Bega 5 New Zealand 6 "Close To You"
7 Simon Fuller 8 Reg Presley 9 22 10 A Little Night Music

Underwater World

Can you identify these eight sea creatures?

1

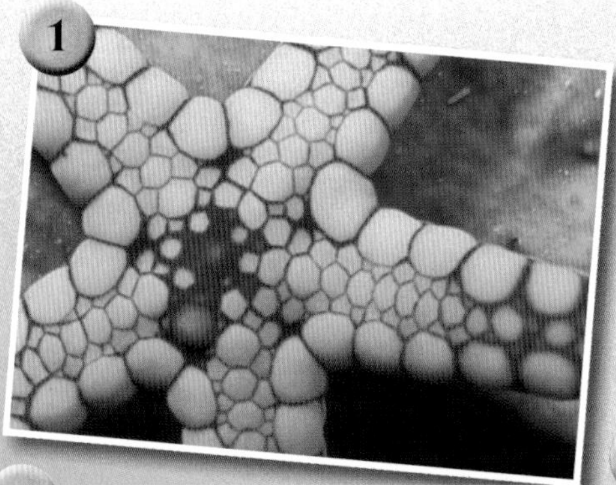

2

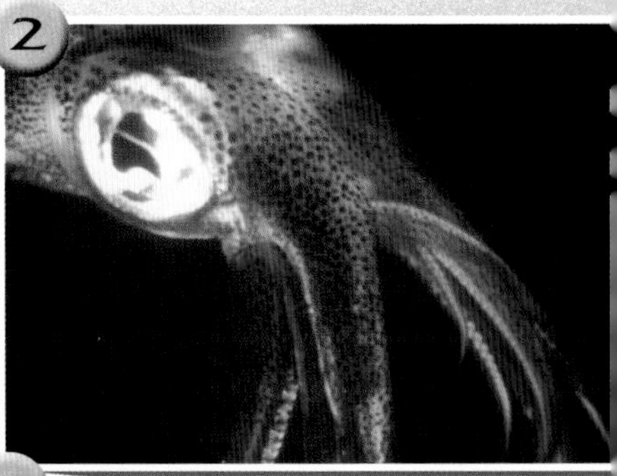

3

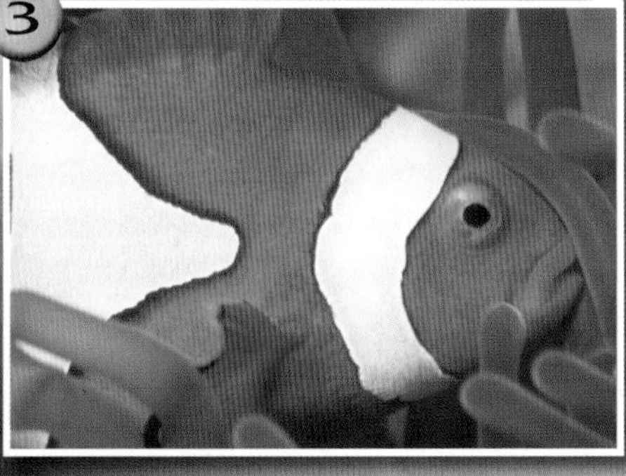

4

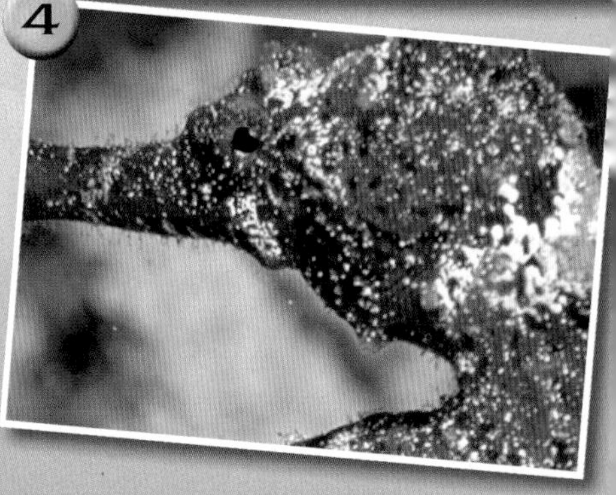

5

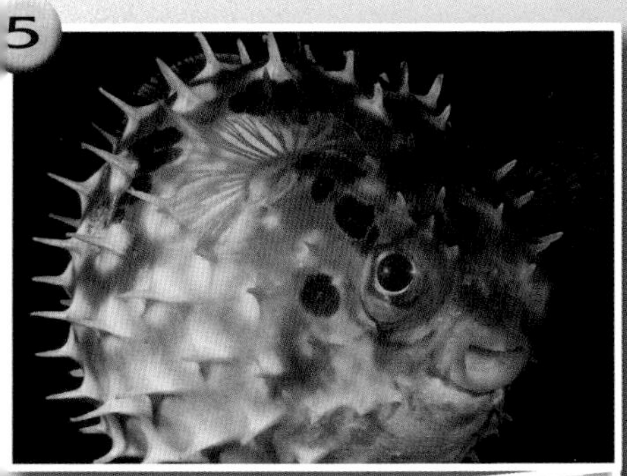

6

7

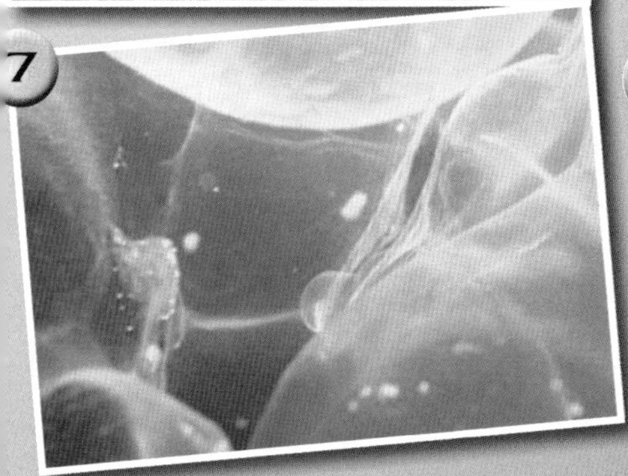

8

ANSWERS

1 Starfish 2 Squid 3 Clown fish 4 Seahorse 5 Puffer fish 6 Lion fish 7 Jellyfish 8 Angel fish

Total Trivia

Q 9

BACKGROUND BONUS

In 1958, which character was played by Tommy Steele in a Rogers and Hammerstein production?

1 Which is the driest desert in the world?

2 What kind of animal is a Heffalump in the *Winnie the Pooh* tales?

3 What is the largest lake through which the Equator passes?

4 What is the world's largest gulf?

5 Who is the central character in the novel *The Thirty-Nine Steps*?

6 On which river does the city of Budapest stand?

7 In World War II, which year witnessed the attack on Pearl Harbor?

8 What was the Roman name for Ireland?

9 What is the name of the cow in *Jack and the Beanstalk*?

10 How many pawns are on a chessboard at the beginning of play?

ANSWERS
1 Atacama Desert **2** Elephant **3** Lake Victoria **4** The Gulf of Mexico **5** Richard Hannay
6 Danube **7** 1941 **8** Hibernia **9** Old Buttercup **10** 16
Background Bonus Buttons in *Cinderella*

Global Matters

1 What name is given to an inhabitant of the Orkney Islands?
2 Which country has the highest population of Roman Catholics?
3 Which country was formerly called Dutch East Indies?
4 What is the closest bridge to the Houses of Parliament?
5 What is the second-highest peak in Africa?
6 What is the nationality of a Helvetian?
7 What is the closest French Channel port to Dover?
8 The hill known as Arthur's Seat overlooks which British city?
9 Which city is home to the Bollywood movie industry?
10 Which city was the first capital of the United States?

LEVEL 4 • QUIZ 230

Q 2

ANSWERS

1 Orcadian **2** Brazil **3** Indonesia **4** Westminster Bridge **5** Mount Kenya **6** Swiss **7** Calais **8** Edinburgh **9** Bombay **10** Philadelphia

Scientifically Speaking

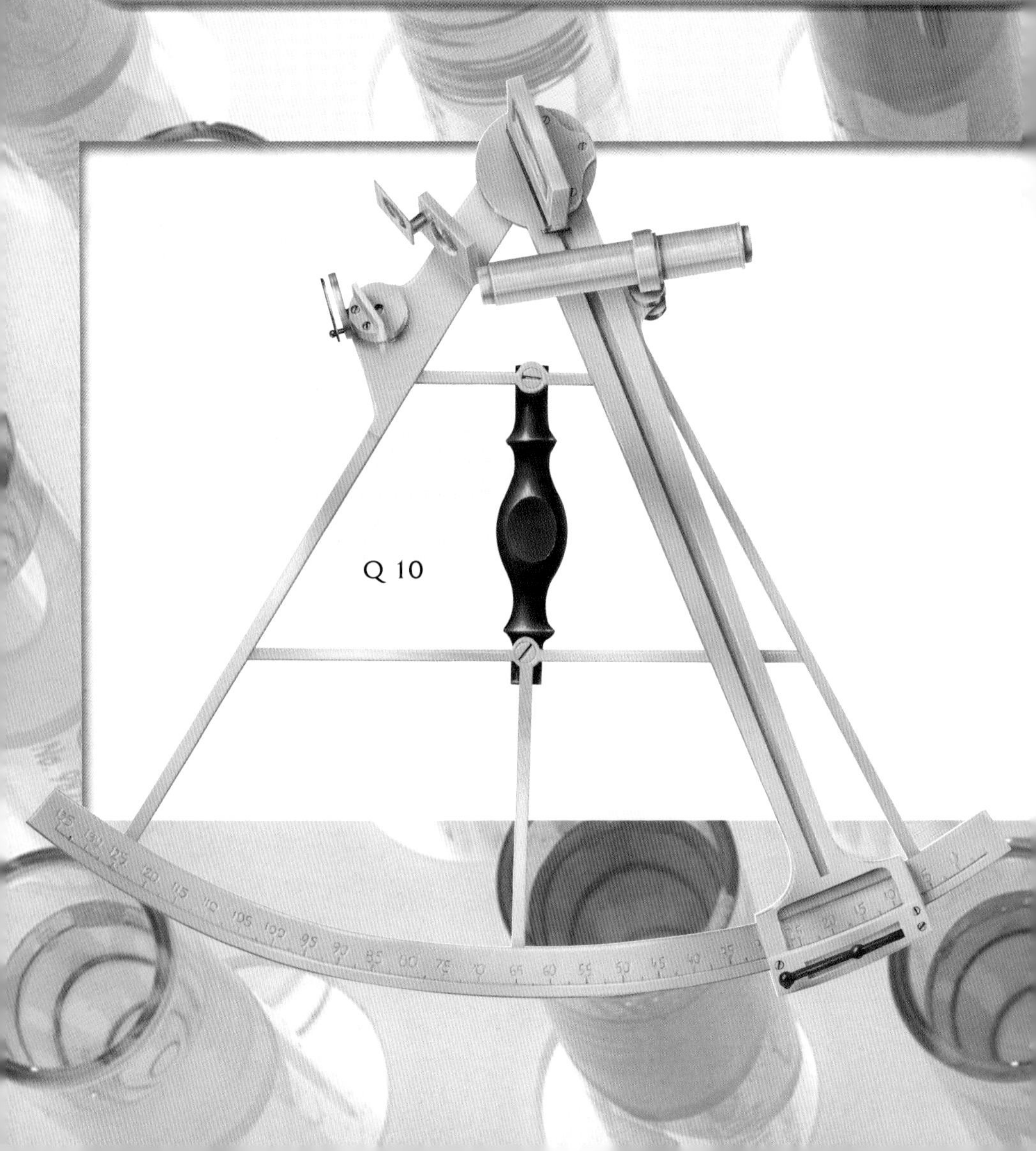

Q 10

LEVEL 4 · QUIZ 231

1 What is the more common name for seasonal allergic rhinitis?

2 Ba is the chemical symbol for which element?

3 What is the lightest metal?

4 Which planet was originally called Georgian?

5 Which bone in the body is named after the Italian for flute?

6 What is the alternative name of the disease herpes zoster?

7 What is the more common name for the ailment renal calculi?

8 Which two-word term describes the temperature of -273° C?

9 What was the name of the first space shuttle?

10 Which S is a scientific instrument for measuring latitude?

ANSWERS

1 Hay fever **2** Barium **3** Lithium **4** Uranus **5** Tibia **6** Shingles **7** Kidney stones **8** Absolute zero **9** Columbia **10** Sextant

Great and Famous

1 The movie *Sweet Dreams* was a biopic of which country and western star?
2 Who was Richard Nixon's first Vice President?
3 Who was the first movie star to win a Best Actor Oscar in consecutive years?
4 Who was the second movie star to win a Best Actor Oscar in consecutive years?
5 Whose autobiography is entitled *The Naked Civil Servant?*
6 Which British Prime Minister won a Nobel Prize for Literature?
7 Who directed his wife, Julie Andrews, in the movie *S.O.B.?*
8 Whose business card read "Secondhand furniture dealer"?
9 Who was BBC TV's first female national newsreader?
10 Which singer's daughter was crowned Miss World in 2003?

Q 6

ANSWERS
1 Patsy Cline **2** Spiro Agnew **3** Spencer Tracy **4** Tom Hanks **5** Quentin Crisp **6** Winston Churchill **7** Blake Edwards **8** Al Capone **9** Angela Rippon **10** Chris de Burgh

Sporting Chance

1 At which public school did the sport of squash originate?
2 Who was the first American cyclist to win the Tour de France?
3 The Joe Robbie Stadium is the home of which American football team?
4 In which Australian city is the Ballymore Oval cricket stadium?
5 In which city was Diego Maradona born?
6 Who was appointed manager of the England soccer team in 1990?
7 Who was named World Athlete of the Year in 1972 after collecting seven gold medals in Munich?
8 In which decade was the Winter Olympics first contested?
9 In which sport is the Stableford scoring system used?
10 Who managed Wimbledon FC to FA Cup glory in 1988?

BACKGROUND BONUS

In 2001, in which sport did Austria secure both the men's and women's gold medals?

LEVEL 4 · QUIZ 233

Q 3

ANSWERS

1 Harrow **2** Greg Lemond **3** Miami Dolphins **4** Brisbane **5** Buenos Aires **6** Graham Taylor **7** Mark Spitz **8** 1920s **9** Golf **10** Bobby Gould

Background Bonus Donhill skiing World Championships

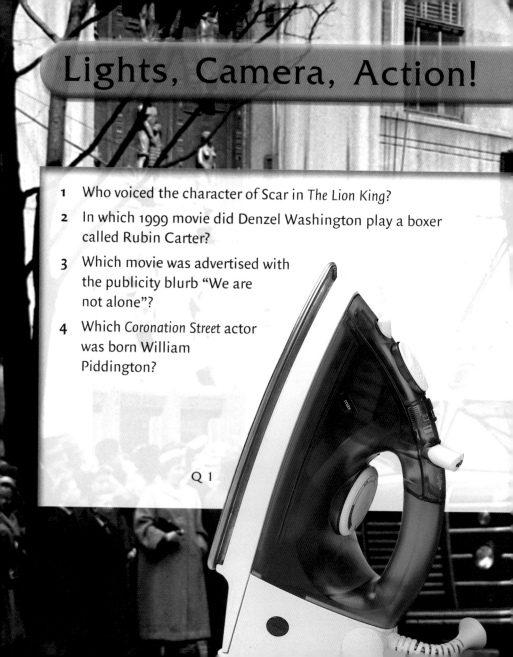

Lights, Camera, Action!

1 Who voiced the character of Scar in *The Lion King*?

2 In which 1999 movie did Denzel Washington play a boxer called Rubin Carter?

3 Which movie was advertised with the publicity blurb "We are not alone"?

4 Which *Coronation Street* actor was born William Piddington?

Q 1

LEVEL 4 · QUIZ 234

5 Who played a policeman called Roy Slater in *Only Fools and Horses* and went on to become an Oscar-winning actor?

6 In which 1967 movie did Julie Andrews play a flapper girl?

7 Who was the first actor to step out of the TARDIS?

8 When John Goodman played Fred Flintstone, who played Barney Rubble?

9 Who played the title role in *Carry On Cleo*, and went on to star in *Coronation Street?*

10 Which movie company was founded in 1919 by Charlie Chaplin, Douglas Fairbanks Snr., Mary Pickford and D.W. Griffith?

ANSWERS

1 Jeremy Irons 2 *The Hurricane* 3 *Close Encounters of the Third Kind* 4 Bill Tarmey 5 Jim Broadbent 6 *Thoroughly Modern Millie* 7 William Hartnell 8 Rick Moranis 9 Amanda Barrie 10 United Artists

Natural Selection

Q 2

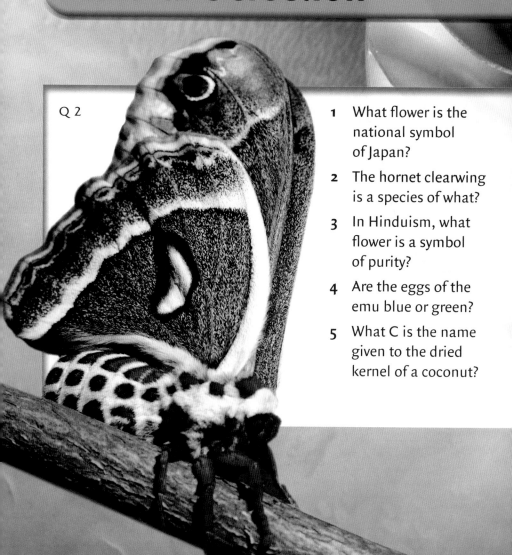

1. What flower is the national symbol of Japan?
2. The hornet clearwing is a species of what?
3. In Hinduism, what flower is a symbol of purity?
4. Are the eggs of the emu blue or green?
5. What C is the name given to the dried kernel of a coconut?

LEVEL 4 · QUIZ 235

6 Hooded, hognosed and striped are all species of which mammal?

7 Which US state is nicknamed the Beehive State?

8 What is special about yaks' milk?

9 What is the fastest-swimming bird?

10 The tarantula hawk is a species of what?

ANSWERS

1 Chrysanthemum 2 Moth 3 Lotus 4 Green 5 Copra 6 Skunk 7 Utah 8 It's Pink 9 Penguin 10 Wasp

Making History

1 In which city was Bobby Kennedy assassinated?

2 According to Shakespeare, which historical figure said "Cry havoc and let slip the dogs of war"?

3 Who was crowned King of England on a battlefield in 1485?

4 Which metal was first hallmarked in the UK in 1913?

5 The Rye House Plot was a plan to assassinate which British monarch?

6 According to the Bible, who was the first king of Israel?

7 Near which Scottish city is the site of the Battle of Culloden?

8 Which country was once ruled by Papa and Baby Doc?

9 From which country did Bulgaria gain its independence?

10 Who was British Prime Minister at the time of the General Strike in 1926?

Q 1

ANSWERS

1 Los Angeles **2** Marc Anthony **3** Henry VII **4** Platinum **5** Charles II **6** Saul **7** Inverness **8** Haiti **9** Turkey **10** Stanley Baldwin

Music Mania

1 Which Irish group recorded the album "In Blue" in 2000?
2 Which musical features the song "Seventy-six Trombones in a Big Parade"?
3 What is the surname of the brothers who founded the Beach Boys?
4 What does the musical instruction "fortissimo" signify?
5 Who did Ringo Starr replace in The Beatles?
6 Which 1956 musical featured the song "You'll Never Walk Alone"?
7 In which country is the musical *Miss Saigon* set?
8 What is the name of The Who's pinball wizard?
9 What nationality are the pop duo Roxette?
10 Which singer was born David Cook?

BACKGROUND BONUS

Lionel Hampton was the first jazz virtuoso of which instrument?

Q 6

ANSWERS

1 The Corrs **2** The Music Man **3** Wilson **4** Very loud **5** Pete Best **6** Carousel **7** Vietnam **8** Tommy **9** Swedish **10** David Essex

Background Bonus Vibraphone (vibes)

Total Trivia

1 What do the initials ZIP stand for with regard to zip codes?

2 What is the official language of Syria?

3 What is Hal 9000 in the movie 2001 *A Space Odyssey*?

4 The Sun of May is on which country's flag?

5 The song "If I Ruled The World" features in which musical?

6 Which country has the longest border with England?

7 Which Greek god is half-man and half-goat?

8 Which mythological creature has the head of an eagle and the body of a lion?

9 In India, what is the profession of a durzi?

10 According to legend, which bird was bestowed with the 100 eyes of Argus?

Q 6

ANSWERS

1 Zone improvement plan 2 Arabic 3 The name of the ship's computer 4 Argentina 5 Pickwick 6 Wales 7 Pan 8 Griffin 9 A tailor 10 Peacock

Global Matters

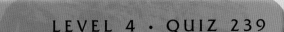

1 What was the 18th state of the United States, named after a French King?

2 Which country is home to the Gaza Strip?

3 Which Scandinavian city is known as The Daughter of the Baltic?

4 Dungarees are named after a region in which Asian country?

5 What is the state capital of Alaska?

6 In which country is the most northerly point of Africa?

7 How many spikes are on the crown of the Statue of Liberty?

8 Which country is surrounded by Argentina, Bolivia and Brazil?

9 What is the capital of Lebanon?

10 In which country did Venetian blinds originate?

ANSWERS

1 Louisiana 2 Israel 3 Helsinki 4 India 5 Juneau 6 Tunisia 7 Seven 8 Paraguay 9 Beirut 10 Japan

Movie Magic

Can you identify eight famous movies from the scenes below?

1

2

3

4

5

6

7

8

ANSWERS

1 Breakfast at Tiffany's **2** The Magnificent Seven **3** Butch Cassidy and the Sundance Kid **4** When Harry Met Sally **5** The Usual Suspects **6** Crouching Tiger, Hidden Dragon **7** Casablanca **8** Easy Rider

Scientifically Speaking

1 What is the more common name for the medical condition talipes?

2 Which H is the medical name for rabies?

3 What does a graphologist study?

4 Which P is the medical term for whooping cough?

Q 6

LEVEL 4 • QUIZ 241

5 Which five-letter U word is the name given to the shadow cast by the Earth on the Moon?

6 What is the generic name for natural gas, coal and oil?

7 Which is the only internal organ of the human body that is capable of regeneration?

8 The ore calamine is obtained from which metal?

9 What is the more common term for the ailment heliosis?

10 Where is the mound of Mars positive?

BACKGROUND BONUS

Bevel, helical, worm and planetry are all types of what?

ANSWERS

1 Club foot **2** Hydrophobia **3** Handwriting **4** Pertussis **5** Umbra **6** Fossil fuels **7** Liver **8** Zinc **9** Sunstroke **10** On the palm of the hand

Background Bonus Gears

Great and Famous

1 Who played the wife of Dustin Hoffman in the controversial movie *Straw Dogs*?

2 What is the middle name of Margaret Thatcher?

3 In what year was John Lennon assassinated?

4 Which singer was born Nathaniel Adams?

5 Who wrote the play *The Odd Couple*?

6 Who retired as Chancellor of Germany in 1998?

7 In which movie did Arnold Schwarzenegger first say "I'll be back"?

8 Which astronaut returned to space in 1998, as a 77-year-old passenger of a space shuttle mission?

9 Who provides lead vocals for Frankie Goes to Hollywood?

10 Who became leader of the PLO in 1969?

Q 9

ANSWERS

1 Susan George **2** Hilda **3** 1980 **4** Nat King Cole **5** Neil Simon **6** Helmut Kohl **7** *Terminator* **8** John Glenn **9** Holly Johnson **10** Yasser Arafat

Lights, Camera, Action!

1. What is the name of the baby in the movie *Three Men And A Baby?*
2. Who played the role of Frank Poncherella in the TV show CHIPS?
3. Which musical features the song "Colonel Buffalo Bill"?
4. Which Mel Brooks comedy is a parody on Hitchcock's thrillers?
5. Which 1962 movie tells the story of the Hudson sisters?
6. What does a foley artist add to a movie?
7. What is the name of the politician played by Paul Eddington in the sitcom *Yes Prime Minister?*
8. What is the name of the hospital in St. *Elsewhere?*
9. On whose novel was the movie *Trainspotting* set?
10. In which US soap did Jane Wyman play the role of Angela Channing?

LEVEL 5 · QUIZ 243

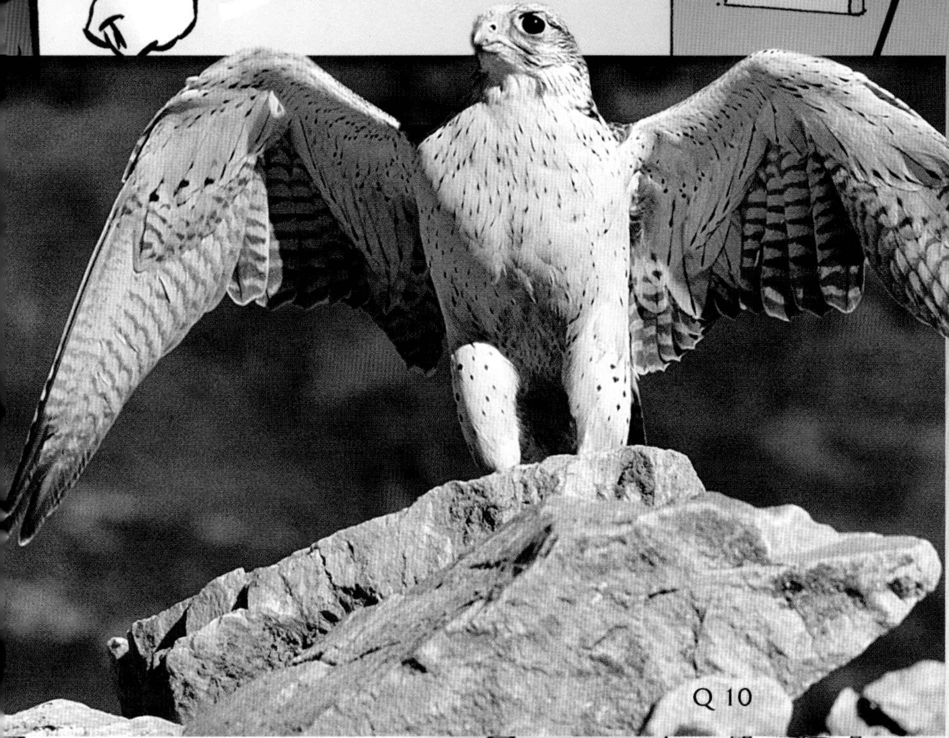

Q 10

ANSWERS
1 Mary **2** Erik Estrada **3** Annie Get your Gun **4** High Anxiety **5** Whatever Happened to Baby Jane? **6** Sound effects **7** Jim Hacker **8** St. Eligius **9** Irvine Welsh **10** Falcon Crest

Natural Selection

1 What is the only animal with retractable horns?

2 Pallid, brown and bumblebee are all species of which mammal?

3 What G is the official state animal of Minnesota?

4 Nutria fur is obtained from which animal?

5 A Pacific sea wasp is a species of which marine creature?

6 Which plant family does the fig belong to?

7 What is the only animal that has oval blood cells?

8 What bird is greeted by the poet Shelley with the words "Hail to thee, blithe spirit"?

9 What is listed in the Red Data Book?

10 When threatened, which animal ejects an inky substance to help it escape its attacker?

Q 3

ANSWERS

1 Snail **2** Bat **3** Gopher **4** Coypu **5** Jellyfish **6** Mulberry **7** Camel **8** Skylark **9** Endangered species **10** Octopus

Written Word

Q 2

1 In the Shakespeare play *The Taming of the Shrew*, which character tamed the shrew?

2 What bird did Geoffrey Chaucer refer to as "A prophet of doom"?

BACKGROUND BONUS

Which letter of the alphabet is used most frequently at the beginning of words?

3 Which novel saw the death of Inspector Morse?

4 Who created the literary detective Sam Spade?

5 The novel *The Moon and Sixpence* was based on the life of which famous artist?

6 Which Kent village is the home of the Larkins in *The Darling Buds of May*?

7 Who penned the novel *The Name of the Rose*?

8 Tom and Maggie Tulliver are the lead characters in which novel?

9 Which play features the characters of Lady Bracknell and Miss Prism?

10 *Greenmantle* was a sequel to which novel?

ANSWERS

1 Petrucchio **2** Barn owl **3** The Remorseful Day **4** Dashiel Hammett **5** Paul Gauguin **6** Pluckley **7** Umberto Eco **8** The Mill On The Floss **9** The Importance Of Being Earnest **10** The Thirty-Nine Steps **Background Bonus** S

Making History

Q 7

LEVEL 5 • QUIZ 246

1 When in battle, which part of a knight's body was protected by the gorget?

2 Name any year that Robert the Bruce was alive.

3 Who was the last English monarch to be born abroad?

4 Hafnia is the Roman name for which European capital city?

5 In which war did the Duke of Wellington drive the French out of Spain?

6 Which European capital city was founded in the 1560s by the Knights of St. John?

7 Who was the first Viceroy of India?

8 What year witnessed the General Strike in Great Britain?

9 In which castle was Edward II murdered?

10 Who was the first Pope to abdicate?

ANSWERS

1 Neck or throat 2 1274 to 1329 3 George II 4 Copenhagen 5 Peninsular War 6 Valetta 7 Warren Hastings 8 1926 9 Berkeley Castle 10 Celestine V

Music Mania

1 *The Witches Curse* is the alternative title of which Gilbert and Sullivan operetta?

2 Which song has been a hit for David Bowie and Aimi Stewart?

3 What was the nationality of the composer Antonin Dvorak?

4 In which city did the world's first public opera house open?

5 What is a paradiddle?

6 Nicely Nicely Johnson is a character from which musical?

7 Under what name do the Russian pop duo of Lena Katina and Julia Volkova perform?

8 Which musical instrument has a name that means "bell play"?

9 Which group topped the UK charts in 1975 with "Barbados"?

10 Which No. 1 hit contains the line "And the papers want to know whose shirts you wear"?

Q 4

ANSWERS

1 Ruddigore **2** "Knock On Wood" **3** Czechoslovakian **4** Venice **5** A drum roll **6** Guys and Dolls **7** Tatu **8** Glockenspiel **9** Typically Tropical **10** "Space Oddity"

Total Trivia

1 On what object is the number one flanked by the numbers 20 and 33?

2 Alphabetically, what is the last element?

3 Bathsheba Everdene is the heroine of which classic novel?

4 What is the name of Postman Pat's son?

Q 6

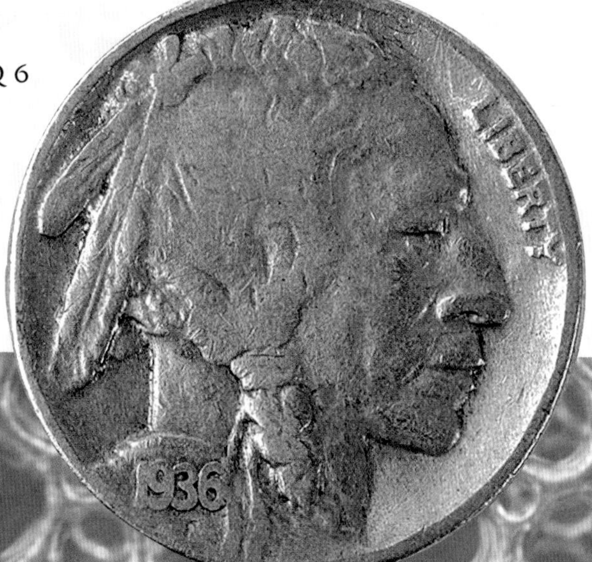

5 Lack of which acid is one of the main causes of anaemia?

6 The name of which element is derived from the German for "Devil's copper"?

7 What substance causes the blood to clot?

8 How is 990 written in Roman numerals?

9 Which goddess is depicted on the U.S. Medal of Honor?

10 Name any year that Joan of Arc was alive?

ANSWERS

1 On a roulette wheel 2 Zirconium 3 *Far From The Madding Crowd* 4 Julian
5 Folic acid 6 Nickel 7 Fibrin 8 XM 9 Minerva 10 1412 to 1431

Global Matters

1. What is the most highly populated city that lies south of the Equator?
2. On which river does the city of Mandalay stand?
3. In which European capital can citizens cross the Bridge of Segovia?
4. What is the capital city of Bhutan?
5. Which capital city lies nearest to the Equator?
6. What is the highest island in the world?
7. Which Australian city is named after the queen of William IV?
8. Roskilde was the capital of which European country until 1443?
9. Which mountain is nicknamed The Tiger of the Alps?
10. What is the deepest sea in the world?

Q 9

ANSWERS

1 Sao Paulo **2** Irawaddy **3** Madrid **4** Thimpu **5** Quito **6** New Guinea **7** Adelaide **8** Denmark **9** Matterhorn **10** Caribbean Sea

Acknowledgements

The publishers would like to thank the following sources for the use of their photographs:

Quiz 9 Warner/Alexander Salkind/pictorialpress.com;
126 TCF/Lucasfilm/pictorialpress.com; 153 P/Paramount/Lucasfilm/pictorialpress.com;
216 pictorialpress.com; 240 Paramount/pictorialpress.com;
UA/Mirisch-Alpha/pictorialpress.com; TCF/Campanile/pictorialpress.com;
Palace/CastleRock/Nelson Entertainment/pictorialpress.com;
Polygram/Spelling/Blue Parrot/Bad Hat Harry/Rosco/pictorialpress.com;
Columbia TriStar/UCV/SPC/Good Machine/Edko/Zoom Hunt/pictorialpress.com;
Warner/pictorialpress.com; Columbia/Pando/Raybert/pictorialpress.com

The publishers would like to thank the following artists for their contribution to this book:

Julie Banyard, Syd Brak, Chris Buzer, Steve Caldwell, Vanessa Card, Jim Channell, Kuo Kang Chen, Denise Coble, Peter Dennis, Richard Draper, Nicholas Forder, Mike Foster, Terry Gabbey, Luigi Galante, Peter Gregory, Terry Grose, Alan Harris, Ian Jackson, Cecilia Johanssan, Andy Lloyd-Jones, Kevin Maddison, Janos Marffy, Diana Mayo, Debbie Meekcoms, Alessandro Menchi, Andrea Morandi, Terry Riley, Steve Roberts, Martin Sanders, Mike Saunders, Susan Scott, Guy Smith, Roger Smith, Sarah Smith, Graham Sumner, Rudi Vizi, Mike White

All other pictures Corel; Digital STOCK; ILN; PhotoDisc;
Sony Computer Entertainment